'After Andy: SoHo in the Eighties'

Paul Taylor

Portraits by

Timothy Greenfield-Sanders

Introduction by

Allan Schwartzman

Schwartz City MELBOURNE

FOR PAT TAYLOR BARTELS

AND DAVID E. JOHNSON

PAUL TAYLOR 1986

PHOTOGRAPH BY ROBERT MAPPLETHORPE

© COPYRIGHT 1986 THE ESTATE OF ROBERT MAPPLETHORPE

ACKNOWLEDGMENTS

Paul Taylor gave his indefatigable stamp to this project.

His untimely passing makes us realize all that we have lost.

To be thanked are Allan Schwartzman for agreeing to write the

introduction to this volume, as well as Timothy Greenfield-Sanders

for allowing the use of his celebrity portraits.

The editing has followed the published versions. Acknowledgment goes

to Jane Rankin-Reid who transcribed the Tony Shafrazi interview and

generally assisted in preparing the manuscript for publication.

Except for a few relatively minor changes and one addition, the finished text

follows the guidelines laid down by Paul Taylor before his death.

Paul Foss ensured that his wishes were fulfilled.

Throughout, assistance was provided by a grant from the

Visual Arts/Craft unit of the Australia Council, which generously

gave the book its posthumous endorsement. Such official support

would have gratified the author no end.

Gratitude must be expressed to the following people

for their contributions to this project: David Johnson, Carol Squiers,

Noel Frankham, Gregory Taylor, Anna and Morry Schwartz,

and most of all Pat Taylor Bartels for her unfailing encouragement.

Contents

Introduction

Allan Schwartzman

Art in the eighties was an opulent feast. Artists, dealers, and collectors were the most prominent diners, filling the dais and ringside tables, while writers were scattered about the back of the room, among the distant cousins and household staff. With success determining the menu, money fueling the fire, and celebrity coloring the place-settings, the written word had become of little importance. Critics, like curators, were forced to try to keep up, to find a place on the gravy train. Some exiled themselves in a theoretical world, others slowly set about to redefine criticism for a postmodern age, and still others opted to become agents of celebrity.

But Paul Taylor didn't share the indignation, angst, or subservience which seemed to propel most of the others. He was drawn straight to power, plunking himself down at the most powerful and glamorous tables. I can think of no other art writer who better understood the period, how it ticked, and how to make himself a part of it. For this he was singularly prepared – a dandy of the highest order, a fun and exciting person, who had a magical ability to be in the most happening places. Paul truly lived every moment to his fullest, and he would go to great lengths to make it all seem effortless.

By the time he arrived in New York in the fall of 1984, Paul had strategized every detail of his ascent, down to reducing his age by several years in recognition of the premium the art world then placed on youth. But he was no greenhorn. In his native Australia he was already a celebrity, having founded and published *Art & Text*, the first Australian art journal to effectively enter the international dialogue. In the early eighties, fresh out of school and working in Melbourne, Paul developed a precocious and valued voice in theoretical circles. He had written perceptive essays about the semiotics of culture, about the common ground of art, fashion, music, and sexuality that was then the intellectual's milieu.

But Paul soon saw that the history of art in the eighties was being written not on the page, but at the box office, and he was determined to ride that wave. So he moved to New York, and used *Art & Text* as his calling card, even as he propelled himself out of its academic world. Instead, he cultivated the journalist's voice, and set about writing some of the wittiest, most knowing essays about the art world. He had an uncanny sense of timing, always writing about the hottest up-and-coming artists and dealers at their most crucial public moments. And Paul also had a knack for insinuating himself into the most powerful publications of the day, waltzing right into the very situations others would spend lifetimes approaching. Within just a few months of his arrival in New York he had become the main art writer of Tina Brown's *Vanity Fair*. Soon he was writing features for *The New York Times*.

However much Paul reveled in celebrity, though, he was not seduced by it. He had too much ego to be a cog in someone else's scheme, and he was too clever to be used against his will or awareness. He understood that celebrity was, at the time, the art world's most powerful tool, and he chose to examine it, much as Cézanne would examine a mountain. Paul would play along with the myths of artistic genius that the machinery was frenetically spinning, but he refused to reinforce them. Instead, he relished in disarming them, rendering them powerless or silly, pointing at their holes, magnifying their contradictions, indicating just where the makeup had been applied, slicing the whole machinery open with a surgeon's economy. Paul had an eternal sense of mischief. He delighted in tripping up the rich and powerful, letting them hang themselves with their own words, pitting one against another and then sitting back so that we could see how they would behave. He could infuriate people. Many took offense at things he had written, some certainly detested him, but that didn't stop even the most singlemindedly success-driven people in the art world from telling him their scandalous tales, confiding in him their most intimate thoughts, somehow always forgetting that nothing would stop Paul from using a good line no matter where or how he heard it. Paul had the amazing ability to seduce even the most protected people to tell stories about the foibles of power. When you read their quotes you can imagine the intimacy he could so seamlessly establish. The more outrageous he made them appear, the more eager they were to talk to him.

From his deft discussion of Andy Warhol's so-called "piss" paintings to his portrayals of the era's key superstars, the articles and interviews assembled here form what is in essence the first book about the art of the eighties. They do a brilliant job of capturing the period, its lustre, and its shortcomings.

Paul placed a lot of importance on the fact that he conducted the last interview with Andy Warhol. Personally, I find the fact more interesting than the interview itself, its purported significance more revealing of Paul than of Andy. Even so, it remains that the entire eighties art scene operated in Warhol's shadow, each and every artist a vehicle of Warhol's prediction that everyone would be famous for fifteen minutes. And look how Paul documented it all: analyzing hype in the name of Julian Schnabel; exploring the formidable merger-marriage of art dealers Mary Boone and Michael Werner; examining how the Italian "Three C's" were marketed; getting the art dealer Tony Shafrazi to try to defend his spray painting atop Picasso's *Guernica* as an artistic act; profiling the superstar artists Kiefer, Mapplethorpe, Salle, even Stallone! Sometimes Paul went too far – defining Cindy Sherman by her boyfriends comes to mind. But usually he got right to the heart of the matter, asking the questions few others would dare. In his profile of Brice Marden, Paul got Mary Boone to make the most shocking statement I have ever read about the artistic process: "Boone says she 'inspired' the slow-working Marden to speed up and make more and reveals her strategy for getting artists to produce: 'Get them into debt. What you always want them to do as an art dealer is to get the artist to have expensive tastes. Get them to buy lots of houses, get them to get expensive habits and expensive girlfriends and expensive wives. That's what I love. I highly encourage it. That's what really drives them to produce.'"

The art world launched its stars, and one by one it shot them down. But unlike so many artists and dealers who were victimized by celebrity, Paul knew when to move on. He understood that celebrity is a language, a tool, and, for art, not much of an end in itself. His unaligned journalist's stance gave him a fluidity that enabled him in 1990, just when the art market was collapsing and the celebrity machine began to disintegrate, to turn his attentions to activism, and to links between homosexuality and the visual arts. He wrote about ACT UP, Gran Fury, and about Robert Indiana, the neglected Pop artist, and how his openness about his sexuality contributed to his comparative obscurity. He talked with Jasper Johns about repressed imagery, and he got the artist to display just how cagey it is his nature to be; he also got Robert Rauschenberg to talk about the difficulty of talking about homosexuality in his day. These pieces are important documents for a nascent area of historical study.

Unlike the artists of the fifties, Paul's homosexuality wasn't a source of conflict in any discernible way, and I believe this is why the activist in him wasn't awakened until his own immune system began to break down noticeably. Paul cultivated an air of invincibility, always appearing in public at the top of his form. His need to be in the public eye intensified when he progressed to AIDS. It pained him to be perceived as vulnerable, so after a few weeks of illness he would push himself to write another article for *The New York Times*, to keep up his public profile. This contradiction between reality and appearances, about which he had written with such cutting finesse, now had personal resonance. Now he wrote with a certain degree of agitation about the decline of the powerful, and he celebrated subversives. But Paul was no longer satisfied writing a string of articles. He entered a new phase as a writer when in the last year of his life he began work on a novel – a *roman à clef* about the art world. He didn't get beyond the first couple of chapters.

Because Paul died just a week after his 35th birthday, at an age when most writers are just beginning to hit their stride, we are left to imagine what he would have gone on to do. In my fantasy, Paul completes his novel and therein finds his true calling as a social satirist, something our times sorely need, and something for which he was singularly prepared. Again people pore over every word of his confection as carefully as they did the diaries of Warhol. In it Paul captures the sparkle of celebrity, of which he was so enamored, but he also intercuts it with the tragedies that beset us, building monuments and then blowing them up, dazzling us, and then peeling back the curtain. I'm certain lots of people would detest him for this, and if he lived to begin a second novel, even more of them would invite him to their parties.

Paul was masterful at tying his juicy articles together with a final, spectacular bow that never ceased to bring a smile to my face. But nowadays when I think about Paul I am haunted by his dying, by the vulnerability he then revealed, by the anger in his heart and the fear in his eyes, by his ability to still conjure grace under pressure. We have been denied a keen observer and a shrewd writer. Additionally, many of us have been denied a great friend who despite his sharp tongue and fierce competitiveness could be extraordinarily giving. ●

Part One

Exit Andy

ANDY WARHOL 1977

Warhol's Piss Paintings

VANITY FAIR FEBRUARY 1985

Anyone who thinks that Andy Warhol's society portraits of the seventies verge on piss-elegance will find something more literal in a little-known but significant series from 1978, the so-called piss paintings. Each entitled *Oxidation*, they have been exhibited only in galleries in Paris and Zurich, and at Documenta 7, in Kassel, West Germany. Nonetheless, they are, along with last year's Rorschach-test pictures, exceptional works in the canon of this saint of twentieth-century art.

Green and orange blots, the figures look like suns in a distant galaxy. They are seemingly anything but Pop art, yet they are arguably Warhol at his purest, and actually help us to redefine Pop. While the artist's spectral traces form a pastiche of the whole idea of authorship and authenticity in modern painting, the usual Warhol mystique surrounds the pictures. Whose piss is it anyway?

Warhol – or an assistant – made these "urine and copper paint on canvas" abstract paintings at a moment when everyone else (either with irony or in deadly earnest) appeared to have rediscovered figurative art. Warhol out-ironized them all by releasing more of himself over these pictures than any scatological Neo-Expressionist would dare. Not since Yves Klein has any major artist made such theatrical art by self-immersion.

We think, when pondering these outrageous assaults on our taste, of the whole genre of splatter movies, or of the infamous piss-painting sequence in Pasolini's film of ten years earlier, *Teorema*, whose themes bear an uncanny resemblance to Warhol's and which is perhaps intended to convey, like the work of Warhol and postmodernist painters in general, the disintegration of our established values. We recall as well Ruskin's accusation that Whistler's paintings were "flinging a pot of paint in the public's face"; the titan in Warhol's movie *Lonesome Cowboys* who relieves his bladder over such seat-shifting duration that even Gulliver's output as a fire fighter is Lilliputian by comparison; and Jackson Pollock's legendary emission into Peggy Guggenheim's fireplace.

Indeed, anyone who has read Warhol's poignant *POPism* is aware of his creative angle on the action painters, the real-men artists who dominated the bravado art world prior to the dawn of the Warhol era. Thus Pollock, for whom any substance was apparently admissible on his canvases, is an obvious target for Warhol's irony. Pollock was said to have lived in his paintings, to have performed them; but in 1978, Warhol certainly pissed all over Pollock's gestures. And the result? Abstract Expressionist paintings, of course.

In all his best art, Warhol celebrates meaning on many levels. Given the composition of the piss paintings, allusions to alchemy are unavoidable when discussing them. Adhering to the postmodernist ethos, Warhol simultaneously upheld and ridiculed the notion of the artist as alchemist or shaman. Even cynics would grudgingly agree that the paintings achieve that which has eluded the grasp of both Marcel Duchamp and Joseph Beuys. What better contemporary demonstration is there of an elevated individual transforming base materials into gold?

The *Oxidations* are also deft analogies for what photography is at its most basic: chemical reaction, light exposure, the trace of a now absent subject – elements that, to primitive minds, are the stuff of a soul-destroying magic. It is possible that the paintings are actually votive offerings to the photographer's art.

Chemically and spiritually, these pictures are among the most ethereal to come out of the Factory, for Warhol has minted his gold with a touch that would make King Midas jealous. There is no fingerprint, as it were, of the organ that painted these images, which is an infinitely more distanced tool than the manual implements of the traditional painter. And though it's an instrument loaded with connotations of the corporeal and the sexual, Warhol has emitted from it only his spirit. He has simply aimed and shot, a technique more in the manner of a boy at play than of the paint-splattered hero of old. But if we agree with anthropologists that urinating and naming are archetypal ways of marking out space and of staking territory, the stains on these pictures are Warhol's autograph; the image is the signature.

With the *Oxidation* series, Warhol contemplated the blur between the unpalatably cheap shot and the sublime masterstroke. One day he may do a series of piss drawings, on blotting paper cut into little round wafers, to be offered to the entire post-Warhol generation. Yet this would only be Andy's newest miracle. ●

Andy Warhol – The Last Interview

FLASH ART APRIL 1987

PAUL TAYLOR **You are going to be showing your *Last Supper* paintings in Milan this year.** ANDY WARHOL Yes. **When did you make the paintings?** I was working on them all year. They were supposed to be shown in December, then January. Now I don't know when. **Are they painted?** I don't know. Some were painted, but they're not going to show the painted ones. We'll use the silk-screened ones. **On some of them you have camouflage over the top of the images. Why is that?** I had some leftover camouflage. **From the self-portraits?** Yeah. **Did you do any preparatory drawings for them?** Yeah, I tried. I did about forty paintings. **They were all preparatory?** Yeah. **It's very odd to see images like this one doubled.** They're just the small ones. **The really big one is where there are images upside down and the right way up.** That's right. **It's odd because you normally see just one Jesus at a time.** Now there are two. **Like the two Popes?** The European Pope and the American Pope. **Did you see Dokoupil's show at Sonnabend Gallery?** Oh no, I haven't gone there yet. I want to go on Saturday. **It might be the last day. There you will see two Jesuses on crucifixes, one beside the other.** Oh. **And he explained to me something like how it was transgressive to have two Jesuses in the same picture.** He took the words out of my mouth. **You're trying to be transgressive?** Yes. **In America, you could be almost as famous as Charles Manson. Is there any similarity between you at the Factory and Jesus at the Last Supper?** That's negative, to me it's negative. I don't want to talk about negative things. **Well, what about these happier days at the present Factory? Now you're a corporation president.** It's the same. **Why did you do the *Last Supper*?** Because [Alexander] Iolas asked me to do the *Last Supper*. He got a gallery in front of the other *Last Supper*, and he asked three or four people to do *Last Suppers*. **Does the *Last Supper* theme mean anything in particular to you?** No. It's a good picture. **What do you think about those books and articles, like Stephen Koch's *Stargazer*, and a 1964 *Newsweek* piece called "Saint Andrew," that bring up the subject of Catholicism?** I don't know. Stephen Koch's book was interesting because he was able to write a whole book about it. He has a new book out which I'm trying to buy to turn into a screenplay. I think it's called *The Bride's Bachelors* or some Duchampy title. Have you read it yet? **No, I read the review in *The New York Times Book Review*.** What did it say? **It was okay.** Yeah? What's it about? Stephen Koch described it to me himself. He said it was about a heterosexual Rauschenberg figure in the sixties, a magnetic artist who has qualities of a lot of sixties artists. He has an entourage. I don't know the rest. I've been meaning to call him and see if he can tell me the story and send me the book. **Who's making a screenplay?** We thought that we might be able to do it. **It's a great idea. Would you be able to get real people to play themselves in it?** I don't know. It might be good. **Do you have screenwriters here?** We just bought Tama Janowitz's book called *Slaves of New York*. **Does that mean you're going back into movie production?** We're trying. But actually what we're working on is our video show which MTV is buying. ***Nothing Special*?** No, it's called *Andy Warhol's Fifteen Minutes*. It was on Thursday last week and it's showing again Monday and it'll be shown two more times: December, and we're doing one for January. **Do you make them?** No, Vincent works on them. Vincent Fremont. **Do you look through the camera on these things at all?** No. **What's your role?** Just interviewing people. **If there was a movie made out of Stephen Koch's novel, what would be your role in it?** I don't know. I'd have to read it first. **It's not usual for business people to talk about these deals before they make them.** I don't care if anyone ... there's always another book. **I saw Ileana [Sonnabend] today and asked her what I should ask you, and she said, "I don't know. For Andy everything is equal."** She's right. **How do you describe that point of view?** I don't know. If she said it she's right. *(laughs)* **It sounds Zennish.** Zennish? What's that? **Like Zen.** Zennish. That's a good word. That's a good title for ... my new book. **What about your transformation from being a commercial artist to a real artist?** I'm still a commercial artist. I was always a commercial artist. **Then what's a commercial artist?** I don't know – someone who sells art. **So almost all artists are commercial artists, just to varying degrees.** I think so. **Is a better commercial artist** one who sells more work?   I don't know. When I started out, art was going down the drain. The people who used to do magazine illustrations and the covers were being replaced by photographers. And when they started using photographers, I started to show my work with galleries. Everybody also was doing window decoration. That led into more galleries. I had some paintings in a window, then in a gallery.   **Is there a parallel situation now?**   No, it just caught on so well that there's a new gallery open every day now. There are a lot more artists, which is real great.   **What has happened to the idea of good art?**   It's all good art.   **Is that to say that it's all equal?**   Yeah well, I don't know, I can't ...   **You're not interested in making distinctions.**   Well no, I just can't tell the difference. I don't see why one Jasper Johns sells for three million and one sells for, you know, like, four hundred thousand. They were both good paintings.   **The market for your work has changed a little in the last few years. To people my age – in their twenties – you were always more important than to the collecting group of people in their fifties and sixties.**   Well, I think the people who buy art now are these younger kids who have a lot of money.   **And that's made a difference in your market.**   Yeah, a little bit.   **How important is it for you to maintain control?**   I've been busy since I started – since I was a working artist. If I wasn't showing in New York I was doing work in Germany, or I was doing portraits.   **What I mean is that as more and more artists come up, and as new galleries open every day, the whole idea of what an artist is changes. It's no longer so special, and maybe a more special artist is one who maintains more control of his or her work.**   I don't know. It seems like every year there's one artist for that year. The people from twenty years ago are still around. I don't know why. The kids nowadays – there's just one a year. They stay around, they just don't ...   **You were identified with a few artists a couple of years ago – Kenny Scharf, Keith Haring.**   We're still friends.   **But I never see you with any of this season's flavors.**   I don't know. They got so much press. It was great. I'm taking photographs now. I have a photography show at Robert Miller Gallery.   **And there's going to be a retrospective of your films at the Whitney Museum.**   Maybe, yes.   **Are you excited about that?**   No.   **Why not?**   They're better talked about than seen.   **Your work as an artist has always been so varied, like Leonardo. You're a painter, a film maker, a publisher ... Do you think that's what an artist is?**   No.   **Can you define an artist for me?**   I think an artist is anybody who does something well, like if you cook well.   **What do you think about all the younger artists now in New York who are using pop imagery?**   Pretty good.   **Is it the same as when it happened in the sixties?**   No, they have different reasons to do things. All these kids are so intellectual.   **Did you like the punk era?**   Well, it's still around. I always think it's gone but it isn't. They still have their hard-rock nights at the Ritz. Do you ever go there?   **No. But punk, like Pop, might never go away.**   I guess so.   **How's *Interview* going?**   It's not bad.   **You're going to be audited soon for the Audit Bureau of Circulations.**   Yeah, they're doing it now.   **What difference will it make?**   I don't know.   **It will be better for advertising ...**   Yeah.   **What's the circulation now?**   170,000. The magazine's getting bigger and bigger.   **What magazines do you read?**   I just read everything.   **You look at everything. Do you read the art magazines?**   Yeah. I look at the pictures.   **You've been in trouble for using someone else's image as far back as 1964. What do you think about the legal situation of appropriated imagery, and the copyright situation?**   I don't know. It's just like a Coca-Cola bottle – when you buy it, you always think that it's yours and you can do whatever you like with it. Now it's sort of different because you pay a deposit on the bottle. We're having the same problem now with the John Wayne pictures. I don't want to get involved, it's too much trouble. I think that you buy a magazine, you pay for it, it's yours. I don't get mad when people take my things.   **You don't do anything about it?**   No. It got a little crazy when people were turning out paintings and signing my name.   **What did you think about that?**   Signing my name to it was wrong but other than that I don't care.   **The whole appropriation epidemic comes down to who is responsible for art. If indeed anyone can manufacture the pictures of those flowers, the whole idea of the artist gets lost somewhere in the process.**   Is that good or bad?   **Well, first of all, do you agree with me?**   Yes, if they take my name away. But when I used the flowers, the original photograph was huge and I just used one square inch of the photo and magnified it.   **What do you ever see that makes you stop in your tracks?**   A good display in a window ... I don't know, a good-looking face.   **What's the feeling when you see a good window display or a good face?**   You just take longer to look at it. I went to China, I didn't want to go, and I went to see the Great Wall. You know, you read about it for years. And actually it was great. It was really, really, really great.   **Have you been working out lately?**   I just did it.   **How much are you lifting now?**   105 pounds.   **On the benchpress? That's strong.**   No, it's light. You're stronger than me, and fitter and handsomer and younger, and you wear better clothes. **Did you enjoy the opening party thrown by GFT at the Tunnel?** I had already been there before.

In the sixties you mean? *(Laughs)* No – the manager or someone took me around it a few days ago. **It's a very convenient club for the Bridge and Tunnel people – they'll be able to come in on those tracks from New Jersey.** I don't know whether it was my idea to call it the Tunnel or whether it was someone else's idea that I liked, but I think it's a good name.

And lots of people turned out for Claes Oldenburg's show that night. He looked happy. A lot of people said he looked happy. I always liked Claes actually. *You* looked great the other night. I took lots of photos of you in your new jacket. **Yes? How did I turn out?** They haven't come back yet. Next time you come by I'll take some close-ups. **For the "Upfront" section of *Interview* perhaps?** Except that I'm not accomplished enough. You could sleep with the publisher. **If you were starting out now, would you do anything differently?** I don't know. I just worked hard. It's all fantasy. **Life is fantasy?** Yeah, it is. **What's real?** Don't know. **Some people would.** Would they? **Do you really believe it, or tomorrow will you say the opposite?** I don't know. I like this idea that you can say the opposite. **But you wouldn't in this case?** No. **Is there any connection between fantasy and religious feeling?** Maybe. I don't know. Church is a fun place to go. **Do you go to Italy very often?** You know we used to make our films there. **And didn't you have a studio in the country for a while?** Outside of Rome. **And did you go to the Vatican?** We passed by it every day. **I remember a polaroid you took of the Pope.** Yeah. **Did you take that from very close up?** Yes. He walked past us. **And he blessed you?** I have a photo of him shaking Fred Hughes's hand. Someone wanted us to make a portrait of the Pope and they've been trying to get us together but we can't and by now the Pope has changed three times. **Fred said he used to feel like the Pope in the old Factory in Union Square. He used to go out on that balcony and wave at the passing masses underneath.** He has a balcony now. **Yes, but from the current Factory he can only see the reception area.** He can wave. **And sometimes it's just as busy as Union Square too.** ●

More Andy

THE NEW YORK TIMES BOOK REVIEW AUGUST 1990

When Bob Colacello met Andy Warhol in 1970, the great artist was entering his famous period of decline. He had been shot, had announced that he had given up painting and had quit directing movies. He had also just launched *Interview* magazine (or *inter/VIEW* as it was first called), the movie fanzine that grew into a successful and offbeat mix of fashion, literature, movies, politics, high society and low life that has inspired others in its wake. Having transformed the face of modern art, Warhol in the 1970s found himself up to his neck in money, power and celebrity, and it is the gossip about this world – as well as an anecdotal account of the rise of *Interview* – that is covered in *Holy Terror: Andy Warhol Close Up* (HarperCollins). In this insider's portrait, Colacello shows that, for Warhol at least, being in decline was the best fun.

For thirteen years, Colacello worked as a columnist and editor at *Interview*; he also procured subjects for Warhol's portraits, observed his master at close range and took copious notes. Seven years after parting ways, he portrays Warhol – unflatteringly – as an eccentric millionaire with bad skin who would suck on chocolates, then spit them out for health reasons; as a "business-artist" who barely distinguished between portrait commissions and advertisements in *Interview*; as one of the limbs of the "Halston-Liza-Bianca-Andy" party animal that lived at Studio 54; as a dizzy gay voyeur, gossiper, shopper and hoarder, and, ultimately, as more interested in precious stones than in art. Warhol was also, he says, "a closet control freak, who deviously pretended he didn't know what was going on," a tightfisted boss and a bad father figure who loved no one and who eventually, in a stroke of divine justice, died alone in the hospital, supposedly from neglect.

Still, Warhol gets all the best lines. Thanks to Colacello's diary, Warhol's deadpan one-liners and irreverent stage whispers are rendered intact. The comments of both men in the company of Warhol's 1970s cronies – among them Elizabeth Taylor, Paulette Goddard, Jacqueline Onassis, Diana Vreeland, and Truman Capote – are played back humorously, revealing an excited pair of dilettantes who are happy to be "up there" with the stars while gently mocking everybody, including themselves, along the way. In *Holy Terror* Warhol manages to be funny almost all the time. Even when he is not brilliant, he is droll. And when both wit and buffoonery fail him, he is funny by being camp. The only drawback to some of these anecdotes is that Colacello has already narrated them in *Exposures*, the book he wrote with Warhol in 1979.

· · · · ·

To counterpoint the story of Warhol in the seventies, which does not really go anywhere except in search of more and more "victims" to buy portraits, Colacello weaves a tale of his own, a kind of *Gulliver's Travels* among big-timers and little people, but lacking in irony and social criticism. In this lengthy subplot, Bob Colacello stars as a talented and wide-eyed film school graduate who fell in with the Warhol gang in his early twenties and impressed them by being fast on his feet—and not only on the dance floor. By 1974 he had risen to the status of *Interview*'s executive editor and was accompanying Warhol almost everywhere. In 1975, when the best-selling issues of *Interview* were featuring their "best friends" on the covers— Liza Minnelli, Cher, Raquel Welch, Ryan O'Neal, Jack Nicholson, Anjelica Huston, and Mick and Bianca Jagger—they realized they "were sitting on the most exclusive scoop of all: the opportunity to document life among the rich and famous from the inside." *Interview* promptly set out to capture "social history in the making"—the parties that were packed with "all the elements of the fashionable new society that would dominate the decade, and merge with the rich Reaganite group in the eighties."

Colacello adjusted to the quickening pace, alcohol, cocaine and social climbing and, by 1979, had turned *Interview* into a financially self-sufficient, pro-Republican rag whose advertising slogan declared, "We please some of the people all of the time." In 1981 he netted Nancy Reagan for an exclusive interview and the cover (to which Warhol the Democrat feigned indifference). But in 1983, after asking Warhol for a large slice of the pie, he was frozen out of his job and resigned. Appropriately enough, he landed as a contributing editor at the new *Vanity Fair*, a glossier, richer version of *Interview* whose advertising slogan, echoing *Interview*'s, became "All things to some people."

Warhol made a comeback as an important artist at the end of the seventies. Yet, when he is not undermining them, Bob Colacello gives scant credit to Warhol's uncanny artistic gifts. The entire Warhol sixties are dealt with in only one chapter, and the numerous and important European retrospectives of his work throughout the seventies are hardly mentioned. Colacello also fails to shed light on Warhol's artistic relationships and to observe the renewed interest in his art in the early eighties. But he has gone to great ends to kiss and tell.

Indeed, he finishes up by going through Warhol's bathroom cabinet and listing the acne creams and lotions he found there. Such behavior is bound to rankle those who look down on bathroom cabinet peepers. Yet it will titillate everyone who is fascinated by Warhol trivia and the chinks in his armor—the thousands who care about what Andy ordered for dinner, whether he masturbated and when, if ever, he was seen to cry. *Holy Terror* is their kind of book—a very close-up portrait, pimples and all. The problem is that, like Gulliver in Brobdingnag staring into the face of a giant, Colacello in contemplating Andy Warhol is fixated on the enlarged pores. ●

Part Two

The Superstars

ROBERT MAPPLETHORPE 1982

Robert Mapplethorpe

AMERICAN PHOTOGRAPHER JANUARY 1988

As aesthetic epiphanies go, Robert Mapplethorpe's must have been one-of-a-kind. How many other serious art photographers would claim they found their true calling on New York's raunchy 42nd Street?

"The first time I went there," Mapplethorpe says, "I didn't know that pornographic male magazines even existed. I was sixteen, straight, and working as a bank messenger. I'd stare at those pictures in the window and get a powerful feeling in my stomach. They were wrapped in cellophane and you couldn't get at them. God," Mapplethorpe remembers thinking, "if you could only get that feeling across in a piece of art."

That, of course, is exactly what he went on to do. Mapplethorpe, who came from an upright Catholic home on Long Island, discovered a lot about himself while trying out life on his own in New York City in the late 1960s — going to art school, living in the legendary Chelsea Hotel, and taking up with intellectual free spirits like punk poet and rock singer Patti Smith. Along the way he acquired a camera and, among other things, began capturing the sharp sensation of backroom erotic male desire in stark, classically composed black-and-white photographs. The pictures were strong — so strong that even before he had his first showing in a SoHo art gallery in 1976, Mapplethorpe's aggressive pictures of male eroticism were the talk of the New York art world. It is a buzz that has surrounded his name ever since, such that today, with some twenty books and exhibition catalogues devoted to his work — only a portion of which dwell on homosexual themes — the controversy surrounding Mapplethorpe has never waned. Once a bad boy, it seems, always a bad boy.

Much has been written about Mapplethorpe over the past decade, and there has been much discussion about the clever way he has manipulated his career by assiduously nurturing connections within the New York art scene. What can't be denied is the originality and magnetism of his work, and the way he has drawn patronage from a number of far-flung sources.

Consider that during the early days of New Wave rock and roll in the mid-seventies, Mapplethorpe produced austere black-and-white album covers for musicians like Patti Smith and the group Television that helped define the artistic ambitions of the movement. Yet he could also turn sophisticated uptown heads with his flattering, delicate portraits of celebrities and socialites like John Paul Getty III, Carolina Herrera, Arnold Schwarzenegger, and Sam Wagstaff, the late photo collector who figured prominently in Mapplethorpe's personal life.

Then, too, Mapplethorpe has for years been a darling of the flamboyant downtown art scene, whose longtime monarch, Andy Warhol, was an admirer. Mapplethorpe's links with Warhol are worth noting, for besides working as a staff photographer for Warhol's *Interview* magazine since the mid-seventies, Mapplethorpe shared with Warhol the singular ability to mix the sacred with the profane. Yet whereas the pope of Pop ironically celebrated the crude and banal, Mapplethorpe was more the worshipping type. Who else would have dared to offer an exquisite, oversized image of male genitals resting atop a marbleized pedestal, as if such bodily goods were the gods' gift to art? With sensibilities like that, it's no wonder that Mapplethorpe emerged a full-blown sensation.

In recent years the lines around Mapplethorpe have begun to soften a bit. Although some of his work is still thoroughly aggressive, if not hard-core, he has taken to photographing almost traditional still lifes, replete with drapery and skulls, and has also begun shooting commercial advertising and fashion imagery. Then again, as he maintains close connections with major galleries, collectors, and curators, fetching some of the highest prices of any living art photographer, the cult of acceptance has widened considerably. These days, the photographer once lauded by such high-minded critics as Roland Barthes and Susan Sontag may even be seen relaxing in a series of magazine ads for a modish brand of lime-juice mixer.

More than ever, 1988 figures to be Mapplethorpe's year. In line with the international acclaim enjoyed by certain big-league painters, he is being honored in major European and American museums. The Stedelijk Museum in Amsterdam will feature a Mapplethorpe retrospective in February, followed by an exhibit of his portraits in April at the National Portrait Gallery in London. New York's Whitney Museum of American Art is rumored to be planning a separate Mapplethorpe show in the spring, making him only the second photographer (after Cindy Sherman) so honored by that museum. Meanwhile, the Institute of Contemporary Art in Philadelphia is organizing its own Mapplethorpe retrospective, scheduled for December.

Typically, Mapplethorpe responds to the prospect of so much exposure rather coyly. "I just want to be written about as a normal artist," he grumbles, knowing full well how preposterous a suggestion that is. Yet that, too, is part of the Mapplethorpe mystique. In addition to the taboo subject matter for which he is famous (including highly graphic depictions of sex acts), Mapplethorpe has made his way by virtue of a charismatic but contradictory personality. "Robert really knows how to draw people in," says one New York critic and curator who has known him off and on for decades. "After seeing his early shows, which really were quite explicit sexually, and then encountering him at downtown parties and clubs dressed head to toe in black leather, I was nervous about meeting him for the first time. But in person he was incredibly charming – soft-spoken, sensitive, good-humored, and self-deprecating. He wove a web around you and made you feel like you were absolutely central to his life – and that that was the most important place to be. But," she continues, "once you fell out of the web you were out forever. Robert is very black and white. In his eyes, you're either *for* him or *against* him."

In recent months, Mapplethorpe has again found himself at the center of speculation—though not for the content of his imagery. Only 41 years old, he is rumored to have recently overcome a serious bout of pneumonia. His slim frame seems more frail than ever, and his azure blue eyes have paled to a curious champagne color. That the eternally youthful Mapplethorpe may be in fading health is a question that's been raised at more than one gathering of New York artists and scene setters.

Still, visitors to Mapplethorpe's sleek, creamy-colored loft and studio in the Chelsea section of Manhattan find its owner and his possessions more composed than ever. His living room, sparely decorated with late-nineteenth-century Arts and Crafts vases, also sports a Mapplethorpe-designed coffee table that is all angles and plate glass. Large black-and-white prints of his own images grace the walls, overshadowed by a portrait of Mapplethorpe himself, taken by Andy Warhol. The rest of the space is smartly functional. At one end is a stagy set, hung with pristine black seamless paper, where the photographer poses his subjects. (Mapplethorpe's darkroom and business office are housed in another, comparatively unpolished space downtown.) With pride, he shows off the more intimate den at the other end of the loft. It is dark and crowded with *objets*

d'art – amateur and master photographs, detailed drawings by homoerotic illustrator Tom of Finland, some small paintings, mirrors, and curious selections from Mapplethorpe's early collection of satanic artifacts. Outwardly shaky, yet as calm and organized as ever, he appears as a man who is putting his worldly affairs in order.

. . . . .

"I never wanted to be a photographer," Mapplethorpe claims. "It was sort of a mistake really. I only wanted to make a statement and photography ended up being the vehicle." Of all the declarations he is prone to make, this one may carry the most credibility.

Mapplethorpe was born in Floral Park, Long Island, in 1946. The town was then, as it remains today, an unassuming middle-class hamlet on the Long Island Expressway, just across the Queens border. Mapplethorpe's father was an electrical engineer and the family was devoutly Catholic. Today Mapplethorpe is reluctant to discuss any aspects of his family or childhood, saying that his Catholic upbringing shaped some of the more "iconographic" elements of his later work.

What does seem clear is that for Mapplethorpe life truly began when he left home in 1962, at the age of 17, and enrolled at the Pratt Institute in Brooklyn, one of New York's best art schools. His desire then, possibly fueled by his inner awakenings on 42nd Street, was to become vaguely, intensely, an "artist." That photography may have offered an outlet never entered his mind, for, as he recalls, "in the 1960s, to be a photographer was not to be an artist. At Pratt anyway."

That it took Mapplethorpe eight years to make his way through art school is not so important, for it was during his years meandering through Pratt that he fell under the spell of a wide circle of influence – not the least of whom was a contrary young artist and poet named Patti Smith.

In 1970 Patti Smith represented something quite new to New York cultural life. An aspiring rock-'n'-roller, she built her act not around music but around poetry, the sort born of the city's intellectual and drug bohemia and personified by the likes of William Burroughs and Allen Ginsberg. Her true model, however, was Arthur Rimbaud, the nineteenth-century French bad-boy poet, who set out to create lofty forms of verse by indulging in visionary ecstasies brought on by drugs, alcohol, sexual perversity, and almost any other extreme experience he thought could lead to illumination. If Mapplethorpe needed aesthetic justification for his own darker yearnings, Rimbaud and Smith provided it in abundance.

Smith met Mapplethorpe by accident, strolling into his bedroom in Brooklyn one day a perfect stranger. "She was looking for a friend and just wandered into my ground-floor apartment," Mapplethorpe recalls. "I was in bed and woke up – and there was Patti Smith."

It wasn't long before the two became lovers, living wherever they might here and there (including the Chelsea Hotel), "infiltrating the New York art scene," as Mapplethorpe puts it, and captivating people. A friend who knew them then recalls "an incredibly beautiful couple always inventing themselves for the rest of the world." Mapplethorpe credits Smith with helping him embolden the homosexuality of his early imagery; she also proved a compelling picture of androgyny as a frequent sitter for Mapplethorpe's camera throughout the 1970s. It is probable that Mapplethorpe began to create his dual persona – as naughty leatherboy and visionary photographer – during his years with Patti Smith. Around this time he began making collage-like constructions that incorporated pornographic images of men, which he now describes as "altarpieces from some bizarre religion."

Mapplethorpe's taste for extremes in pursuit of his art has been no secret to those who have watched him move deftly through the subcultures of New York the last ten years, the gay community especially. The photographer has taken portraits of numerous muscle-bound models and has been known to advertise for them in the personals sections of gay newspapers. Recalls one frequent sitter and boyfriend, who claims he often procured other men to pose for Mapplethorpe, "I had noticed Robert for about a year on the street, but was put off by the leather-and-boots image. Then one day I saw him in a tuxedo carrying a corsage, and I thought there was probably more to this guy than I realized."

Hardly an apologist, Mapplethorpe is proud of having exposed his sexual adventures through his photography. "Let's face it, most photographers are living their lives vicariously by taking pictures," he reasons. "When they get into sex or pornography, it's often a sort of cover-up for their own sexual inactivity or inadequacy. They'd rather do it through the camera and sublimate their desires in order to take pictures." In short, Mapplethorpe believes himself exempt from such venality because of the openly confessional nature of his work – an attitude as Catholic as it is Rimbaudesque.

· · · · ·

If Patti Smith was the one who helped Mapplethorpe idealize his demons for art's sake, it fell on several others to pave the way for the photographer's acceptance in more fashionable circles. Critical here was John McKendry, a New York art historian who, until his death in 1975, was curator of prints and photography at the Metropolitan Museum of Art. More than a scholar, McKendry was a grand connoisseur, devoted to the cause of photography as art. He was also a great animator of the social scene. With his socialite wife, Maxime de la Falaise, McKendry sat at the pivotal point where the art world met the *beau monde* of fashion and high society.

"John was my closest friend for two years," Mapplethorpe says. "He bought me my first camera and persuaded me to take up photography full time." Just as important, McKendry took Mapplethorpe to Europe and introduced his protégé to the sorts of glamorous jet setters who would soon come to populate the photographer's portraits. Mapplethorpe's eye for elegant composition was unquestionably cultivated by McKendry, but there were other influences. "John was interested in fantasy and content," comments an old friend. "He was drawn to whatever conveyed excitement, especially if it was exotic."

Whatever role John McKendry played as Mapplethorpe's patron was ultimately overshadowed by Sam Wagstaff, the aesthetic tastemaker who helped create much of the market for fine-art photography in the last fifteen years. The two met and became fast friends in 1971, while Wagstaff was still known primarily as a respected curator of modern art. Eventually the two men became lovers and tore into the photography world together – as fervent collectors making the rounds at major galleries and auction houses, but also in the abiding role of professor and student, impresario and star performer. For besides being erudite, wealthy and handsome, Wagstaff was 25 years to the day older than Mapplethorpe.

There are some within the art world who maintain that Mapplethorpe was essentially created by Wagstaff, who tirelessly devoted himself to promoting the career of the young photographer. Given Mapplethorpe's strong personality and the wide arc of his social and artistic orbits, that is an unfair judgment. Nonetheless, Mapplethorpe's great surge as an art photographer to be reckoned with by curators and gallery owners dates from his close association with the influential collector.

The two shows that really put Mapplethorpe's name on everybody's lips occurred in 1976 and 1977 – one a mixed bag of portraits, flowers, and still lifes at the Holly Solomon Gallery and the other an eye-opening display of male nudes and men dressed in sadomasochistic paraphernalia exhibited at the Kitchen, a noncommercial space in SoHo that was as much a home for New Wave concerts and performance art as it was for photography.

Even with the stir created by some of the work, Mapplethorpe's images were selling for as low as $150 after his initial showings, a situation that prompted Wagstaff to move Mapplethorpe uptown to the prestigious Robert Miller Gallery on 57th Street. According to noted dealer and collector Harry Lunn, an ardent Mapplethorpe supporter since the mid-seventies, "Sam simply believed that Miller could do more for Robert's career, and he was right. It's not just the splashy exhibit that counts – it's what goes on every day of the week between buyers and sellers. Robert Miller was geared to distribution in a major, if very selective, way."

With Wagstaff and Miller carefully building market interest, Mapplethorpe was then given his first exhibit at the new gallery in 1979 – a joint exhibit actually, since alongside his own portraits and stills was a quiet collection of drawings by Patti Smith, who had recently released her first record album and was herself becoming a big ticket. The opening was a mob scene, the exhibition a media and art-world event: more importantly, by shrewdly controlling the availability of original prints for purchase, the gallery ensured that the growing demand for Mapplethorpe's work would be met with limited supply.

Although photography was still considered an upstart within the art market in 1979, Mapplethorpe saw prices for his imagery rise steadily over the next several years. In 1981 prints went for $2,000, a figure that rose to $5,000 three years later. By then, however, Mapplethorpe's studio was minting only special editions of his photographs restricted to three prints. As of last year, his platinum-on-linen prints were produced in single editions only, retailing for $15,000 apiece.

It is interesting to speculate just how far Wagstaff's help may have carried his protégé – but speculation it has to be. In 1986, after months of rumors that he was seriously ill, Wagstaff died of pneumonia. The bulk of his $5 million estate – much of it coming from the sale of his prized collection to California's Getty Museum in 1985 – went to Mapplethorpe, for whom the inheritance came as small consolation. "I watched him die," Mapplethorpe says grimly. "It was awful."

Time does heal, however, at least certain losses. With his upcoming round of international shows, new commercial accounts, and the still-climbing prices for his pictures, Mapplethorpe gives few hints that life is anything but good these days, despite his recent health concerns.

He is especially at ease in assessing his contribution to the culture around him. That he would like some credit for pulling photography into the spotlight of the art world is understandable. Yet Mapplethorpe considers it no less significant an achievement for having broken through on the force of images that border ever so close to flagrant pornography. What better vindication indeed than museum retrospectives for raising to new heights "that powerful feeling in my stomach."

On the one hand, Mapplethorpe is liable to quip, like some latter-day Oscar Wilde with a Hasselblad, "Photography is not that important. My life is important." Then he admits, "I guess I'm glad to have been a part of the art world – it's allowed me to have lived the lifestyle I wanted." ●

*This article was
based on original reporting by
Carol Squiers and Steven Koch
and edited by Allan Ripp*

Julian Schnabel

THE NEW YORK TIMES BOOK REVIEW JANUARY 1988

Julian Schnabel, the artist who once told a reporter for *The New York Times* that he never reads books, has written one. The work of this 36-year-old painter, whose exhibition at the Whitney Museum of American art is just closing, always attracts the written word – at least since his "broken plate" paintings caught the eyes of magazines and newspapers in 1980. These ambitious, impressive, but mostly just fashionable, tasteful paintings were a calculated affront to the prevailing regime of artistic austerity. Schnabel negotiated the storms of protest that followed their appearance with infuriating flair, and he bristled heroically with disdain for the art world. Recently, however, notoriety has left him as quickly as it found him, and the artist's movie-star antics and his pose as a Romantic genius are becoming old news.

Invited by a wily literary agent to tell his own story, Schnabel rose to the occasion. Compiled from his notebooks, as well as from tape-recorded anecdotes that were boiled down and spiffed up by his ghostwriters and editors, the narrative of *CVJ* (Random House) resembles the fragmentary, discontinuous surface of his paintings. The hero of this autobiography is a far cry from the overconfident artist depicted in the press. He is an impassive, dispirited character, exactly like those found in blank-generation (post-Bret Easton Ellis) literature. But behind its modest and self-effacing vignettes, *CVJ* is a smug success story. The subtitle of *CVJ* – readers are not told what these initials stand for, though apparently they refer to his wife – is *Nicknames of Maitre D's & Other Excerpts From Life*. Perhaps it should be *The Rise and Rise of Julian Schnabel by Julian Schnabel*.

The book tells of a young, Brooklyn-born, pot-smoking Jewish boy who moves with his family to Texas when he is 14 years old. He harbors feelings of yearning and alienation. Then, in 1974, he and his girlfriend run off to New York. The downtown art scene provides a colorful background to the romantic and artistic adventures that follow – including, inevitably, his drunken fights with other painters, cheap housing, part-time work as a short-order cook, poverty and hunger (for chocolates). Finally, he finds satisfaction in outrageous fortune and wedded bliss in 1980 or 1981, and the narrative stops. By then Schnabel had almost hit the top of the New York and international art worlds and was, as he says regally, "starting to get used to being treated well."

. . . . .

Toward the end of the seventies, while he was still serving his apprenticeship to superstardom, the artist hit on his plate-painting technique. His trademark became paint applied to surfaces of broken plates that were glued to mammoth masonite supports. To the art world, his technique was as catchy as the poured paint of Jackson Pollock had been (Pollock's spirit is invoked throughout the book). Schnabel's bravado creations – he refers to the first one as Frankenstein – were held together with liberal amounts of adhesive. To novelty seekers and a few serious critics alike, they were brutally thrilling, scabrous and jewellike in equal measure, easy contestants for instant notoriety. Similarly outrageous were enormous paintings made of oil and antlers on ponyskin, black velvet and other cultural detritus. He has even painted on used Kabuki theater backdrops. Schnabel tackled the big subjects – Death, God, Art and Julian Schnabel. Yet his gift for combining high and low themes and gnarly materials should not be underestimated. In one gesture, his paintings made history kitschy and kitsch historic.

CVJ also recounts Schnabel's forays into Europe. While his travels do not familiarize him with the correct spelling of important European names (perhaps his editors do not read either), they did inspire his art; the Texan responded to the ascendant Continental trend in gestural, figurative painting. His imagery and strident surfaces were inspired by the work of a variety of European artists who were little-known here in the seventies, such as Sigmar Polke, Anselm Kiefer, and Joseph Beuys. These works he inflated to classic Abstract Expressionist size, and his own brazen style was born. In *CVJ*, however, all of his paintings have the status of background scenery. The author does not try – perhaps does not know how – to explain them.

He did know that an increasingly nostalgic America was waiting for a big old-time painter. By 1980, when Schnabel and his young dealer, Mary Boone, arrived on the scene, they hit the right note in the euphoric new era. The prices she lassoed for his paintings were as shocking as the pictures,

JULIAN SCHNABEL 1980

and the publicity was scandalous. And, for the first time since the fifties, gauche painting became the rage. Just as Schnabel's art returned to the aesthetics of the immediate postwar years, *CVJ* appeals to the popular conception of the unruly artist. Schnabel's account of his early days mimics stories about people like Jackson Pollack who were renowned for beery artistic arguments that frothed over into fisticuffs. His descriptions of his life at Max's Kansas City, however, depend heavily on poetic license. Unlike Pollock at the Cedar Tavern, the young Schnabel at Max's was a marginal presence; and anyway, the bar closed soon after he came to New York.

CVJ is sometimes picaresquely funny, as in its descriptions of Italian artists, critics, and curators (of the artists he writes: "They were all wearing white linen suits with Campari stains") and of habitués of the downtown clubs in New York. But the artist's tales of angst are included, it seems, just for color and tone. They don't ring true. Reflecting on a trip to Venice with his wife-to-be, he writes: "I remember sitting in Harry's in a teal-blue linen suit with a tie on that Jacqueline had bought for me that day (and she hardly knew me) and having my shirt buttoned up, feeling like I had no neck, feeling like my face was a pumpkin and wondering how she could love me." What that really means is that, pumpkin head or not, Schnabel can still land fine women and clothes and suffer in good restaurants. (Of course, he also knows the nicknames of maitre d's.)

Unsuccessful artists resemble one another, but successful ones are successful in their own way. Schnabel's account should have furnished a fuller narrative of how he cut away from the pack, but he is stubbornly vague. And by ending his story around 1981, he can avoid discussing business and therefore keep the myth of the young genius intact. Leo Castelli once lent his prestige to Schnabel and Mary Boone by exhibiting the artist, yet he remains in the shadows here. And there is no mention of the artist's departure in 1984 from the Castelli galleries, as well as from Mary Boone's. Schnabel's handling of the mass media and his reactions to the recent backlash against his work in the art world are also not discussed, nor are his rocky relationships with European critics and curators which led to his exclusion from the important Documenta exhibition in Germany in 1982 — was he victimized? Finally, he writes without context, as though he were the only thing that mattered in the art world.

CVJ will be consulted by many for its reproductions alone. Thanks to the more than a hundred pictures, a handsome document has been made out of a slim text. But, while nourishing the myths about himself, Schnabel takes pains to conceal the fascinating politics of success in the contemporary art world. It remains for a more important book to consider the contradictions of the position of the Romantic artist in New York in the eighties, and the way careers, such as Schnabel's, have been financed and sustained. Julian Schnabel, an admitted Romantic, would never write it. But then again, he probably wouldn't read it either. ●

MARY BOONE 1986

Mary Boone and Michael Werner

Manhattan, Inc. June 1986

A good man is hard to find, but Mary Boone has found her share of them – her artists, boyfriends, clients, former collaborator Leo Castelli, and her current beau, German art dealer Michael Werner. While Boone is well known to New Yorkers through magazine articles, art-world gossip, and the image-conscious antics of her gallery and its artists, Werner is still a mystery to most Manhattanites. If, in the racy international scene, Boone is considered coltish, Werner is more akin to cultish. But this great European success story has now become of more than specialized interest in New York. The German painters in his close-knit stable – Georg Baselitz, Markus Lüpertz, A.R. Penck, and Jörg Immendorff – have been among the most controversial, and best-selling, artists on the market from the beginning of the eighties right up to the recent past. Furthermore, Werner has not only charmed one of America's favorite daughters and moved his artists into her gallery, he has also announced their intention to marry later this year.

Werner, at 47, is thirteen years Boone's senior. Until 1980 he was not well known on the international scene and lived in only moderate comfort in Germany. His beginnings were humble, both as a gallery owner and as a human being: the son of an electronics engineer, he describes his background as "very narrow, very petit-bourgeois. This class is worse than the working class because the working class has a certain freedom, whereas the next higher step is really tense and very narrow. I decided at 17 to become an art dealer. It was just about doing this beautiful, great thing. The other alternative I saw then was in being a diplomat."

"For me it's been very simple," he says of his rise to the top in Germany. "I happened to be in a certain situation and just found out what the best way to work it is." And he adds confidently, "I'm sure for myself that I'm going to be able to deal with the situation in New York the same way."

Today Werner is a real force in the American art world as well as a cultural titan in Germany – just as his artists, originally termed the German Neo-Expressionists (because of their heated, gestural, and historically backward-looking, painting styles), are ensconced in both their native land and in the States as the artistic status quo. Although mid-size paintings by his artists now go for an average of $25,000 to $70,000, ten years ago there was little demand, even in Germany, for the group at all. And despite early bids by such established and important New York dealers as Ileana Sonnabend to represent them, they have entered the Boone gallery, making Boone and Werner the most commercially powerful couple on the international art circuit.

Werner's friends say that, above everything, he loves what he thinks of as real quality – good wine, good food, good cigars, and good art. "Don't tell them how good-looking Michael is," implores Boone coyly. "I don't want everybody chasing after him." But it's surely Boone who, with the combined help of her tan skin, total Chanel wardrobe, and cascading coif, is the good-looking one. She's smart, variously bullying and flattering in conversation, in possession of the most flexible vocabulary of any New York art dealer, and she oozes, quite naturally, self-assurance and success.

Boone, in short, is a hit. She has an intense, if socially preordained, sense of style that is strictly observed, extending from the biggest, bluntest items, like the paintings she sells, all the way down to the smallest details, like the points of the pencils in her gallery, which, one insider says, must be kept needle-sharp. Boone seems to be obsessively tidy. Her pens are divided in gallery pen drawers according to color – three red, three green, and three blue. And if a pen is missing, "Well, she wouldn't kill you," says one source nervously, "but ..."

Werner, on the other hand, can appear carefree and easygoing. During a New York visit he may sit around his fiancée's gallery browsing through old catalogues and waiting for her to finish up. His own gallery, on Cologne's Gertrudenstrasse, seems, compared with the Boone monument, a casual drop-in affair. His personal appearance is also a very different proposition from the neatly packaged bundle that is Boone. Werner's Savile Row suit clothes a typically formless postwar German body. He can be either attentive and charming ("You have the most beautiful eyes") or, according to certain teeth-gritting reports, tough and cynical. Whereas Boone is a commercial success story, Werner is a connoisseur, and like all connoisseurs, he is fundamentally old-fashioned. Yet despite their differences, Werner has found for his artists a wonderful medium in Boone.

A few years ago Boone was her own message. She painted an image of herself as slick and glossy as her painted toenails in the pages of *Life* magazine. Her artists – most notably Julian Schnabel – painted huge canvases as rough and shoddy as the chances of her competitors. From 1979 to 1982, the art world looked like it was Boone's oyster. Then in the fall of 1982 a remarkable thing happened. Boone met Werner at an exhibition called "Zeitgeist" in Berlin. It seemed a match made in heaven, or at least on Mount Olympus where all art-world demigods reside. And their union did not pass unnoticed. Schnabel, who was at the scene at the time, remembers: "Michael saw Mary. Mary saw Michael. They were consenting adults."

"Zeitgeist," an enormous and outrageous show of contemporary art, was, in terms of artists and works of art included, a professional coup for Boone and Werner individually. Boone describes it as "one of the most significant exhibitions of the artists who have since then come to define this generation." Since then, Boone and Werner's efforts have been a coup for them jointly. Their collaboration started in 1983 when Werner sent Mary Boone Gallery an exhibition of paintings by the early twentieth-century eclectic Francis Picabia. These were works that suddenly looked current, due to their similarity to the paintings of Sigmar Polke – a German on the fringe of the Werner stable – and of David Salle, Boone's present top dog. Following Picabia, in carefully measured increments, came the so-called Michael Werner artists. Within two years of the meeting of Boone and Werner at "Zeitgeist," Baselitz, Lüpertz, Penck, and Immendorff all found their works deposited behind Boone's glass-fronted fortress at 417 West Broadway. (In the process, other German artists Boone had already shown – Rainer Fetting, Helmut Middendorf, Walter Dahn, and Georg Dokoupil – landed comfortably in the galleries of her American rivals.) Werner is now beginning to return the favor to Boone with exhibitions in his Cologne gallery of works purchased from her artists – Salle, Jean-Michel Basquiat, and Eric Fischl.

. . . . .

The significance of Werner's German invasion extends beyond the narrow boundaries of the art market. To call Werner simply an art dealer is like saying, simply, that the international art game is about art. Werner and his group of painters are nothing less than international ambassadors for German culture. Werner appears to have marketed them, much to the acquisitive glee of nostalgic American collectors, as the heirs of the Abstract Expressionists (many of whom were born in Europe). There are those who consider Werner and his contingent a sort of mafia, inasmuch as they have been successful in shaping the way German art of the eighties has been seen by the rest of the world. Boone sees Werner's American ambitions as part of a significant cultural tendency. "No German artist after the war ever had a major museum exhibition in New York before Joseph Beuys, and that was in 1979 at the Guggenheim," she says. "This to me shows a kind of cultural aversion or suspicion or selectivity about what we're letting in, because we were showing the French, the Dutch. It was clear why it was happening. And in much the same way that Beuys opened a kind of dialogue between Germany and the rest of the world, Michael aided with the artists that followed."

Certainly by the time Werner established his first gallery, in Berlin in 1963, German horizons were cruelly limited by American "cultural imperialism," as the explosion of postwar Abstract Expressionist and Pop art came to be known. The Americans, according to Werner, "were big heroes in Germany, freeing the country with CARE packages and all that. They didn't bulldoze – they did their usual educational program. They always are very educational. I remember when I saw the first black man. It was a sensation for me. He gave me chocolate. They were like gods. That carried the whole emotion of German people; we were very much on the Americans' side. But that all has changed since Vietnam."

During a discussion around the big table in Boone's library (which is referred to as "Michael's office" when he's in town), Werner states, on behalf of all Germans, that "from our point of view there is a very strong wish to get out of the regional situation into an international situation. Anyway, maybe it's too long an explanation ..."

"No, don't say it's too long, Michael," says Boone, getting up to make a telephone call.

"Well, for the last 300 years," he begins, lighting a cigar, "the German artist had no chance to get out of the country, and it's a stigma. Even earlier, Dürer went to Italy and everyone laughed at him, more or less. The Germans only have this historical wish to get out over the border and out of their own narrow circumstance ..."

Apprenticed to Galerie Rudolf Springer in Berlin from age 17 to 22, the young Werner was eager to set up his own gallery. When sacked from Springer's, he opened a gallery with a friend, Benjamin Katz, in rented rooms directly opposite Springer's on the Kurfürstendamm, West Berlin's swish main shopping street. There they showed Georg Baselitz, who has remained with Werner (and other dealers) ever since. But despite an outlandish publicity stunt, in which Baselitz's

MICHAEL WERNER 1988

1963 exhibition at Galerie Werner & Katz was closed by police for obscenity, Werner and Katz were broke after only a few months. With Katz's uncle as the source of funds for the gallery, the locks were changed and Werner was forced out. So he set up his so-called "First Orthodox Salon" the following year, at first in a storefront and then in his apartment.

Each day at noon, Werner would fold his bed behind a screen and prepare for the rare visitor. He exhibited Baselitz, wrote manifestos and sarcastic attacks on local art critics, and, not surprisingly, still failed to make it into the black. During these years Werner learned about Markus Lüpertz, whose works he bought and eventually exhibited in 1968. (He also took a liking to Lüpertz's wife, who moved in with Werner in 1969 and married him seven years later.) But riots and "left-wing activism" in Berlin in 1968 induced Werner to move to Cologne. "Emotionally, I was involved," he maintains, "but I left because it was just too stupid." Werner opened his third gallery – his first in Cologne, the city that was to become the center of the German art world in the eighties – in 1968.

Another artist in Werner's stable was A.R. Penck, a pseudonym for Ralf Winkler, an East German painter and art-world personality. Penck remained in East Germany until 1980, by which time Werner's clever dealing had helped bring him to the verge of an international art celebrity that could no longer be administered across the Iron Curtain. "Penck was in Berlin the day the wall went up, visiting Baselitz," says Werner. "But he decided to go back home to Dresden. Now he lives in Ireland and has a studio in London."

For ten years, Penck was "managed" by Werner in a way that yielded the artist a seemingly bountiful monthly stipend. Werner had to struggle to meet these payments, but eventually he made enormous profits from Penck. Today he still pays Penck a stipend, although it is more like an advance – about $15,000 per month – with an annual amount appended to even their accounts. Unlike most American dealers, Werner likes to buy paintings outright from his artists and pay them a stipend based on a 50 per cent commission. (Boone's artists are on stipends as well.) Werner also finances and publishes *Krater & Wolke*, an expensive magazine edited by Penck as a hobby and published in an edition of 200. "The agreement is that I do not interfere and that I make no money limits." Werner adheres to this condition and yet also, admirably, keeps the venture afloat.

When he is in Germany, Werner visits his artists and friends frequently, which means driving to whichever city they live in and staying for a few days. He visits art collectors the same

way. "In Europe," he says, "most clients deal with just one dealer who builds up their collections. Because I know their taste, I know what they need. But the American dealers just hang the paintings on the walls and wait for the clients to come in and decide if they want them or not." As an example of his dedicated methods, there is the story of a collector from Kassel, a chemist named Jost Herbig, with whom Werner would jog. According to David Nolan, a former gallery assistant for Werner and now a private dealer from a showroom on lower Broadway, "Michael didn't go running because he liked running. He went running because his collector wanted to run, and he wanted this collector to buy from him. One day Herbig turned around and said to Michael, 'You know that Oldenburg I just got?' Michael said yes, he really thought it was a wonderful piece. The collector said, 'I'm going to race you, and if you beat me, you get the sculpture.' At that stage, the piece cost about DM100,000, expensive even then, and for Michael it really was a lot of money. So they had this race, and Michael was even given a head start. As he says, he has never worked so hard for anything in his life, and he sweated so much he almost killed himself, but he lost."

In 1969 Werner first exhibited a young Maoist painter from Düsseldorf, Jörg Immendorff, and four years later he enlisted a special artist who would become his great defector, Anselm Kiefer. Werner showed many other artists, but these five – Baselitz, Lüpertz, Penck, Immendorff, and Kiefer – epitomized what was to become a rather incestuous stable. Although Werner strongly denies it, some dealers say that he "ranked" his artists for promotional purposes and marketed them either as a group or as individuals to local and international museums and private collectors. Boone says, "They were all generating their art in a climate of extreme indifference for eight years, then moderate indifference for another eight years. This led to the artists and Michael becoming quite close. There was a lot of discussion, not about sales, because there was no one buying these artists, but about the content of the work and the aesthetic direction. In one sense they were working very strongly against a general trend, not just against American dealers showing American artists but also all the European dealers who were showing American artists."

Apparently Kiefer eventually came to see himself as the most important artist in Werner's stable, which may have caused friction. Whether or not Werner actually ranked the painters, an artist's position in his estimation over the years, says Nolan, "would mean that literally he would get more money per month, that Michael would push the work in a different way, that he wouldn't try to get it in with the other artists but would say, for instance, 'This is Kiefer. He's important.' And Kiefer wanted all that to change." By 1981 Kiefer had left Werner's gallery.

Kiefer is now the hottest-selling German artist anywhere. With a long waiting list for his work at Marian Goodman Gallery on 57th Street, he needs to make only a few paintings a year. "I was painting when people didn't want painting – when Conceptual art was the thing," he said in his studio in Germany's Oden Forest earlier this year. "Now they want paintings and they can't have them."

"I sort of made Kiefer leave the gallery," claims Werner, "by constantly criticizing him. I didn't want him to leave. It's just that I went really hard on him to make him change his direction. I believe that his work is not about painting anymore, and he is doing an 'idea art.' The big things about American art in general," Werner theorizes, "are enlargement and emptying-out. This is what American painterly culture is about. It is enlargement and emptying-out, and since Kiefer is involved with America he is doing exactly this. Now it makes no difference where he shows or what he shows. The thing is just set. Nobody is even interested anymore in how it looks."

In 1980 Kiefer and Baselitz represented Germany at the Venice Biennale. A year later "A New Spirit in Painting" in London's Royal Academy also put Kiefer in the spotlight, and Documenta 7 in Kassel in 1982 was his crowning achievement. American dealers had already begun to swarm around the Michael Werner artists – and Kiefer. Boone recalls that "there was an incredible push to show any or all of these artists." Werner already had worked with galleries throughout Europe – Nancy Gillespie in Paris, Galerie Maeght in Zurich, Leslie Waddington and Anthony d'Offay in London – but he was looking for the right outlet in New York.

In 1981 Ileana Sonnabend made the trek to London, along with hundreds of others, to see "A New Spirit in Painting." "There I met Baselitz and Hans Neuendorf, whose gallery in Hamburg was also dealing Baselitz, and I declared my interest," she recounts. The next day Neuendorf and Werner turned up at her hotel, the Westbury, to discuss the possibilities of a New York show. At that time the outcome was negative, but eventually Sonnabend got Baselitz, as did Xavier Fourcade. That happened because, Sonnabend says, "Xavier Fourcade was also in that hotel. He'd also seen that show. We had both been interested in the works since the Venice Biennale."

Fourcade says he did all of his dealings with Baselitz through Neuendorf. He says he bought the paintings he showed and was never forced to take any work that he didn't want. Werner

tells a rather different story: "I thought I should find not only a traditional dealer but someone who was involved with some big names, at least, because I took Baselitz extremely seriously. So I went to Xavier Fourcade because he was involved with traditional art dealing with big names. He told me he was involved with the Arshile Gorky estate, the Barnett Newman estate – glamorous things – and de Kooning. That's enough already, right? So we set up that he will do a show. Ileana was a little upset – but she is a great person."

Fourcade promptly sold two large paintings by Baselitz to the Tate Gallery in London and the Pompidou Center in Paris for more than $60,000 and $40,000 respectively, which, he says, "made Baselitz very happy. I got his work out of Germany, which nobody else had been able to do." Baselitz had, of course, already been gotten out of Germany, exhibiting in solo and group shows, but by 1981 the hunger for his paintings had become rife.

For her part, Boone began to think about showing Baselitz, Kiefer, and Sigmar Polke as early as 1979 – "that's when I first went to Germany. But I thought it would be impossible. I was a small gallery then. I had a very modest space. I was about 28 years old and didn't know Michael Werner. The idea of being so audacious as to go up to him and ask him to show such important artists seemed absolutely like I must be nuts!"

Boone had met Werner once before "Zeitgeist," in January 1981, at the German exhibition in the Musée d'Art Moderne de la ville de Paris. She was introduced to him there by a friend, Barbara Jakobson, the same gregarious woman who had earlier introduced Boone to Leo Castelli. Castelli's subsequent interest in Julian Schnabel, of course, helped establish Boone's place on the art map. "Leo and I bridged generations," she quips, "whereas Michael and I bridge miles. I thought Michael was great-looking. I already knew what a great dealer he was. The first thing I remember thinking about him was that I was shocked he was so young. I expected him to be Leo's age. You know, I expected an old stately gentleman." Werner remembers their meeting in Paris as a slow start. "Barbara Jakobson introduced me to her and I said, 'Hi, nice to meet you,' but I was very nervous and upset because I had all kinds of problems with the show."

. . . . .

About two years later, in October 1982, it was "Zeitgeist" (literally the spirit of the times), the brassy Neo-Expressionist exhibition in Berlin – another triumph for Werner and a good show for Boone's artists David Salle and Julian Schnabel –

that finally brought Boone and Werner together. The painter Sigmar Polke threw them into a taxi after the opening of the show. "We were all kind of in a big bunch," says Boone. "It was Helen van der Meij and Kiefer and I, because that fall I was doing a big Kiefer show, and by this time he and Michael are friendly again, at least superficially friendly. And it was Julian and David, who were still friendly then too, and Markus Lüpertz and Georg Baselitz and Sigmar. We were all kind of together, and then all divided up into cabs to go to the various things, because it was a whole four-day period of openings and parties. It was Sigmar who grabbed us both, and it was then that we really started talking."

Shortly after "Zeitgeist" Boone opened a Kiefer exhibition at her gallery. Knowing what she stood to gain from the artist's burgeoning reputation, she had entered the race against two other galleries — Sonnabend's and Marian Goodman's — that had an equal interest in Kiefer. Sonnabend was beaten to the post by Boone — she says she thought they were planning a simultaneous two-gallery exhibition. Goodman refuses to comment on Boone's show.

One persistent, and quite baffling, rumor has it that Boone had difficulty getting enough works by Kiefer to make up an entire exhibition. The story is that Boone went to Charles and Doris Saatchi, Britain's preeminent collectors of contemporary art, for help in filling out what would otherwise have been a rather empty gallery. To date, the Saatchis own 23 Kiefers, and they intend to continue to collect his paintings. They supposedly lent five of them to Boone.

Charles Saatchi says he can't remember if he lent Boone any paintings, although his curator, Julia Ernst, says that five of the seven paintings in Boone's exhibition "went from London to New York." But Ernst, who did not work for Saatchi at the time of Boone's exhibition, adds that "only Helen van der Meij knows how many of those came from Saatchi." Van der Meij and Kiefer both say that some of the works in Boone's show were from the Saatchi collection, and Kiefer says that only two paintings were for sale.

Boone denies that she borrowed any paintings from Saatchi. "That's a rumor that was started at the time of the show," she says. "I heard it too." And indeed, it is impossible to reconcile the assertion that Boone had only two works for sale with her records, which indicate that she sold four: one now hangs in the Virginia Museum; one is in the Stedelijk Museum in Amsterdam; one went to Asher Edelman and Adrian Mnuchin; and one was traded with Julian Schnabel. Moreover, only one of the paintings in Boone's show appears in the catalogue of the

Saatchi collection, and that picture was purchased after her exhibition.

Of course, the real point to be made about Boone's Kiefer exhibition is that it proved that she could present the top European artist at the pinnacle of his fame. The show opened at the Mary Boone Gallery in November 1982, immediately after Werner's and Boone's careers collided at "Zeitgeist" but before they started collaborating. Although Goodman remained Kiefer's U.S. dealer, Boone's was the most talked-about gallery in town during the Kiefer show. And much of the talk was about Werner — what was his relationship with Boone?

Ileana Sonnabend had once been in a situation similar to Boone's. She had been married to Castelli, and for many years afterward continued to work with him, although her gallery maintained a more pronounced European inflection. As a decades-old bridge between contemporary European and American art, Sonnabend arguably knows more about working with foreign dealers than anyone in New York. By 1983 she was representing Baselitz (whose 1963 show at Werner's Berlin gallery she saw the day before the police raided it), Penck, and Immendorff. On the subject of Werner, she cautions that "although Michael thinks he is more powerful than he actually is, he is forceful, he is stubborn, he is ruthless."

In any negotiations with an American gallery, adds Antonio Homem, Sonnabend's gallery director, "Werner proceeds from the point of view that you are a lost cause. His idea is that he doesn't give you what you want, if he can help it. You get what he wants you to get."

"Michael underestimates the American art scene," rejoins Sonnabend. "You know, he sees Americans as just people who drink bad coffee and are gullible, like children. He is a great manipulator, and so is Mary Boone. It is difficult in this case to know just who is manipulating whom."

Actually, the pair's gains seem to be reciprocal. Werner landed an American showcase for his stable, but with Werner, Mary Boone Gallery purchased a new lease on life, and though neither formal partners nor spouses, Boone and Werner became a formidable pair — an eighties version of the famous Castelli-Sonnabend alliance.

Seven months after Boone's Kiefer show, in 1983, came "Expressions," a large exhibition that toured the United States and that was in many people's minds the first and last word in "New Art from Germany," as it was subtitled. "Expressions" presented the works of only five Germans — Baselitz, Immendorff, Kiefer, Lüpertz, and Penck — and its catalogue offered, "Unless otherwise noted, the illustrated works ... are courtesy of, or property of, Galerie Michael Werner, Cologne."

Kiefer says he was reluctant to be included in the exhibition with Werner's other artists and was "tricked" into it with works borrowed in most cases from private and museum collections. But the exhibition, one dealer remarked, "could not have been done without Kiefer, because everyone knew about his stature at that point." As for Werner, "Expressions" and his new arrangement with Boone were the twin trumpets that heralded his arrival in the U.S.A. He prepared to reclaim his artists from the American galleries that had so profitably nursed them during the boom in German art that had begun three years earlier.

Sonnabend lost Baselitz, Penck, and Immendorff all at once. "I was heartbroken," she says. "In any case, Michael had a very perverse attitude about success. He explained to me that we were doing too well for these artists. First of all, we were selling too much. Secondly, he said we were selling on a misunderstanding, because no one could understand these artists, so if people liked them it must be because people misunderstood them. Mary and Michael took me out to lunch and told me they were grateful for the work I had done and that we should all work together. They said that they wouldn't want to take the artists away, and the next thing I knew was that there was an Immendorff show at Mary Boone across the street, so I didn't feel too good about that. I felt pushed out."

Werner went to lunch with Fourcade too, to Mortimer's. "It was a discussion among businessmen," Werner says. "I told him — I'm not orthodox in this sense. I'm willing to work with you on an *equal level*. So you can continue to show Baselitz if you let me participate in de Kooning. I hadn't asked Mary if she was interested in de Kooning, but I thought she would be. (*laughs*)" Fourcade recalls the meeting this way: "He said that if I wanted to have Baselitz then I should give him de Kooning. But it was more than de Kooning. He also wanted John Chamberlain and Malcolm Morley. I told him to go to hell."

The next notable episode in the Boone-Werner alliance takes place at the 1985 Paris Biennale. It's a double whammy involving both Boone and Werner and the work of an American artist they have both exhibited, David Salle. By this time Salle has finally exhibited in Werner's gallery in Cologne, in a show of works that were handpicked and purchased in advance by Werner over the last two years and that were for sale at high American prices, like the one that went to the Carnegie Institute in Pittsburgh for a handsome $75,000. Many of Werner's friends call him a "traitor" for showing a famous American artist — "about 70 per cent of my audience told me

that," Werner estimates. But Salle is one American about whom Werner and Boone both feel very strongly, and they don't care who knows it.

"In the last ten years," Werner says, "the power of the dealer has diminished in a great way. The artists are much more powerful. They do the politics, more or less — that is, the artists who are in the game, the ones on top. Today the famous artists distribute their paintings strategically." The dealers have to show the artist that they care, as did Boone when she donated $300,000 to the Brooklyn Academy of Music toward the cost of mounting *The Birth of the Poet*, for which Salle was scenery designer. Or they try to make sure their artists have prime locations in important exhibitions. In Paris, both Boone and Werner felt that the Americans, Salle in particular, were given low priority, and this, according to one observer, is what they did about it.

It's two days before the opening of the Biennale when Boone flies in to Paris. She is visibly disturbed. The worry is that Salle has been betrayed, that his paintings are stuck in a second-rate space. With the help of Werner, who hopes he can influence the curators, Boone thinks the disaster can be averted. It is Werner who hits on a solution: "Immendorff, Immendorff" — their cries fill the Paris air. The proposed solution is to reinstall Salle's paintings, to put them with Immendorff's works in the latter's large open space on the ground floor. Immendorff is contacted and doesn't raise any objections. But the Biennale curators — one German, one Italian, one American, and the arrogant French — take a vote and decide not to budge. The Salles will stay put.

The next day a story begins to spread. Late the night before, a Biennale official was awakened by an urgent phone call — the persistent couple still wanted to rearrange works in the exhibition.

Boone says they did try to get the paintings reinstalled. "Michael, you can tell the story."

"I don't know what Mary did, but I talked to the curators," begins Werner. "It was not just a bad space for David. It was like he was just stored away. I don't know what happened. The whole thing kind of escalated."

Did they try to move the paintings?

"You mean touch the paintings? No ... but we were really mad because they played around with us for two days. [Then] it was finished. We just dropped the issue and went back to our hotel."

On the telephone twelve hours later, Boone adds that, with one of Baselitz's assistants, she did return to the exhibition hall the night before the press opening. But, she says, they only wanted to hang the Salles, not move them.

The buzz about their efforts on behalf of Salle is typical of the sort of talk that seems to attach itself to Werner and Boone. Perhaps this is unavoidable, given their obsessive devotion to their stables and Werner's well-recognized clout, both cultural and commercial. At the "German Art in the 20th Century" show at London's Royal Academy last October, at least one observer suggested, albeit obliquely, that Werner's heavy hand had influenced the exhibition. *Time* magazine's art critic, Robert Hughes, wrote in a review of the exhibition that "it is not hard to suspect that art-market pressures have been playing on the curators, since nearly all the recent artists in the show ... are in the stable of one German dealer, Michael Werner." To be sure, the exhibition did show off Werner's group and upset Kiefer, who was represented with only three, early, works. Yet Werner was not happy either. "It throws me back three years, by creating an aggressive 'anti' situation of my clients toward my artists. They have 35 Beckmanns in it. The Beckmanns, in square centimeters, are half of what Baselitz had there. The exhibition is very bad for me. And if this guy Hughes [suggests] I manipulated, this is ridiculous. The organizers are so vain, they wouldn't even talk to me. The only one who came out great was Kiefer, because everybody was asking, 'Why are there only three paintings?'" Moreover, as exhibition co-organizer Norman Rosenthal, who was *also* one of the organizers of both "Zeitgeist" and "A New Spirit in Painting," swears, "I'm not pressurable by anybody. Actually, Michael Werner didn't like the show very much. He said it was positively dangerous. He is genuinely melancholic."

Now that Werner has chosen to wed himself to the American market, New Yorkers will no doubt form their own opinions of the enigmatic dealer. Some will side with those colleagues who see him as a crusader, others with those who call him an impresario, an engineer of artistic careers, a cultural inseminator, and even a trainer of sorts. In the end, all of that is only to say that behind Michael Werner, as behind any successful breeder, stands not just a good woman but an entire thoroughbred stable. ●

David Salle

THE NEW YORK TIMES MAGAZINE JANUARY 1987

David Salle's loft in the TriBeCa area of Manhattan is divided into two: his work studio is downstairs; his living quarters upstairs. His studio, where he spends most of his time, is sparse and industrial-looking, whereas one floor above, everything is bright and jazzy. His paintings are usually also in two distinct parts – left and right, top and bottom and, recently, outside and inside – with one of the panels set inside another. Salle's name is pronounced with two syllables, as in the name Sally. And when he talks, he can't help faulting his own argument; he says he always sees both sides.

He describes his upstairs loft equivocally. Renovated by architect Christian Hubert, it is elegant, with a touch of the fifties about it. "You could say that it's a low-ceilinged, lightless room that feels rather claustrophobic," he says. "You could say it's a space with some architectural distinction and is quite sculptural. You could say that it's just another downtown loft space wanting to be a civilized house."

"It looks like the loft of someone who made his money fast," quips Robert Mapplethorpe, who photographed it recently for an interior design magazine. An impoverished young artist when he arrived in New York eleven years ago, Salle has risen to the top of his profession within a remarkably short period of time. His paintings now fetch as much as $85,000. He makes about twenty of them a year and they are sold by two of the city's best-known art dealers, Mary Boone and Leo Castelli.

The work of this 34-year-old artist is included in the collections of London's Tate Gallery, the Pompidou Center in Paris, the Museum of Contemporary Art in Los Angeles, and New York's Whitney Museum of American Art and the Museum of Modern Art. Next Saturday, a survey of Salle's paintings from 1979 to 1986 will open at the Whitney and continue through March 29. With this exhibition (which is a more extensive version of the one that recently ended at the Institute of Contemporary Art, University of Pennsylvania), Salle follows in the footsteps of many other American artists who have been similarly honored, including Andy Warhol and Jasper Johns.

For the last two years, half of Salle's efforts have been spent designing sets and costumes for his friend, the choreographer Karole Armitage. His designs – bearing the disjunctive stamp of his paintings – have appeared in Armitage's *The Mollino Room* for the American Ballet Theater, and in a dance work they created, *The Elizabethan Phrasing of the Late Albert Ayler*, which will be performed at the Brooklyn Academy of Music later this year.

Salle's paintings are notoriously complex and erotically charged. In many works, a figure and an interior, or a portrait and a landscape, are enigmatically layered atop one another. He "quotes" liberally from existing imagery, from Brassaï's photographic nudes to spunky dancing crocodiles to Géricault's paintings of human cadavers, and actually incorporates objects, such as coffee tables with their tops punched out. Salle's imagery is variously brooding and lighthearted; the colors, lurid and melancholy – dirty yellows, envious greens, and brothel reds.

Often conjuring up feelings of longing and alienation in the viewer, Salle's pictures are reminiscent of the paintings of the Pop artist James Rosenquist and sometimes of the later work of the French painter Francis Picabia. "But," says the art critic Clement Greenberg, "Salle's paintings are like those of his forebears only insofar as the way they are put together. They're not pressured; they're put together meretriciously."

Salle's supporters, however, include quite a few in the art and design worlds. For many, his offbeat combinations of painting and sculpture, drawing and photography – laced with humor and irony – hit the mark. "He has taught me a new way of looking at a picture," says the architect Philip Johnson. "Salle is my favorite among the young ones because of the mastery with which he handles his abrupt content. I like the violent contrasts and the ways the continuity is broken, though what they signify – I don't know."

Over the last few years, Salle's consistently high performance has won over many critics. When John Russell, chief art critic of *The New York Times*, saw Salle's paintings four years ago, they "seemed dingy, incoherent, and absurdly pretentious. I liked them even less because they were spread all over two of the best galleries in town." But, he continues, "I came to see that aggregation need not spell aggravation, and that by working with impacted idioms and apparently incompatible images, Salle was able to maneuver fast and freely where others would have struggled to find 'a coherent voice.'"

David Salle stands 5 feet 8 inches tall, is wiry and muscular (a weight trainer goes to his loft to supervise his workouts) and his clothes are well-tailored. His gaze is direct, intense; wide saucer ears tremble like antennae as he talks, and one listens. He likes to theorize about his art, but his speech, like his paintings, is laden with non sequiturs and neologisms.

His interest in art began when he was growing up in Wichita, Kansas, and at age 18 he headed for the newly founded California Institute of the Arts (Cal Arts) in Valencia, near Los Angeles. There, he shared a studio with fellow painter Eric Fischl, and one of his teachers was the artist John Baldessari, who recalls the "incredible batch of students at that time." He says: "David was certainly one of the best. He had an inquiring personality and omnivorous appetite for information about art. He was very shy, but one was aware that he was always watching you — your every move, your every action."

When Salle ventured into New York in 1975, during the city's financial crisis, he was 22. By the following year, he was forced to declare himself bankrupt. And in 1979 be married, only to separate shortly thereafter. He recalls: "When I came to New York, it was dead and on the verge of bankruptcy. There was not just a lack of money, but also a lack of spiritual resolve."

During those first years in New York, he was just one more artist in a crowd of smart young artists, many from California. They colonized TriBeCa because SoHo was already filled to brimming with countercultural, Minimalist, and Conceptual artists, and set up their own scene. It was then that Salle first saw the self-consciously New Wave dances of Karole Armitage.

A hallmark of New York's New Wave was the generous "quoting" from past styles, and this distinguished all the arts. New Wave music, fashion, and art shared a willingness to re-use. In particular, Salle discovered the B-grade sensibility, or film noir. Because the heyday of the New York School — which included artists from Jackson Pollock to Bruce Nauman and spanned the forties through the early seventies — was over, Salle's work was inspired by other cultural forms, such as "the movies of Douglas Sirk and, to a lesser extent, of Sam Fuller and Fassbinder," he says.

The quoting from past styles and popular culture is known, in the argot of the art world, as appropriation. It's an age-old tradition for artists to lift images from the works of their forebears — or from non-art sources. "Manet painted a number of conspicuously corny pickups of earlier art," notes Nan Rosenthal,

a curator of twentieth-century art at Washington's National Gallery. "Conceptually, in his approach to painting, Salle is a collagist. He quotes a set of disparate images and layers them — creating both attention to surface and illusions of depth."

Like his Cal Arts teacher John Baldessari, Salle juxtaposes already existing images to create new meanings — but the comparison ends there. Even in his paintings and in the photographs he took at Cal Arts, Salle's coupling of text and images appears strikingly unorthodox. Salle also experimented with video art and published limited editions of small illustrated books.

Two paste-up jobs in the art departments of magazines — first in Wichita and later in New York — were a curiously appropriate training for Salle, and many of his graphic female nudes were "appropriated" from a pornographic magazine called *Stag*, for which he worked in 1976 and 1977. Salle plays down the work experience: "I was a very bad layout artist and I never tried to get good at it."

The gridded plan of a magazine page, however, is something that is shared with his paintings, just as the split format of his pictures resembles the double-page spread. The various elements in Salle's pictures — say, a black-and-white figure, an inset landscape, a stained color, even text — are spatially arranged on a blank field, as in magazine design.

Salle's own depictions of women since that time have rarely curried favor with those in the art world who see in his work a traditional, sexist dichotomy of the woman as fetish and the man as voyeur. Others, such as Philip Johnson, contend that "sex should be in pictures — why not? That slight tumescence that you feel sometimes is part of seeing."

Sherrie Levine, an artist and a feminist, thinks that the issue is more complicated: "David was a very good friend and it was always interesting to me that he was capable of being friends with women, unlike many other artists, many other men. Especially in his early work, where there are images of women smoking — looking contemplative and contemplatively — I had the idea that they were pictures of a man looking at a woman looking at a man. And I thought that was pretty interesting, because I've always seen the self-portraits of Cindy Sherman as pictures of a woman looking at a man looking at a woman. His are pictures that posit a man's consciousness in relation to a woman's consciousness."

In terms of art history, Salle's nudes are no more explicit than Courbet's or the Surrealists'. Furthermore, he rejects the whole idea of an artist's responsibility to the morals of his audience: "One of the reasons that one makes art is because

DAVID SALLE 1991

one is dissatisfied with the prevailing ways of naming and describing. Making art is not making policy, and there's not necessarily a congruity between them."

. . . . .

By 1979, figurative painting was looming everywhere one looked, and Salle's idiosyncratic pictures piqued interest — at the same time that they scandalized. No one knew what to make of them. During her first few visits to Salle's studio, Mary Boone was "pretty shocked," she recalls. "The pictures were a combination of strange, comical, awkward, and unwieldy. The most flattering thing I can say is that they were unexpected. This is a man who has all the underpinnings of Conceptualism and was making paintings of nude girls!"

Leo Castelli, who first saw Salle's work at a client's home, "didn't understand the use of props in his paintings, like chairs and tables. I thought of Rauschenberg and was puzzled."

Today, Boone and Castelli are both devoted enthusiasts. "I love his work," says Boone. "It's my lifeblood. It's changed my life. It's been absorbed into my whole being."

Salle held a sell-out exhibition in the loft of two private art dealers on West Broadway in 1979. The show's success freed him from debt (although he was not legally solvent until 1983) and it allowed him to quit his part-time jobs. Other than working as a paste-up artist, he was, at various times, a teacher at the Hartford Art School in Connecticut, a restaurant cook (with Julian Schnabel, his friend and fellow artist) and a reviewer of exhibitions.

Soon after the 1979 show, Boone, who had opened her gallery almost two years earlier, invited Salle to join her. Salle accepted and waited for more than a year for his first exhibition. In the meantime, Julian Schnabel — the Muhammad Ali of the art world who fearlessly proclaimed himself "The Greatest" — was bursting on the art scene. Schnabel was also represented by Boone, and the two quickly became the most talked-about artist-dealer pair in memory.

Many, like David Whitney, curator of Salle's exhibition at the Whitney Museum, were totally put off. "I was very confused by all the PR, so I wasn't aware of David's work for a very long time," he recalls. "I think the publicity about Mary and Julian was immensely harmful to begin with, and Mary still has her detractors because of it."

Salle himself recognized an artist's need to stand apart in a crowd. Helene Winer, the first to exhibit Salle's art in New York (in the nonprofit Artists Space in 1976), saw that in many ways "David was ahead of the others. He was aware of public

exposure. His studio was always tidy, he invited people over and always had something to say about his art — and writing reviews became a quick way to become separate from the mob and to be invited places." She maintains that "if artists deny that they're interested in how the system works, they're either going to have to find someone else to take care of them, or they're going to fail."

Salle's own reactions to the publicity surrounding Schnabel and Boone were mixed. "I had two feelings about it," he recalls. "On one level, the media spectacle was disgusting. On another level, I thought it was just fine, because everyone is always curious about the new kid on the block."

In 1980, he and Schnabel arranged to exchange paintings. Salle gave Schnabel a typical diptych titled *Daemonization*. Then one day Schnabel phoned Salle, asking him over. He sat Salle down in one of two chairs facing a white sheet; he was going to unveil the painting he had made in exchange.

Although the two artists had always approached painting with the belief that nothing was necessarily out of bounds, Schnabel was nervous, Salle recalls, and on drawing aside the sheet said, "I've done something that will join us together in art history!" It was the same painting that Salle had given him, with the panels reversed, and a dour portrait of Salle himself superimposed on the left. Later, the painting, retitled *Jump*, was sold jointly for $16,000 (midway between the 1980 market value of the two artists' work).

Like other details of their friendship, their eventual falling-out also became news. "Julian and David split up because Julian was under the impression that David was stealing imagery from him, and he made this quite clear publicly," says Ross Bleckner, a mutual friend who also studied at Cal Arts. "David just got tired of trying to maintain his good feelings." (Now, however, Schnabel is silent on the subject. And, in retrospect, the differences in their works can be seen to outweigh their similarities.)

Before his first show, Salle's paintings were priced between $1,000 and $2,000; by 1981, they ranged from $3,500 to $6,000. In March 1982, Boone swung a two-gallery show for Salle: at Leo Castelli's and at her gallery simultaneously, a ploy that had previously been successful for Schnabel. The Salle show was a hit. "This show," wrote Peter Schjeldahl, the art critic, "would be an Event if catered with a box of Chiclets and held in a subway toilet." Salle's two-gallery exhibition was only his second with Boone, although the top price for a large painting was already as high as $20,000. In alternative years, Salle began showing at the two galleries, across the street from each other on SoHo's West Broadway.

In 1984, the price range for a David Salle was between $25,000 and $35,000, but it quickly became clear to Boone that the secondary market – the prices reached for resale of his paintings – was becoming, as she says, "outlandishly disparate with the primary market."

One painting in Salle's 1985 exhibition, titled *The Bigger Credenza* (which will be in the Whitney show), is what Boone calls a "difficult" painting. It is big, with a monochrome recumbent nude in the right panel, and a handful of ropy blobs, like spilled cream, on the left. Its retail price was set at $45,000. Boone sold it to the Texas Gallery in Houston, with the conventional dealer's discount, for $33,750, believing that the Texas Gallery was trying to place the work in the collection of Dominique de Menil. The following year, through the Manhattan gallery of Luhring, Augustine and Hodes, the Texas Gallery sold the painting to a young New York businessman who was willing to pay $80,000. By the end of the transactions, the middlemen took in $46,250; Boone got $13,500, and Salle was paid a little over $20,000.

. . . . .

Not everyone is happy with the direction art is headed in nowadays, especially when seen in the work of practitioners like Salle.

"The art world suffers from demoralized taste in general," says the critic Clement Greenberg. "People don't trust their own reactions anymore, so they go by extraneous factors, like trends and publicity. You have to go back in time to the early sixties, when the so-called far-out in taste triumphed. No one wanted to miss out on the next Pollock or Cézanne or Manet, so Pop art and now Salle and Schnabel and the Italians and the Germans come along, and everyone's intimidated about missing out."

There are few modern artists who cannot be dubbed Salle's predecessors: from Rauschenberg to Jasper Johns, from Picabia to James Rosenquist. In fact, Salle uses the imagery of older artists so extensively that in some ways his pictures are a catalogue of modernist art motifs. And like many of the Pop artists who preceded him, including Rauschenberg and Warhol, Salle has been sued for appropriating images. (For his use of a picture of flowers from *Modern Photography* magazine, Warhol, for example, paid out royalties and art works worth more than $50,000.)

In the summer of 1984, Mike Cockrell and Judge Hughes, two Brooklyn artists, observed that David Salle had appropriated one of their drawings in his large canvas titled *What Is the Reason for Your Visit to Germany?*. They brought suit for copyright infringement while the work – which had been sold to the German chocolate magnate Peter Ludwig and which will be in the Whitney show – was on display at the Leo Castelli Gallery.

The image in question was already widely known. Cockrell and Hughes had made a drawing from Robert H. Jackson's Pulitzer Prize-winning photograph of the shooting of Lee Harvey Oswald, and Salle considered it public property. "I didn't think about it," he says. "I just did it, as they say, in the heat of creative passion. I just wanted that image for my painting." Cockrell and Hughes, who were about to have their own exhibition, won a $2,000 out-of-court settlement (Castelli and Salle each paid half).

Roy Lichtenstein, earlier an idol of Salle's, now a fan, believes that Rauschenberg, and Salle after him, "quoted from the past, from Titian and newspapers, because each has a different meaning, and when you put them together they kind of talk to one another. In Salle's work, the quotations set up a kind of vibration. He was the first to use blatantly different styles. The interesting thing is his use of inconsistent styles in the same way you might have contrasts in color and texture. Of course, this could have made for very bad art, but he does it so that it looks exactly right in the paintings."

Salle casts the difference between his work and that of his forebears in the postmodernist new-wine-in-old-bottles light. "There is nothing technically ground-breaking in my work at all," he says matter-of-factly. "But while technically it might not be innovative, it looks and feels different."

Salle, like Rauschenberg, uses many different media, but there's no mistaking the two. Rauschenberg's paintings are joyous and take on the whole world; Salle's are moody and introverted. Indeed, if the bottles are Rauschenberg's, the contents evoke Jasper Johns.

Like those of Johns, Salle's pictures have something deadly and awesome about them. Johns added a new dimension to modern painting – a dimension of brick-wall superficiality. In his paintings of the fifties and sixties, he pulled down a blind between the artist and the viewer, and then painted flat images, like flags and targets, on that blind. The world of both artists is out of view, only occasionally peering through like light through a tear in the curtain, or in readymade imagery presented as surrogates for the artists' own feelings.

. . . . .

Salle is becoming more reclusive as he spends longer hours working. He paints with the door shut on his two assistants every day till at least 9PM, walks down the street to dine and then reads till early morning (presently, he is reading Edmund Wilson's diaries, *The Fifties*).

"Everyone changes when they become successful," says the artist Ross Bleckner. "David's become more insular. He always exhibited a certain edge that came from his fear that people didn't like his work. When you become successful, you lose that fear." But Salle's paintings are becoming more ambitious. If his choice of imagery is any measure, he is thinking more of the greats in art history — about the old and modern masters — and less about the cheap, about pornography. Yet he retains the ability to pluck hidden gems from the neglected mineshafts of culture, especially of the fifties.

"When people refer to the fifties aspect in my work," he reflects, "perhaps they're thinking in terms of the mass-produced aspect of the culture, like boomerang tables. But when I think about the fifties, I think of Balanchine's abstract ballets, of great abstract paintings, of humanely innovative architecture, of improvisational comedy, and of *Lolita*."

In one way or another, all these elements are found in his new paintings and theater collaboration, as if by quoting the past he can invoke it. In an era when almost anything goes, it would seem that the role of artists like Salle is no longer to invent but to synthesize. His paintings are the most potent fusion of discord, wit, and drama. ●

Anselm Keifer

The New York Times Magazine OCTOBER 1988

Anselm Kiefer's paintings are big, thickly painted, operatic. Many of the unreal, nightmarish landscapes are so vast, in fact, that viewing them is like entering a theater. From a distance, they resemble stage sets. Up close, the "vistas" turn out to be churned paint, burned straw and molten lead, the surfaces stained with what looks like blood and strewn with hand-written German words. It is only after all this has been deciphered that their full impact is felt. These are paintings of apocalypse and redemption.

The West German artist is often criticized in his own country for exhuming history's painful memories. Unblinking studies of the terrors both of the present and past — nuclear destruction, the Holocaust, war in Europe, Fascism — his paintings provoke and even horrify. Many of their subjects have been out of bounds for artists since they were used for propaganda by the Nazis, and some of his vast architectural spaces are modeled on Albert Speer's actual Nazi designs. Kiefer, it seems, wants some of their power.

Megalomania is another of his dominant themes, and he portrays, without passing judgment, such tyrants as Nero and Hitler as the heroes they were in their own time. "I do not identify with Nero or Hitler," the artist says. "But I have to reenact what they did just a little bit in order to understand the madness."

In these days of *Historikerstreit* — the shocking German debate about whether Hitler's Reich was worse than other European dictatorships of his day — Kiefer's art has a special resonance. Sympathy for his subject matter has become widespread, especially among younger Europeans disenchanted with Europe's role as the battleground for the superpowers. Two years ago, a survey of Kiefer's art opened at the Stedelijk Museum in Amsterdam to capacity crowds. The attendance (112,000 people in less than seven weeks) was about three times that of the museum's other shows of contemporary artists.

Although he rode the Neo-Expressionist wave into the United States, Kiefer's art is neither figurative nor self-expressive. He is not even strictly a painter. His works synthesize photography, painting and linguistic devices, and so are closest to the art of pastiche. It is a process that imitates the "alchemic" fusion of chemicals, light, and paper that makes a photographic image.

The art critic Roberta Smith observed in 1982 that the "emphasis on history and the land itself — its very materials — takes Kiefer's art outside painting, both emotionally and in terms of recent art." His unconventional materials, she wrote, "evoke early seventies non-painting: Conceptual, Process, Earth art — strategies that wrenched art out of its usual context and attempted to give it new meaning."

These days, of course, Kiefer is known not so much for the unconventionality of his painting materials as for his Garboesque avoidance of the press and for his iron control over the distribution and exhibition of his work. As though distinguishing an actor from his role in a play, he insists that the lives of artists should not be mistaken for the content of their art. So he is reluctant to pose for photographs or to give interviews. In the post-Pop era, this strategy adds to his mystique.

"You know, I don't allow myself to be photographed because that kind of genius behavior really is nineteenth-century," he says. "It was then that the bourgeoisie needed heroes. The Industrial Revolution meant that ordinary people could do everything, that they could be omnipotent, so they invented geniuses. I don't think I'm so important."

Even as more and more contemporary artists resign themselves to the manipulation of art by dealers and entrepreneurs, Kiefer goes to great lengths to maintain control of his work. He has retained the right to sell from his own studio, and only a select number of galleries in Europe and the Marian Goodman Gallery in New York are permitted to show his work. When his large paintings do appear in a gallery, he has a say as to who can buy them. Kiefer refuses to sell to corporations and speculators, as well as to anyone whose interest is exclusively financial or propagandistic.

Today, Anselm Kiefer is probably the most sought-after contemporary artist in the world. He is also one of the wealthiest. Last year, *Germany's Spiritual Heroes*, which was denounced for its subject matter when it was first shown at the Venice Biennale in 1980, changed hands in the United States for almost $1 million.

Since last December, Americans have been able to see a major retrospective of Kiefer's paintings, photographs and hand-made books, which are as big as Gutenberg Bibles. Organized by the Art Institute of Chicago and the Philadelphia Museum of Art, the exhibition has made stops in Chicago and Philadelphia, and arrives today at New York's Museum of Modern Art. The show can be seen through January 3, 1989.

. . . . .

Visitors to Kiefer's studio in Buchen, a remote town in West Germany's Oden Forest, must drive for two hours from Frankfurt along a narrow country road. If they travel by rail, they must change trains from town to town until the train to Buchen arrives on a single-carriage track. In Buchen, one of Kiefer's young studio assistants leads the way through muddy, industrial streets and then past the electronically controlled security gates to the artist's "factory," which houses his paintings, a photography laboratory and a metal foundry.

Very few people are allowed into the studio. Some art dealers make it, but most art critics and journalists have no luck. I met Kiefer and his wife, Julia, by chance in a Pittsburgh hotel lobby in 1985. I had just published an article on him in my journal, *Art & Text*, and I happened to have a copy of it with me. Over gin and a cigar, he read the article and subsequently invited me to visit his studio, which I did the following winter. I have talked with him several times since.

When I visited him, his work clothes were too big for him, but the smile fit. Resembling a German student of the 1960s, the tall, balding man in wire-rimmed glasses made the surprising comment that his favorite artist was Andy Warhol.

"Andy Warhol was doing perhaps the same thing as I'm doing," he said later, after Warhol's death, "but his medium was the surface. He was so extremely superficial that he was saying there is something behind it. I can see that he was looking into the depths, like me."

Although his paintings have much of the *Sturm und Drang* of archetypal German art, Kiefer does not consider himself a nationalistic artist. Contending that nations as we know them have become obsolete, he said, "In the past, there were a lot of wars between towns. After that there were wars between nations, and after that, war is no longer necessary.

"This is a time of velocity, you cannot protect yourself from other people. The most important thing to learn about Germany is that traditional geographical borders do not exist. Most of the population thinks in national and geographical terms. I think this is all over since the new weapons and nuclear power

stations. What happens in China happens to us. For this reason, what Reagan wants from the S.D.I. is very atavistic."

Even though the Kiefer retrospective that is now at the Museum of Modern Art represents the triumphal march of contemporary German art into American museums, his success is something of a paradox. The two artists he considers most influential in his work — Andy Warhol and Joseph Beuys, a founder of West Germany's Green Party — received a cool reception in most of America's modernist academies during their lifetimes.

Few American curators detect the influence of these two high priests of art in Kiefer's work. Mark Rosenthal, the co-organizer of the retrospective, sees echoes of the Abstract Expressionists, particularly Jackson Pollock. The agitated surfaces, large-size and simple frontal formats of paintings evoke the New York School in the forties and fifties. "He is such a rich painter," says William Rubin, director emeritus of painting and sculpture at the Modern. "His paintings have a combination of art and poetry that is specifically his own. I don't think that any of the contemporary American or European painters is as good as Kiefer. He is my bet."

Anselm Kiefer was born in Bavaria, Germany's conservative south, in March 1945, two months before the end of the war. Like Beuys and Warhol, he was raised as a Roman Catholic. When he was growing up, huge slabs of his country's recent past — the entire Nazi era, the division of the nation — were *verboten*.

In 1966, after dropping out of studies in law and French, Kiefer went to France. He visited the monastery in La Tourette that was designed by Le Corbusier, the modernist architect and visionary. The monastery is a text-book example of the translation of spiritual ideas into concrete forms, and Kiefer was eager to learn from it firsthand. He lived there as a guest of the Dominican monks for three weeks and participated in their rituals. He returned to Germany determined to become an artist, and enrolled in art school.

As he had at La Tourette, Kiefer became one with the objects of his investigations. In a 1969 series of photographs originally titled *From Summer to Fall of 1969 I Occupied Switzerland, France and Italy* (the series is now known as *Occupations*), the artist appears in front of various historic and monumental outdoor sites in riding breeches and boots and with one arm outstretched in the Nazi salute. Had these images been photographed within Germany, Kiefer would have transgressed a postwar prohibition against the gesture. Just as outrageously, two photographs, captioned *Walking on*

Water – Attempt in the Bathtub in the Studio in my House, showed Kiefer standing in his bathtub in the same uniform and salute.

His attempts at irony were lost on his instructors, and he left art school. In 1970, he was accepted to study informally with Joseph Beuys in Düsseldorf. On weekends, he would load his neo-Symbolist paintings and handmade books into the back of his car to show Beuys. (In his books, he combined many of the hefty materials of his larger works with his technique of painting over photographs. "My books are films in a way," he explains. "In the books, time is important. There is a type of cinematography, as in films. But in looking at paintings there is no time. They are a kind of apparition.")

"We all thought Kiefer was crazy," recalls Walter Dahn, one of Beuys's full-time students at the Düsseldorf Academy of Arts at the time. "The academy was in turmoil," he says, referring to Beuys's attempts to organize the students against the school's supposed suppression of creativity. In 1972, when Beuys was sacked, "the students were raging mad," Dahn continues, "and in would come this Kiefer with his odd-looking paintings that looked as though nothing in the world was changing." But Beuys silenced their derision. "I could see later that Kiefer was doing something Beuys himself had attempted in his drawings of the fifties," adds Dahn. "They were both dealing with the ghosts of German history."

Kiefer was encouraged by Beuys to paint, even though painting had been abandoned around the world in favor of experimental art forms, such as Conceptual and Performance art. Kiefer also learned about alchemy from Beuys, who believed that the artist, like a shaman, can transform base materials into mystical touchstones.

In 1977, for a catalogue of his work, Kiefer wrote a one-page autobiography that was actually a list of people and places. The names of Rilke, Rodin, van Gogh, Genet, Le Corbusier and Hitler appear, as does the simple entry: "1971 Marriage to Julia." Six years earlier, Kiefer and his new wife, a schoolteacher, had moved into a stone schoolhouse in the small town of Hornbach, near Buchen. (The couple is still there, and now have three children.) The attic and basement of the house became his studios and the settings for his strange experiments in paintings and photographs.

In a number of paintings of the mid-seventies, the Trinity of Father, Son, and Holy Spirit are represented by three eternally burning fires on the floor, with a snake, representing Satan, close by, while the attic recedes in an exaggerated theatrical perspective. Kiefer also began to employ the dramatic effects of Baroque religious paintings that drew the viewer into the pictures.

Holy saints spiraling to heaven were typical subjects of Baroque art, but figures of any kind (other than the busts of German "heroes" in one series) were soon to be expunged from Kiefer's art. As his paintings began to resemble vast stage sets, they were emptied of characters, and figures were replaced with mesmerizing perspectives. Kiefer painted landscapes with extraordinarily high horizon lines and densely matted surfaces, giving his viewers the illusion of looking down on the ground while they are, in fact, looking up into his pictures.

. . . . .

During the 1970s, young German painters had little expectation of international success. The art scene, centered in Düsseldorf, was dominated by American Minimal and Conceptual artists and Joseph Beuys. The so-called Neo-Expressionists – including Georg Baselitz and A.R. Penck – had emerged in Berlin, but that city and its art were widely regarded as provincial; these artists won some national recognition after 1969, when Michael Werner, their dealer, moved his gallery from Berlin to Cologne, near Düsseldorf. Ten years later, Werner (currently married to Mary Boone, the American dealer) was the most powerful gallery owner in Germany, and his Neo-Expressionists were the most celebrated on the international scene.

Werner says that in 1972 he was visited by Katharina Sieverding (a student of Beuys), who told him about Kiefer. Some of the artists in Werner's stable had also shown interest in the young painter. Within a day or two of Sieverding's visit, Werner says, he received an invitation from Beuys to dine at his home. This was Werner's first and last invitation there. At the end of the evening, the host approached Werner and handed him a large envelope. Inside were Kiefer's résumé, slides, and telephone number.

A year later, Kiefer held his first show at the Michael Werner Gallery. It was titled *"Nothung"* – the name of Wotan's sword in Richard Wagner's opera *The Ring of the Nibelung* – and comprised only one painting and a series of related books. Werner says he initially found Kiefer's work hard to sell, and the painting went for DM3,500 (about $1,750). In 1974, the artist showed more of his handmade volumes. The following year, he showed his books together with a single painting, *Nero Paints,* an important early work that depicts a furrowed field dripping in blood, on which is superimposed the outline of a large, burning painter's palette. The title and image refer to the Emperor Nero's destruction of Rome.

According to the historian Suetonius, Nero had watched the disaster with tears of joy. Dressed as a tragic actor, he sang of the destruction of Troy, and looked forward to building a new, greater city on Rome's ashes. Nero's "cleansing" of Rome by fire was the gesture of a megalomaniac; to Kiefer, it is also suggestive of the purgative powers attributed to fire by alchemists. Both interpretations became recurrent metaphors in Kiefer's work, continuing in his paintings *Painting = Burning* and *Painting of the Scorched Earth*, through his recent works dealing with the simultaneously creative and destructive power of nuclear energy.

"Scorched earth is a technical term used in the army," Kiefer has explained. "Retreating troops set fire to the area they are leaving so that the enemy won't be able to grow crops there anymore. I don't want to illustrate an ordinary military operation, but to depict the problem of the contemporary art of painting. If you like, you might view it as a new start that every painting has to make. Each work of art destroys the one before it."

In the mid-seventies, Michael Werner increased his influence throughout Europe by building a network of gallery contacts in other cities for his artists. One of his methods was to suggest to museum and gallery directors that if they wanted to exhibit one of his artists they had to have at least one of the others.

During those years, Kiefer's career gained in momentum, and by 1977 Werner had Kiefer's work shown in, among other galleries, the Galerie Helen van der Meij in Amsterdam. Yet the cohesion among the artists that resulted from Werner's tactics gave the impression that they were a movement, which later became irksome to Kiefer. Moreover, Werner's demands operated according to a rating system in which Baselitz was always at the top and Kiefer at the bottom.

The relationship between Werner and Kiefer became increasingly strained. When he visited Kiefer's studio, Werner's insults were common. He has complained to me since that Kiefer's art "is not about painting anymore – he is doing an idea art." Finally, in 1979, when Kiefer was invited to hold a one-man exhibition at the Van Abbemuseum in Eindhoven, across the German-Dutch border, Werner stayed away during both the installation of the show and the opening. He did tiptoe into the museum the following morning, but Kiefer was waiting. Within minutes, the artist quit Werner's stable.

Wary of dealers, yet financially destitute, Kiefer started to sell works directly from his studio. Helen van der Meij became his agent, but few of his paintings were sold. It wasn't until the Venice Biennale in 1980, when Kiefer gained sudden notoriety, that the artist assumed center stage.

Baselitz and Kiefer had been selected to represent West Germany at the Biennale, and Kiefer decided to commemorate in his paintings some politically ambiguous "heroes" of Europe's recent history, such as Frederick the Great and Richard Wagner. A storm of protests quickly followed. "The reaction of the German newspapers was very bad," say Klaus Gallwitz, West Germany's commissioner for the Biennale. "Germans and Austrians alike attacked him for his work, *Germany's Spiritual Heroes*. They were against his hidden and overt quotations of the stages of Germany's past. What Kiefer made was directly against what people wanted to see."

Kiefer countered in a rare early interview that he was "not primarily concerned with the persons who are portrayed. Rather, it is the history of the reactions to their work. When I cite Richard Wagner, I do not mean the composer of this or that opera. For me, it is more important that Wagner 'changed,' if you will, from a revolutionary into a reactionary ... the way in which he was used in the Third Reich and the problems associated with this."

For the Americans at the Biennale, the content of Kiefer's art was not the biggest issue. They were more excited by the return to painting in European art. Dealers and collectors, who had exhausted the market for American Conceptual and post-Minimal art, suddenly awoke to what was happening in Europe. And once stirred, they stampeded.

Among the dealers who saw Kiefer's work in Venice were three from New York: Ileana Sonnabend, Mary Boone, and Marian Goodman. Goodman was the first to secure a Kiefer show, but Sonnabend persisted, and she was soon joined by Boone. While the pair was wooing him with the offer of a two-gallery show in their galleries across the street from each other on SoHo's West Broadway, Kiefer was selling to Sonnabend. She bought about 25 paintings directly from his studio, still more from his museum exhibition in Essen, West Germany, and also all of his work that Werner was holding in storage. She immediately sold many of the paintings for prices ranging from $7,000 to $15,000.

Kiefer, however, suddenly rejected the two-gallery idea. Helen van der Meij placated Boone by passing on two works for her to sell. Boone then begged and borrowed five additional paintings, and quickly mounted an exhibition, in 1982, that gave the impression that she had bagged Kiefer, the hottest new name in the art scene. In 1984, Marian Goodman relocated to a larger gallery – comparable in size to that of Boone's or Sonnabend's – and Kiefer finally decided to go with her.

In Cologne, Kiefer chose the gallery of Paul Maenz, whom he had met at the Venice Biennale. The two men had held a lively conversation about a piece of sculpture, although neither knew who the other was, and it was only when they parted that they exchanged names. In London, Kiefer was introduced to the Anthony d'Offay Gallery by Helen van der Meij. She took Kiefer and Baselitz with her when she joined d'Offay in 1982. (She has since left the gallery, but the painters remained.)

As soon as the business arrangements were made, Kiefer's paintings became scarce and their value soared. In galleries today, the cost of a large Kiefer is $300,000; for one of his handmade books, $50,000 to $100,000. Very few of his works appear at auction. One exception was at last year's benefit for London's Whitechapel Gallery. In gratitude for the gallery's retrospective of his paintings in 1982, Kiefer donated a large recent work. The last item on the block, it was sold, after fierce bidding, to Leslie Wexner – the Ohio businessman and owner of The Limited – for £300,000 (or $495,000), at the time the most ever paid for one of Kiefer's works.

. . . . .

Kiefer, who estimates that 75 per cent of his collectors are Jewish, has made several paintings since 1980 that mourn the Holocaust and the monstrous separation of Jews from non-Jews in Germany. Taking his cue from Paul Celan's poem, "Death Fugue," Kiefer's *Margarete – Shulamith* paintings counterpoint Goethe's blonde heroine Margarete (symbolized by yellow straw) with the biblical Shulamith (represented by nothing other than ash mixed into the paintings' blackened surfaces).

On the strength of these works, Kiefer became the first contemporary German artist to be accorded a retrospective at the Israel Museum in Jerusalem, which was held in 1984. The *Jerusalem Post Magazine* commented, "Mourning might be the key to the psyche of Kiefer. It is not a mourning comparable to the mourning of the Jews of our times. Kiefer seems to be mourning the indigestibility of his heritage by battling with it in an ongoing series of waking dreams."

Kiefer's interest in Judaism has also led him to study the cabbala. After visiting Jerusalem in 1983 and 1984, he embarked on a series titled *Departure From Egypt*. He has also left strictly German subject matter behind, and is taking on political themes that have universal implications, such as nuclear energy.

Since the early 1980s, Kiefer has become more outrageous with his choice of materials. Molten lead thrown onto the surface, metal weights hanging from the pictures, and airplane propellers symbolize everything from mystical emanations to the hierarchy of angels in theological lore.

Anselm Kiefer's numerous followers see him as an old-fashioned genius. Certainly, his works pull out all the stops in their search for emotional effect. This, combined with his uncompromising self-management, places German art near the forefront of Western culture and transforms Kiefer himself into another of his country's controversial heroes. ●

SANDRO CHIA 1991

FRANCESCO CLEMENTE 1987

ENZO CUCCHI 1989

MIMMO PALADINO 1991

The Italian Transavantgarde

THE VILLAGE VOICE SEPTEMBER 1987

Sandro Chia was timed to explode. He boiled for fifteen minutes, like an egg in a saucepan, and then was history. Chia's story, and that of Francesco Clemente, Enzo Cucchi, and Mimmo Paladino, is not memorable simply because his paintings threw America's doors back open to European art in general and to European painting in particular. It is memorable, even historic, as an utterly contemporary promotional and artistic campaign. To be sure, the Italian painters did wedge comparatively base, physical sensations into an art world transfixed by the union of the brain and the assembly line. But they also became the first Europeans to be commercially packaged for America, the first heroes in the fragmented art scene of the 1980s.

Pluralism had destroyed consensus in postwar art, the market had restored it, and by 1980 the success of the Italians in New York had restructured the scene along the vectors of international deal-making. The managers of the scene became the deal-makers, art dealers who invested, multiplied, and laundered new money and gave form to a new tendency. This is their story, the story of a setup that is now a blueprint for all emerging so-called avant-gardes.

It's a story that can be traced back twenty-five years, to Pop art, when Leo Castelli planted mines across Europe creating that continent's first commercial art explosion. It was then that his ex-wife, Ileana Sonnabend, set up shop in Paris and promoted and distributed Pop art, and it was then that the first American – Robert Rauschenberg, who was considered a Pop artist – won his controversial prize at the Venice Biennale. It's a story, like almost every other tale of the 1980s art world, that has its origins in Pop.

Yet there is no moral to this story; the new Italian painters now spell business as usual. But if their rise is compared to that of their American predecessors, art criticism has clearly lost out. "For the first time," says Giancarlo Politi, editor and publisher of Italy's *Flash Art* magazine, "this kind of art became popular because it had some elements which everybody could accept. In a way, it eliminated criticism." And nothing since it has restored it. "The critic will be important with the new Conceptual art," Politi continues, "but as an indirect agent of a gallery."

The protagonist of our story is Gian Enzo Sperone, partner of the Sperone Westwater Gallery on Greene Street, the New York gallery that represents Chia, Clemente, Cucchi, and Paladino. Sperone is a charming, edgy, Faustian 48-year-old who has bargained off many old loves to arrive at the recent, unprecedented success of his current crop. Since he opened his gallery twenty-five years ago, he has exhibited American Pop, Minimal, and Conceptual artists, followed by the Italian Arte Povera and, now, the younger Italian painters he gleaned from smaller galleries in the late seventies.

Upon opening his gallery in Turin, Sperone visited Ileana Sonnabend in Paris and arranged to show the Pop artists in Italy. Exactly twenty years later, in 1983, Sperone's young star, Sandro Chia, was showing in both Sperone's New York gallery and Leo Castelli's. Chia's passage from Italy to America – followed by Clemente's, Cucchi's, and Paladino's – was a dazzling piece of artistic entrepreneurship. Yet absolutely everybody involved claims that it was merely good fortune. Calculated or coincidental, the path blazed by Sperone's torch-bearers is now followed by all ambitious newcomers with fiber-optical speed and efficiency.

In 1968, recalls Sperone, "In the so-called revolution of the students and the like, it was written several times in front of the gallery, 'Sperone be careful, we know that you are an agent of American culture and an agent of the CIA.'" Many Europeans wanted to overthrow America's postwar cultural imperialism. According to Jean-Christophe Ammann, director of the Kunsthalle in Basel, Switzerland, "In '73 or '74, American influence stopped in Europe and nobody bought American artists in Italy anymore. I don't know why, but Gian Enzo didn't have an easy time." So when the opportunity to invert the status quo came at the end of the seventies, Sperone seized it.

Amazingly, in 1980, when the Italian painters held their widely publicized shows in New York, their success was presented as *fait accompli* and the artists were greeted – even in the most marginal forums – with a rhetoric similar to that which Americans met in Europe in the late sixties. "Manhattan galleries are undergoing an invasion," said *TWA Ambassador* magazine's art critic Carter Ratcliff. While some observers were perplexed by a decline in American influence, by what Ratcliff heavy-handedly calls "challenging the American hegemony" and "warning of a shift in the balance of aesthetic power," the airborne critic nevertheless assured travelers that the foreigners pose no serious threat to "America's dominance of Europe": "Enzo Cucci [sic] – like so many of the younger European invaders – has learned about large scale and painterly freedom from America. Hence the invasion often feels like a testimonial to the power of American art over the past three decades."

According to the dealers and museum directors who launched the Italians in New York, however, American art at the end of the seventies was its own worst enemy. They all held that Minimal, Conceptual, and Performance art, and the photography boom, had run their course. "In the seventies, the art world in New York was very provincial," claims Edy de Wilde, the former director of Amsterdam's Stedelijk Museum. "They didn't know anything about what had happened in Europe, so it must have been a huge shock to see Europe suddenly getting some vitality again, a vitality which responded to the needs that were alive in America also." Angela Westwater, Sperone's American partner, insists that the impact of the Italians "had to do with the context of what else was going on. The state of mind of a lot of museum people and a lot of buyers was, you know, 'It's kind of boring, nothing's really happening. All this Conceptual art is dying out.' "

Like a row of dominoes, art galleries and museums from the south to the north of Europe and then across the Atlantic capitulated to the bittersweet novelty of the Italian painters. Initially, they were exhibited separately, in local galleries in Modena, Turin, and Rome, but Sperone's efforts to secure them – Clemente in 1975, Chia in 1977, and Cucchi in 1980 – grew in direct proportion to the interest of European collectors. The Cologne dealer Paul Maenz was next to recognize these Italian cultural pariahs as a treasure trove of international interest.

In 1978, Maenz showcased the young painters alongside the established Arte Povera artists in a series of exhibitions that occupied his gallery all year, and in 1979, he followed the younger group's unexpected success with a show called "Arte Cifra." He then organized shows in small museums in Mannheim, Bonn, Wolfsburg, and Gröningen in the Netherlands, which, along with his own gallery, transferred their attention from Conceptual art to new painting.

In addition to such commercial gallery-organized museum shows, Jean-Christophe Ammann in Basel was preparing a

prestigious seven-person exhibition for May 1980 – in which works were for sale and which traveled to the Museum Folkwang in Essen and the Stedelijk Museum in Amsterdam. And a group of European commercial galleries supervised by Hans Jörgen Müller organized "Europe 79" in Stuttgart, which featured the young Italians. Each of these exhibitions was accompanied by a catalogue and degree of speculation that was unmatched by any of the artists' American contemporaries, and it was at these shows that the decisive action took place. Franz Haks, director of the Gröningen Museum, remembers the mood of those transitional days. "There was repetition in everything. It was really an annoying time. Everyone was looking around and saying, 'Christ, why isn't something happening?' Then for me in Stuttgart it was, 'Oh my God, there's a whole generation with new things!' "

In 1978, Paul Maenz Gallery was selling works by the young Italians at $1,000. "Then all of a sudden things happened," recalls Gert de Vries, Maenz's partner. "You know, sometimes you can show things for years and no one's interested. Then you do something and every week something new is developing out of it." The Stedelijk Museum bought the most expensive piece from the Basel exhibition – a Chia painting from Sperone, with a commission going to the Kunsthalle – for 18,000 Swiss francs, roughly $9,000, which was the comparatively exorbitant amount Sperone had written down for insurance. However, de Vries recalls that at Basel, the pictures were "relatively expensive already. But at the end of the year they were three times, five times that."

After Sperone, Maenz, and Ammann, the next significant players were the Zurich dealer Bruno Bischofberger and the Berlin collector Erich Marx and his curator, the critic and publisher Heiner Bastian. The role of Marx and Bastian is simple enough: their interest signaled to other, less confident, collectors that the Italians were for real. Marx put his money where Bastian's mouth was and bought "15 or 17 Chia paintings altogether," estimates Bastion, "and of Clemente and Cucchi, maybe eight." Bischofberger started to collaborate with Sperone in 1979, taking one third of the works to sell, buying others in bulk at reduced prices from the artists' studios, and gleaning still more from museum exhibitions. He placed them quickly into the collections of high-profile art lovers like Günther Sachs, a rich playboy and former beau of Brigitte Bardot, whose interest added the cachet of celebrity to the new stars in Europe.

But it was Edy de Wilde's support – he took Ammann's show from Basel to Amsterdam and made sweeping purchases – that was most meaningful. De Wilde was a particular champion of postwar painting. He speaks of Willem de Kooning as an old friend and remembers the days in New York when one saw the newest works by Barnett Newman, Jasper Johns, and Andy Warhol in their studios. (The first work of Pop art he bought, however, came from Sonnabend in Paris.) Yet "when Minimal art came and went over into Conceptual art and things came further and further from visual art," he explains, "I was less interested." De Wilde's warm reception to the new painting was based largely on his reaction against Conceptualism. He supported the Italians – buying twenty works for the museum and others for himself – even at the risk of inflating their prices. And in 1984 he bowed out from twenty years at the Stedelijk, having fully committed the museum to the return of painting.

The Stedelijk's commitment, and that of the lesser museums, then became the art's selling point in New York. "I remember showing tattered old catalogues to a lot of people," says Westwater, "not so much that they would read the texts but so there was an awareness that the artists didn't come out of the blue. 'Yes, they have had shows in Italy and yes, they were in this group show in Germany or the Swiss and Stedelijk one,'" she would say.

Westwater herself had to be won over to the artists, which Sperone first attempted in 1979. "In order to convince Angela, being such a close friend of Carl Andre and completely devoted to the Minimal generation, I was trying to see what kinds of words I could use to let her feel completely free," he recalls. "So I told her that I think they are authentic, they are painters, they have a great character and I think you should show them. You will not make money for two, three, four years maybe, but in the end you will make a great success."

Sandro Chia, the first to exhibit in New York, was not immediately successful. While Chia's large paintings cost $3,000 at Sperone's gallery in Rome, others were priced from $1,500 to $4,000 at this New York solo debut. Heiner Bastian, who purchased works from Sperone Westwater, remembers that Chia's show met with "very little response. I think most of the works were sent back to Europe." Even at Chia's show two years later, says Sperone, the prices were set at a low $8,000 to $15,000. "A so-called avant-garde gallery cannot survive at these prices," he exclaims.

After Basel and the "Aperto" show at the 1980 Venice Biennale, demand for the artists soared, and Sperone and Westwater pressed ahead with the "Three C's" in New York. Westwater remembers that at first, "Gian Enzo brought transparencies [of the paintings]. Then he brought in a few articles. I could read a little Italian. I was getting into it." But she had not met the artists, and when Sandro Chia's first exhibition arrived – it had been sent over in a roll and was to be put on stretchers in New York – Westwater's face dropped. Today, she is more chipper about it: "I didn't know every piece before it arrived here, but I certainly was very excited ... these huge gorillas in these paintings, these monkeys shooting people and funny things going on."

Their Greene Street gallery still bears a plaque that reads "Sperone Westwater Fischer." Konrad Fischer was and is still a promoter of Minimal and post-Minimal from his gallery at Düsseldorf. Sperone and Fischer had a gallery together in Rome in the early seventies, and when they opened in New York, they brought in Westwater. But when it came to the young Italians, Fischer was unmovable. "With Konrad it was harder because Konrad is a former artist, and that's a problem," says Sperone.

Angela Westwater maintains that relations among the partners were civil, but Sperone's still-volatile temper belies this. "Konrad was drinking a lot during the opening, not the day before, there at the opening," Sperone says, "and through the alcohol saying things that you cannot say, for instance, 'I am sure that Gian Enzo will make good for this gallery showing this art and probably will make a lot of money, but their work is completely vulgar.' So I had to say, 'Konrad, you cannot do that.' We asked him to leave the gallery, otherwise Sandro Chia or Francesco Clemente would leave immediately. If he could have kept his mouth closed, we would have accepted his partnership."

A final line of attack, or persuasion, was launched by Giancarlo Politi's *Flash Art*. In 1979, the magazine became firmly committed to the young Italians and featured them in new bilingual Italian/English editions. In 1980, Politi, who used to sport a large pink Paladino painting in his Milan residence, published a highly illustrated treatise penned by the Italian art history professor and part-time critic Achille Bonito Oliva. To champion an art movement was a long-standing ambition of Bonito Oliva, and these artists were neither his first, nor last, attempt. Yet his sympathy was genuine, and in his essay and subsequent book he christened the new movement with a term that has stuck. *The Italian Transavantgarde* has since been translated into English, French, German, Indian, Portuguese, Spanish, Polish, Finnish, and Chinese. For Politi, publicizing the Italians not only supported his country's most successful international art movement since Futurism; its success also stretched the boundaries of the art world far enough to situate the previously peripheral *Flash Art* magazine comfortably inside.

In what the Europeans deem a significant career move, Chia, followed by Clemente, relocated to New York. Paul Maenz Gallery, for one, started having trouble obtaining new works from the artists. "When Clemente lived in Italy he was easy to contact. New York was different," explains de Vries. "Of course part of his interest was no longer in Europe, he wanted to be successful in America. You can phone three times, four times, five times and say, 'Can we talk about a show?' and he says, 'Yeah, I don't know yet because I have to do this thing and I don't have material available.' You cannot go forever and you wait for a call from that side. Of course you always feel sad because you invest so much of your interest, your energy. I remember sitting at Sandro Chia's bedside when he stayed at my home and we talked for nights. We talked about Baudrillard and Lyotard and the French people. I was surprised, you know. He was able to read them in French. That was in '78 when we did the first show."

Unknown to Maenz and de Vries, Sperone and Bischof-berger had hatched what Sperone calls "a little conspiracy." Sperone says, "I can tell you now because a few years have passed. I was part of that little conspiracy. Sandro had the idea to spend a year in Germany and Paul Maenz was overly confident that he could represent his work during that time. I had several people waiting for major works, including de Wilde, so we told Paul that he couldn't get any more. Paul decided that he was strong enough to show his own German artists and that he didn't need any more disappointment coming from Italy." Indeed, Maenz never stopped playing up his initial foresight and later launched a group of Germans, which he dubbed the "Mülheimer Freiheit." Swiftly, these young Cologne painters traveled the paths blazed by the Italians. (And he recently exhibited a gaggle of New York Neo-Conceptualists, including four from Ileana Sonnabend.)

Success came in 1980 to Chia, Clemente, and Cucchi in the exhibition of the "Three C's" at Sperone Westwater Fischer, and to Paladino at the Annina Nosei and Marian Goodman galleries (he moved to Sperone Westwater in 1983). Sandro Chia had a ball, spearheading, in a way, the American revival of painting. But by 1984 his fans were sick of him. Britain's preeminent collectors, Charles and Doris Saatchi, were ready to dump their holdings of his work at auction, but Sperone Westwater bought them back for the sake of their star's market. Then successive art critics — responding both to the built-in obsolescence of new art and to Chia's hubris — tried to separate themselves from the pack by denouncing him. While their trashings may have been intended in a valiant spirit of independence, they actually showed themselves to be as susceptible to fashion as the collectors.

In 1987, just last season, Westwater did manage to place all of Chia's new works. But while Cucchi is lionized in both Europe and institutions like the Guggenheim Museum as the tortoise to Chia's hare, the exotic art of Francesco Clemente stakes the strongest claim on the American art world's heart, and its wallet.

The triumphant return of European art in the United States is an ironic affirmation of Pop art's conquest of the world, an art world that has reacted to Pop-style imperialism by imitating it. Not since Pop has any trend been so bought out before being unleashed on a large and unsuspecting audience. Art criticism — as opposed to promotion — has been entirely locked out of the process that makes art valuable; unlike his supposed enthusiasm for French theory, Chia's interest in *The Village Voice*'s 1980 feature on the Italians was simply to count the number of times his name appeared. Nowadays, post-Transavantgarde, the system inaugurated by Pop art, is total. Only the objects change. ●

Interview with Tony Shafrazi

JULY 1988

On February 28, 1974, artist and future SoHo art dealer Tony Shafrazi entered the Museum of Modern Art in New York and sprayed the words "Kill Lies All" in red paint across the surface of Pablo Picasso's painting GUERNICA. Picasso, who died in 1973, left the picture on permanent loan to the Modern until the Franco regime was removed from power in his native Spain. At that time, it was understood GUERNICA would be returned to the Spanish people.   Until now, Shafrazi has been reluctant to discuss the incident publicly. Although enjoying insider status in the international art scene, his radical gesture has nevertheless had many powerful detractors. Among them is William Rubin, director emeritus of painting and sculpture at the Modern.   When Paul Taylor spoke to him while researching this interview with Tony Shafrazi, Rubin was emphatic on the subject: "I regret that the Museum did not bring proceedings against Shafrazi and throw him in jail. I argued vehemently with the directors of the Museum to indict him... It was pure chance that he didn't destroy one of the greatest works of art in the history of man. If the conservators hadn't gotten to the picture within three minutes, the paint couldn't have been gotten out. It's still not totally out. If every artist acted this way, there would be no Michelangelos or Leonardos left."
In the following transcript, published here for the first time, Tony Shafrazi presents a markedly different account.

PAUL TAYLOR **Before we begin I want to ask you about a statement I heard you make last week. You said that in 1974, when you did the *Guernica* business, you felt you were totally on the edge and taking an extreme position.** TONY SHAFRAZI Everybody was pretty close to the edge. **Where was the edge in those days?** The edge is your phrase. What was the question again? **Can you give me a sense of what the downtown New York art scene was like then?** I grew up in the late fifties [in Iran] and arrived from London in New York during the euphoria of the early 1960s. What I liked about it then were the trends in culture, both in Pop art as well as in the popular scene, in films, fashion, and so on. This euphoria gave way to a gradual disintegration of hope and a series of shocking events – the assassinations of JFK, Martin Luther King, Bobby Kennedy, Malcolm X ... **The deaths of people like Otis Redding.** Yes, there was a number of unexpected deaths of talented people in popular music as well, such as Brian Jones and Jim Morrison. Youth felt this more than most because they are very connected to the media. Experiencing these shocks via the newly arrived color television was a massive blow to the innocent, hopeful era of the early 1960s. Also, when the Vietnam war really started to grab hold, there was a disillusionment among avant-garde artists with the approach to art-making. Many became concerned with investigating the means of communication as well as language itself. The work of art as an object of beauty had absolutely no place any longer.

What about you in particular? My self-development went from sculpture to Minimal works to the photo-related lectures I did using language. My particular contribution, I felt, was to ask: How can I use language in an effective way? The only production that seemed to make sense was to bring the object of language back into the real world, as opposed to leaving it in the confines of pure abstraction which had come to a complete standstill. One of my pieces was sheets of white paper that I would hand out to people. They contained the phrase "I don't know" as an attempt to get the reader to participate in this state of not-knowing by saying it – catching them in the act of enunciation. Saying the phrase re-questioned the function of language. **Let's get back to 1974. Can you tell me what it was like to go into the museum that day? Tell me why you did it. A lot of people think it was pure vandalism. Did you know then about Laszlo Toth and all that?** No. I don't even want to know. **It's got nothing to do with that?** No, absolutely not. I don't know who the guy was, and nobody else does either. **He belonged to a group of anarchists.** But all this is shoddy in relation to the art world. During my time I have been absolutely dedicated and committed to the central issues of the art world. My commitment has always been to exhibit new artists, to work with museums and organize exhibitions for them. **Let's get back to the Museum. Did you have to smuggle the paint in?** Yeah. Anyway, that idea to write on the painting was insignificant because the address of most major works of art is already a world address, like Smithson's *Spiral Jetty* work in the desert. **You're not answering my question. I want**

TONY SHAFRAZI 1984

to know what it was like when you went to the Museum? A long time after this incident Rauschenberg told me the story about his erasure of a de Kooning drawing. He said that when he got the idea of changing a great artist's work, he began to shake. He knew he had to carry it out. Once he saw its artistic validity, he had to go through with his plan. He knocked on de Kooning's door, praying the artist wouldn't be home so he wouldn't have to go through with it. When de Kooning came to the door, Rauschenberg told him his idea. De Kooning took a long look at him: Rauschenberg was literally falling apart. Then de Kooning started to look painstakingly through his drawings, eventually choosing a very difficult one for him to erase. It took Rauschenberg two weeks of hard work to complete the task. **Since that time the work has become somewhat historical.** Yes. When my "writing on painting" idea came to me, it was uncomfortable and then it dawned on me that it would have to be on the surface of a historical work – an icon that everyone already assumed to be a masterpiece. **Okay.** The repercussions for me were awesome, terrifying. Developing my plan took eight months of isolation, and I couldn't engage anyone else in it. I had to investigate every facet of it on my own. The writer Rudy Wurlitzer later commented that it was like Dostoyevsky's *Crime and Punishment* reenacted. I wrote to my father telling him that whatever he might hear, he should know mine was an act of faith made visible. Living with the terror of the consequences, I was committed to showing the depth of my faith. The time that I did it – the rendezvous – was like walking back into reality and just doing it. Suddenly the world seemed like a frozen stage. **You were alone?** Yeah. The idea was to write with complete clarity and commitment, everything else was secondary. When the guard came up, I just gave him the spray can. **What happened then?** I was naive. I thought that when you're arrested you get a trial. I expected to give a defense or explanation, to be able to bring art to trial and expose it to a larger audience, but that wasn't the case. The way the real law, or cultural law, works is a little different from that. **Were you ever arrested?** I presented my argument to the viewers before being taken to the police station. It was not a subjective act of rage or a political gesture. It was intended as a statement. The story hit the press about an hour after it happened so there was a lot of media attention. The police took me to the Tombs, which was quite grueling. **What's the Tombs?** The old court house and city jail. It houses the most volatile forces from the New York streets – there had been massive riots there a few years before. It was rather scary to be suddenly in that context. **Did you eventually go to court and defend yourself?** I went to court for arraignment rather late that night. The courtroom was packed with close to two hundred artists. **And they were supportive?** Yeah, they thought it was fantastic that a serious artist had done it. Joseph Kosuth was getting on a plane in Sweden when he saw it in a newspaper. In Paris Daniel Buren saw the headlines, saw my name and said, "My god, Tony did it!" He thought it was fantastic. Lynda Benglis was in L.A. and sent me a copy of the *L.A. Times* with a picture on the front page of cops with shotguns aimed at a bull, below a picture of *Guernica* itself. It was on UPI and all the wire services around the world. **What time was this?** I did it at three in the afternoon and by the time I got to the Tombs, it was closer to six. I had no record so it took a long time for me to be processed. The arraignment took place around eleven. As I came out, I saw this massive gallery of artists waiting. I had to stand with my back to them. In front of me as I faced the judge, high up on the courtroom wall, was the sign "In God We Trust." It was quite awesome. I felt responsible for the artists' safety. The judge demanded $1,000 bail. I surrendered my passport but they wouldn't take traveler's checks. It was the only money I had with me. Everyone dug in their pockets and came up with all the money. It was a lot at that time. I was floating, I didn't know what was happening. Later, they all took me to dinner. **Robert Pincus-Witten says that shortly after this you went to a party at Virginia Dwan's with Richard Serra. Pincus-Witten says he remembers saying, "I'm outraged, it's a disgrace that there's a vandal in our community. But no one supported me so I left. Because Tony's action was viewed as an act of Conceptual art, no one thought it was wrong. My sympathies were with Picasso."** This was after Smithson died. John Baldessari arranged for me to lecture at Cal Arts then I went to New Mexico with Smithson. We went to Amarillo. I wanted to stay but Smithson wanted to do another landwork. We went there and he took over. Three days later he died. We had an event in Virginia Dwan's house in New York. **You came with Serra?** I'll tell you the sequence. Smithson had died, we took the body on a plane. Carl [Andre] met us. Then there was the church service which was very emotional. Afterwards, we had dinner at Mickey's Chinese Chance restaurant. Sol [LeWitt] offered to help me with some shows. Richard Serra asked me what I was planning to do now. **The artist Kent Floeter, who used to show with Mary Boone, said that Richard Serra put you up to it. Serra is supposed to have said, "You're always talking about this, so why don't you do it?" Is that true?** Why don't you ask Serra? **You went to court, you got out on bail. Why weren't you**

55

prosecuted?   My lawyer explained that no juror would understand a word of what I was planning to say in my own defense. The MoMA didn't even know what I was doing. When I was arrested, I was searched in a bathroom. I remember William Rubin sticking his head in the door and giving me a hint of a smile. He seems to have understood.   **According to Rubin, he was not even in the museum at the time.**   The MoMA was very concerned with the repercussions of all this. In the late 1940s, Ad Reinhardt had marched outside the building with a placard protesting that the museum was anti-modern. Museums were in a desperate bind. The galleries were in a bind. SoHo didn't even exist except for Paula Cooper. The artists were vanishing from the art scene, into the desert or wherever. In response, the Museum had started offering free admission on some days.   **But what does this have to do with you?**   The painting was on loan, it was a very volatile situation. It was front-page news. The Museum wanted to hush it up. Maybe some people wanted to help behind the scenes.   **Like who?** Perhaps Oldenburg, I don't know.   **Did the State Department or the Shah help?**   When the Shah heard about it later, in 1977, apparently he said, "I wonder why he did that? Obviously this man has great plans for the future."   **But no one assisted you?**   No. But at another party, perhaps it was at Virginia Dwan's, I seem to remember Oldenburg taking me aside and giving me a soft punch. He was appreciative of the scale of the work I'd made. The MoMA wanted to settle out of court. It finally entailed going to hearings with these raging bulls of guards threatening me.   **So it wasn't anything like Kafka or Socrates?**   No, I had a glimpse of that but not much. At certain points, though, the hearings became frighteningly grueling – old rusty pipe-smoking psychologists, with old ideas, giving me ink-blot tests! They were trying to get me to say I was "not guilty" in legal terms, that I didn't do anything wrong. The settlement I got was five years probation.   **They didn't deport you?**   No. I was supposed to report to the probation officer every week, but I was just getting shows in Europe. I was "creative."   **But it's not up to the museum to decide whether to deport you?**   The judge hearing the case – I think his name was Yeargin – was a member of the museum.   **What did you tell the judge?**   I went up the stairs to the landing on the highest floor where there were four or five people looking at the painting and stepped in front of them. It was like walking through an invisible barrier.   **Like going onto a stage?**   Yes. There was absolute silence, everything was completely frozen for a long time. The noise returned as I stepped back. Things started clicking back into place and I saw the guard coming toward me and I gave him the spray can. My arresting officer happened to be next door buying books for his daughter. He called in on the radio. I was taken to a lavatory. The guards looked massive, very powerful. During the five or so minutes that we were in this place there were about twelve people already working on the painting.   **They got the paint off that day?**   Yes. Then in 1977 or 1978, I was having coffee with some friends at the Spring Bar in SoHo. There were some ladies there, giggling. They wanted my autograph. I was embarrassed but they told me it was for the head conservator at the MoMA. Her office was decorated with wanted posters and pictures of the event.   **Can you tell me about the Guerilla Art Action that happened a few days later?**   I wasn't part of that, it wasn't my scene. Poppy Johnson, and I think Jon Hendricks and Mel Kendrick were involved. Have I told you what I did in Leo Castelli's gallery?   **No.**   There was a Dan Flavin show on then, with incredible diagonals that gave three open spaces of light. I saw the perfect location for three words I'd been working on, "Get It Done." I sprayed them on the wall and the director said, "What the hell are you doing?" and dived at me and grabbed me. I was wearing a long leather jacket and he broke a button. I told him, "Look, you broke my button." He shouted back, "We just fucking painted that wall." I said, "So paint it again!"   **How did Leo react?**   To this day he's never said a word about it.   **Can we return to the *Guernica* and your text? Was your intention to renovate an old picture? Was this an instance of early appropriation?**   The paradox of entropy is something that Robert Smithson talked about a lot at that time. He explained that the whole sense of the chronology of art is unreal, a figment of human consciousness. What's important is art's historicity. I recognized this in relation to contextual language.   **That's a Duchampian idea.**   Yes. In my case, having acknowledged the extraordinary value of *Guernica*, that Picasso was a god, it was necessary to "defrock" him, to unhinge him, even at the risk of being punished. I had to imagine what he would say. I think he would have smiled. Wanting to touch the surface had to do with the father and son thing. I was bringing a shine to it, bringing it into immediate relevance, bringing the work of art, via the written word, to the front page, bringing it into the media. I wanted to see a work of art on the front page. It was many years before we had paintings regularly featured in the media as we do today. ●

Interview with Sherrie Levine

Flash Art summer 1987

PAUL TAYLOR **I don't remember reading any question-and-answer interviews with you before – as opposed to articles about you that incorporate some quotes.** SHERRIE LEVINE There have been a couple. **Nevertheless, somebody said to me that if artists were paid according to the amount of criticism written about them, you would be a millionairess.** I guess that's true. *(laughs)* **Has there been an exceptional amount of critical attention for your work, at least in the States?** I guess there has been. I'm really grateful for it. Part of the reason – which I guess you're going to ask me next, right? – is that I consider it my job to be articulate about what my project is. It makes writers' jobs easier. **You use the word "project." Others might say "career" or "calling" or "profession." A project is like an assignment with a definite goal, an end ... Is that the case with your work?** When I said the word, I wondered if that's really what I meant. I guess on some level I think about it like that. It's a game for me – on the one hand. Obviously I have my own obsessions, like anybody else. And they pop up all the time, whether I want them to or not. **You just divided your practice into two: game and obsessions.** There's a compulsion to repeat. In other words, the game is never won. **Has there been a psychoanalytical analysis of your work?** Some of the feminist critiques that are coming out of Lacanian theory. I can't think of anything extensive. **It sounds like a reading that you've made yourself.** Yeah, most recently. In my earlier career there was a lot of Frankfurt School theory being applied. Then as I've rekindled my interest in psychoanalytic theory, the critics picked up on that. **There was the point made about your earlier work which was that you appropriated images from art by men. You were cast as a woman re-making men's imagery.** In the late seventies and early eighties, the art world only wanted images of male desire. So I guess I had a sort of bad-girl attitude: You want it, I'll give it to you. But of course, because I'm a woman, those images became a woman's work. **What does the expression "images of male desire" mean?** It means that you consider the great modernist paintings as images or representations of their desire ... At first I found Lacan extremely difficult, but when I really started to get interested in it I read a book called *Feminine Sexuality* with two very good introductory essays by Juliet Mitchell and ... **Jacqueline Rose.** That was a real turning point for me. **Why did you become interested in Lacan at roughly the same time as everybody else here? Why did Americans and others suddenly become enamored with this work?** Speaking for myself, I found Frankfurt School theory insufficient, and I had an intuition that an answer might be in a more psychoanalytic reading of things. **You're talking about two areas of theory – a psychoanalytical one and then this modern ...** Sociological reading. **As a semiologist asked me the other week, why did the art world suddenly become interested in this stuff?** Obviously, as an artist, I make the pictures that I want to make and I look for theory that I think is going to help me in a different kind of language. It's not that the theory precedes the work. **Certainly, particular theoreticians are incredibly influential – in my case it was Barthes – but I wonder whether in time these names will be flushed out of the art system and go out of fashion like the names Merleau-Ponty and Wittgenstein did. What do you think of the trends of artists indexing their work to particular theorists?** It's probably always been true of artists who read. But I also watch television and eat in restaurants and buy clothes. I do a lot of things, including reading theory. It's not like I'm setting up hierarchy where the theory comes first and everything else comes second. It's an activity that I enjoy, basically. It's another kind of play. I had this idea today – it's a rather unformed idea so I'm reluctant to put it into print, but I'll see what you say about it. I was thinking that what is wrong with a lot of Frankfurt School theory is that it assumes art is about power and that, for me, art is about play. **Isn't play about power too? It does involve oppositions and competition and often a victor and vanquished.** I guess play can be a theatrical representation of power. **Why does the art world, and why do a lot of artists, privilege the intellectual pursuit over those entertainments that you mentioned?** I think it's because we're worried that they won't take us seriously. **So what do you think of journalists who write about an artist's taste in shopping, or movies, or records. Is that valid criticism?** Sure. But I don't think it's true that all critics want to discuss artists in intellectual terms to begin with. All artists don't read – maybe you and I and our friends do, but I don't think that there's a trend. There have always been critics who are intellectuals and artists who are intellectuals, but they are not necessarily the whole situation. And I don't

SHERRIE LEVINE 1987

want to imply that they're in any way better than artists who aren't intellectuals. **You mentioned your obsessions. Of course, you would notice them as they reappear. What are they? What do you call them?** It's funny, I was just reading an interview with Ross Bleckner who said that the reason he makes art is because he can say things that he would never allow himself to say in any other language. I feel pretty close to that. **Do you have names for these things?** Yes, but not for public consumption. (laughs) The thing that's interesting to me about when artists talk about their art is what they don't say. You know, what they think is hidden in the work. **Do artists often withhold the truth about the productive mechanism of their work? Their career moves, what we politely call their "strategies"?** Right. But the unconscious is often what makes art compelling. If we weren't artists we might be hysterics. We would have to somatize these symptoms. **I thought that in art now in New York – not only among artists of your generation but also among the younger ones – the unconscious is virtually all you're allowed to talk about. The conscious aspect of the art production – the realities of its marketing – is what remains unspoken. It reminds me of Warhol's quip in *POPism* – that Pop art put the outside on the inside and the inside on the outside, which is like the situation now in this neo-Pop era: the consciousness of art is the career moves of an artist, but this is hardly ever admitted by an artist.** Right. One of the reasons that I talk about it to you is that you don't get offended by it. Part of it is that we're not really supposed to talk about it. **That's why it's authentically more suppressed than this "unconscious" of yours that you choose not to talk about ... When the stripe paintings of yours first surfaced, you told me on the telephone that you had done these works that you considered to be generic stripe paintings. Later I spoke to the editor of an important American art magazine, and she used the same word. In a sense, there's almost a generic response to your generic stripe paintings. In fact they're generic history paintings referring to the history of the stripe – referring to Brice Marden, Blinky Palermo, Bridget Riley, even Kenneth Noland. Is the act of reference to those artists the content of the paintings?** That's just the modus operandi. The content is the discomfort you feel at the déjà vu that you experience. I think of them as not very different in subject matter from my direct appropriations. The discomfort that you feel in the face of something that's not quite original is for me the subject matter. **So the feeling of looking at something is the subject matter of the works.** The experience, yes – the experience of uneasiness. **Does that mean that you did not have to continue to appropriate photographs and paintings to continue to elicit that response?** What I discovered is that it's even more troublesome when something's *almost* original. **If you're trying to create a feeling of déjà vu, then you are addressing a quite specific viewer – one who knows art history, and one who knows your work.** I guess that's my ideal viewer. Others experience them, I think, as formal paintings. When it comes down to it, I think all artists have a very small, idealized audience, and whoever else likes the work, well, that's great. **That audience is like your alter ego. Do you address a gendered viewer in your works?** I never think about it that way, so probably not – at least not consciously. **It seemed so at Documenta 7. The Egon Schiele appropriations were self-portraits of a male artist that referred curiously to the overall situation. Exactly how much irony was involved?** I guess, like any artist, I'm trying to describe my experience and because I'm a woman my experience is different from a man's. I really thought it was a joke. Schiele always seemed to me the ultimate male expressionist, the ultimate bohemian, so I thought it would be amusing to try on his clothes, as it were. **His birthday suit! You are suggesting that your earlier direct appropriations and your stripe paintings do the same thing, but the history of art has a different role in both of those oeuvres.** Yes. And I seemed to have straddled two very popular movements. That's my public persona. In terms of my private obsessions, nothing has changed very much. **Your next show – at Mary Boone Gallery – will have new photographic appropriations as well as stripes.** They won't be stripes, but they will be some kind of geometric pattern, and there will be knot paintings. I'm not exactly sure yet what the photographic works will be, partly due to legal problems, but I'm researching that now. **Would you appropriate the work of a woman artist?** I never have, but ... **Would you appropriate the work of a contemporary?** Never consciously, though I've been accused of it. (laughs) I am very influenced by the work around me, sometimes I'm even more interested in the people who are not thinking about the things that I am thinking about. I think the original subject matter of my appropriated work was the anxiety of influence. **You say that you have been fortunate to straddle two movements. I guess that you are referring to appropriation and the thing that's happening now.** You mean the "new abstraction"? **Did you know that it was coming around the corner when you started painting the stripes?** Well, I did know that I personally was very bored with figurative imagery. And I suspected that a lot of other people were too, so when I did the drawings after Malevich I just found it so refreshing after this bombardment of figurative imagery that we were all involved in, that it just seemed to me like a nice cool drink of water. So it made a lot of sense that a lot of other people thought that way too. It wasn't surprising to me. **You must have a fickle taste in imagery if you can get "bored" with figuration after a few years and want to go abstract.** I think that people do something for a while, and then they get bored and do something else. Their major concerns probably don't change very much. Certainly the symptomatic aspects change, but I don't think that's a bad thing. It keeps life interesting. "Fickleness" has a pejorative edge to it that I don't think is appropriate. One has to keep oneself interested. One has to keep it fresh, so you do what you can. **So the figurative or abstract face of your work is just the exterior.** Yes. They're not, in my mind, really crucial. **But the interior is invisible.** In a way, yes – the things that I really care about. The struggle for any artist is how to represent what the real conflicts are. **What are they?** In the most abstract sense I think that as a professional artist I've always been involved in issues of representation, what it means to represent some-thing. **It was said that your appropriated photographs played a part in the "End of Painting," but when I first met you when visiting from Australia you told me that you were going to make paintings – show that painting is not the enemy. It seems that if someone says that your work is about this or that, you prove them wrong.** Well, I take criticism very seriously, so when somebody says something that really strikes a wrong chord, then I realize that there must be some truth to it. (*laughs*) I think about it very hard and ask myself – why have I denied that aspect of my work, denied painting in this case? I have a painting up in the back room at Mary's now and it's next to an early Brice Marden. I looked at the painting and said to Mary that it's really funny because I stopped painting because I believed Brice Marden had made the last painting that anyone could make. It's taken me fifteen years to see that endgame art is a field that I can move around in. **The resistance to the idea of art as game theory is based in transcendental notions of the art work. To many, it is a repugnant idea that an artist does something purely in response to the art world.** But when I call it a game, I don't mean that it doesn't have any heartfelt components. One responds to one's environment. For me, it's hard to think of making art any other way. **The stripe paintings are the apotheosis of nonreference, as most abstract painting was in its idealist manifestations, but your direct appropriations refer explicitly – to history, the history of art.** That's what I think is so amusing about the stripe paintings, that ostensibly they are nonreferential, but on the other hand they have all these references. The idea was to make an abstract painting, a nonobjective painting, that in fact had lots of refer-ences. **There's an irony involved, I guess – that while being so "empty," they're so "loaded."** This is the opposite of the direct appropriations, which appear to be so loaded in content but as photographs of photographs, they have no referent in a way. A Walker Evans is the same as an Edward Weston on a certain level, which annoyed a lot of people when I first did them. **How different is one appropriation artist from another, in the theoretical sense?** There's a Barnett Newman quote I really like … I think it's Barnett Newman, maybe Ad Reinhardt. He said, "It's impossible to know if something is creative unless everybody is doing the same thing." **How long did it take for sales of your work to catch up to your critical reputation?** People have been writing about my work since 1977. I've only started living off it in the last few years. **Since 1984. What were you doing before that?** A lot of waitressing and commercial art … teaching. **And laying out *The New York Times Book Review*, too. Did you deliberately change your style for the sake of sales?** It's not that I changed my style, but I changed medium. I was playing one game and decided to play another game as well. **Did anyone respond negatively to this decision?** I'm sure people have. I don't personally experience that much bile about it, but I'm sure it's there. **To play the game of the market entailed greater visibility. What are the stages that an artist passes through in playing this game?** No matter what you do as an artist there are certain parameters, certain choices. The choices and things that curtail your activity are things like how much time you have, how much space, how much money … **You knew that the stripe paintings would make you more money than your photographs.** You're asking why painting is privileged in this way. It's an interesting question. I'm not sure about it. The more I make art, I see the reasons why people use these materials. It's because they've been proven to last. When people try to use new materials, one is never quite so sure. **It sounds very traditionalist.** It's "conservative" in the literal sense of the word, that is, easier to conserve. But I haven't abandoned the photographs. What I realized was that I could make them too. It wasn't an either-or situation, and that was liberating. My decision to paint was a decision on the level of desire as well as a decision to work in a less marginalized area of the art world. I've been an artist since I was a child, and I started out as a painter. I wanted to see what it felt like to allow myself to paint again. I'm enjoying it a lot, and that's important to me. I find that I like painting more than I enjoy arguing with photo labs. **I like the fact that some of your new checkerboard paintings are called "checks" … I guess that going to Mary Boone Gallery was a major step in the market game too.** That's one of those questions like, "When did you stop beating your wife?" (*laughs*) I went there for all the obvious reasons. She's a very good dealer. She knows the business very well. She has very interesting taste and she knows how to keep a career visible ... Mary talks a lot about artists being the Id of the art world which I think is really interesting. It's certainly what my Schieles were about. **What does it mean?** It's the part that acts without inhibition, that follows its own desire. That's what I take it to mean. **Is it destructive?** Obviously we're talking about a theater, a theatrical social space in which artists represent the Id. Artists are members in society so we're subject to all the things that everyone else is, but we're given a kind of – rope (*laughs*) – which allows us to represent parts of ourselves that other people don't allow themselves publicly. **That's the cultural agreement that privileges artists, sure. But what happens if that cultural agreement falls apart, if there's a cultural disagreement? Isn't this what is meant by the notion of an epistemic change?** Yes, then something else will happen. In general, artists are now much better behaved than the generation before us, because we're required to be. **But instead of there being a change of scene, the roles of the artist and so on seem to have been reified in the eighties. In terms of the theater, shouldn't we now be asking who is the theater proprietor, the playwright, the stage manager?** Art now is a collaboration. **Do you want to see those roles change?** Well, one nice thing about having success is that it brings with it a little bit of power. **"Success is the best revenge."** That's obviously true. **But do we lose the will to transform things as we get more successful?** I don't know, I'm not that successful yet. (*laughs*) It's true: somebody asked Ralph Nader once why he didn't run for president and he replied that if he were president he wouldn't be able to do anything. The thing about the art world is that it's not about real power. I think it's highly developed play – for us and also for people who do have real power. **Are other areas of culture – theater, literature, film – about play too? Why is this the case in the art world especially?** It's not that I feel that I have no power. I just don't have the real power that I thought I might have had when I was a few years younger. **The notion of play makes the content of any artistic gesture incredibly empty in certain ways.** I don't think that play is that empty. On the level of the symbolic, it's very important. But it's a different kind of importance from direct political power – the ability to instrument socialized medicine, for example. I think that the artists and critics sometimes confuse the two things and there's a kind of apology for their own limited activity. The notion of an important artist does not have as much meaning to me as it used to. **Some of your new checker paintings look like chessboards too!** ●

CINDY SHERMAN 1980

Cindy Sherman

New York Woman MARCH 1989

If she had lived in another era, Cindy Sherman might have been a circus entertainer, a prostitute or perhaps even a philosopher. In her photographs, her set-up "self-portraits," Sherman mesmerizes her audience with a never-ending strip-tease, dressing up and making up to portray hundreds of different women, a few men, but never her true self. She is a wizard with a camera — and also a bit of a ham — and she is out to prove that surface is everything. The world being what it is today, Cindy Sherman ended up an artist.

In fact, 35-year-old New Jersey-born Sherman has become a fairy tale princess of the eighties art world. Her art, her life and her good fortune can seem dizzyingly unreal. Small black-and-white photographs of herself that she used to sell for $100 now go for at least $5,000 (if they ever come up for resale). Her new photos, which will be shown at Metro Pictures in SoHo at the end of March, sell for between $7,000 and $15,000 each.

From her campy stills of the late seventies of B-grade movie characters to her grossed-out color extravaganzas of today, Sherman plays with what is traditionally considered women's greatest stumbling block, and their greatest weapon — appearance. But because her art deals so patently in female stereotypes, her photographs are portraits not of how she sees herself but of how she sees men seeing women.

"Other people see my work as pictures of myself," she says. "I don't. They're not self-portraits." When she portrays herself in words, as in pictures, she reveals little; it is as though she is simultaneously holding back a secret and telling it for the thousandth time. Painfully shy in conversation, she laughs nervously and frequently. Sometimes her words sound forced, as if she would rather be somewhere else — at the gym or on her farm upstate. This is an effect, she says, of being brought up to always be "nice and polite." Occasionally she displays flashes of confidence and the desire to pin down an emotion precisely, though her tool is normally a camera. Like any artist, she says, she draws from her own experience.

Reluctant to commit herself to any strong statement about the sexes — preferring to let the ambiguity of her images stand — Sherman nevertheless claims that "the male half of society has structured the whole language of how women see and think about themselves." The men in Sherman's life — her father, a string of artist-boyfriends, now her husband — have inspired her to rearrange her self-image, and it is largely in men's eyes that she has discovered the content of her art: the way women are looked at, objectified, resented.

Cindy Sherman first came to prominence in the late 1970s with her 8-by-10-inch black-and-white photos called *Untitled Film Stills*. They showed the artist as a character in a variety of simulated B-movies, pensively smoking a cigarette or looking frightened among the skyscrapers of downtown Manhattan. The pictures had a fifties feel to them, and Sherman was both the director and leading lady. They riveted the art world's attention. According to artist Robert Longo, one of Sherman's closest friends and a former lover, "After we separated, Cindy became a real hot commodity. There were all these fucking idiots who got so turned on by her photographs."

By 1982 her face was appearing all over the place — in galleries, art magazines, even undergraduate art history courses. It was during the same period that the big-boy painters (as she calls them) were hitting the scene. Such artists as Longo and Julian Schnabel were attacking enormous canvases with oil paints, tar, molten lead, and broken crockery. In making art from her own face, Sherman was wielding a much finer brush — her makeup brush.

When Sherman began dabbling in makeup, she was, she says now, "just a normal teenager trying to look older. It was to attract boys." Later, in college, she was reacting to the "natural," no-makeup look that was everywhere at the time. Even then, it seems, she believed that appearances were everything. Slowly, she took the game a step further. "My father has a couple of old photographs of me dressed up as an old lady." (Sherman's father, an engineer, may have influenced her, she says, "in terms of all his technology. He was always collecting cameras and always snapping family photos. By the time I was a teenager, he was into movie cameras.") It didn't take long until the thrill of making up, as any drag queen will testify, became addictive, and painting her face struck a deep chord. Every day she would transform herself, inch by inch, into a new woman. "I would secretively put on makeup at home and turn into a different person. I would put on makeup even when I was sick in bed. I thought, 'You never know who's going to knock at the door. It might be the man of my dreams.'

I was obsessed with being presentable." Before long, she concludes, "I was like someone who drinks in secret."

Sherman mastered the art of self-transformation at college in Buffalo, where she was an art major in the mid-seventies. She was painting and making little photographic narrative scenes starring herself. One early work, a double portrait called *Twins*, shows two Cindy Shermans. She also made mock covers of magazines, such as *Vogue*, *Cosmopolitan*, and *Family Circle*, with her face seamlessly superimposed. The idea was parody, or, as Sherman says, "making fun — with a little bit of anger in there." The difference between her face and the models' on these covers was that her eyes were crossed or her tongue sticking out.

Her early work stemmed from observations that, like actors, women must falsify their appearance to look natural and that one's self-image is a mask permanently encasing one's soul. In their manipulation of this mask, Sherman's photographs raise many of the fundamental artistic questions about reality and representation, surface and depth, seeing and being seen, as well as questions about truth and the impulse that sometimes strikes when one gazes into a mirror — the desire to conceal. Among her great accomplishments is that though she is using modern ways of making images, her work is deeply rooted in the origins of art. Like a primitive, Sherman uses her body to tell stories about our culture.

While she was in art school, Sherman hooked up with Robert Longo, a fellow student. "Looking back," she says, "I wouldn't really choose an artist to be with — just because of the egos involved." Yet somehow she doesn't seem able to avoid them.

Longo, the painter Charlie Clough, and others set up a noncommercial gallery called Hallwalls in an old ice factory in Buffalo. According to Longo, Sherman was a behind-the-scenes presence at the gallery but was turned off by all the talk. As he puts it, "While us men were out in the main area of Hallwalls all waving our dicks at each other, Cindy was in the back room making work. Her work was so fresh compared with everybody else's."

Eager to break onto the art scene, Longo was plotting his move to New York City. Sherman resisted the idea. "I didn't really like the city. I was scared of it. I also thought that people should be able to stay out of the city and make a living without having to move," she remembers. "Now, I don't think that was realistic." But the couple fought over it. "I had this real dramatic ethnic temper. And she was always real quiet. But whenever Cindy would get mad, she would try to kill you," Longo recalls. "I remember one time she threw this big fucking ashtray at me and said, 'I'm going to kill you!' "

One day, after such a fight, Sherman made a silent three-minute Super-8 movie of herself crying, puffy-eyed and contrite. "I had a box with a one-way mirror and a camera inside," she says. "I'd be looking at the camera, and it would film me. And I was telling myself, 'I hate you, I hate you.' " It is a revealing early document, a confession. And immediately afterward, she began inventing herself anew. She started portraying herself in pictures as everything a woman should be.

Sherman and Longo made the move to the big city in 1977, when she was awarded a $3,000 grant by the National Endowment for the Arts. But even this miniature windfall had a price; it was the first of many instances where Sherman's success posed a threat to men. As Longo admits, her getting that grant "was crushing to my male ego."

The pair sublet a loft on South Street, in lower Manhattan, but Sherman was spooked by her new surroundings. She "would get totally made-up, look fucking beautiful, like a knockout, and wouldn't leave the house," says Longo. Her fears, she says, were "totally based on what my father had instilled in me — that in New York City you get raped and attacked and mugged. I was just petrified."

So she began to stage-manage her life and transformed their loft into the background for her *Film Stills*. In one photograph she is leaning in a hallway, dejected and lonely. In others she is deep in thought at the kitchen sink or poring over a letter. A few outdoor pix were snapped by her father, others by Longo. In several, something seems to be happening outside the frame, making her characters look as intimidated by their surroundings as she was.

Longo constituted her audience, and for him she became adept at dressing up and playing the role of a woman. "She'd put on all this fucking makeup," he says, "put my socks in her tits and come over to me looking like a fucking transvestite. 'Ooh, give me kiss,' she'd say. Horrible! But then you'd see the photographs, and she'd look fucking hot."

When Sherman eventually ventured uptown and found a job at Macy's, she lasted a day. The princess was so distressed by the work that she came home and, according to Longo, became hysterical. Longo called a friend of theirs, Helene Winer at Artists Space, who agreed to employ Sherman as a secretary on a temporary basis. She stayed on for years, always refusing to take her job too seriously. She would occasionally don an absurd costume, such as a nurse's uniform, to lighten the day's work. "I was being interviewed for a job somewhere," remembers Winer, "and some people were coming to talk to me. Cindy knew they were coming to the gallery, so she dressed up in this absolutely pink secretary suit, complete with a little hat."

In 1980 Helene Winer opened Metro Pictures gallery with her friend Janelle Reiring, formerly director of the Leo Castelli Gallery. Sherman and Longo had parted (amicably) as lovers, yet they both became the show ponies of the new gallery's stable. Sherman landed one of the first shows, exhibiting her early color works, in which she used projected slide backgrounds. She made them in editions of ten, and they sold out for a low $400 each.

As soon as Metro Pictures opened, its artists were on the cutting edge of the New York scene. They included the cream of the young "post-Conceptual" artists that Winer and Reiring had discovered while working at their respective galleries. Sherman was one of the stars of this group, much like a lead female singer in a New Wave band, and she and her friends lived out their fairy tale aspirations up and down the length of downtown. "A group of us would all meet at the Odeon and have dinner," she says of her life in the early eighties. "It was right at the beginning of our success, and we could afford it. We'd all order food, and drink too much before the food came, and then want to do some drugs. Everyone would go do drugs and then not be able to eat the food. Afterward we'd all go and dance."

But behind this glamorous exterior, Sherman remembers that she felt nervous and brittle. "Before, I was looking for something secure. I wanted some stability, and I wanted to be in love. I think a lot of the socializing was a combination of just being single and thinking that maybe you're going to meet someone at the Mudd Club."

On the scene was Richard Prince, an "appropriation" artist who played in a band with Longo. His art consisted solely of re-photographing other people's photography. In 1980 he made a play for Sherman. Cinderella thought she had found her Prince, and a few months later they were living together. But for the duration of their relationship, which lasted about a year and a half, Sherman stood head and shoulders above Prince, and this created problems. For instance, when he discovered that her art would be included in the prestigious Documenta exhibition in West Germany in 1982, he became, she says, "jealous and destructive" (though Prince denies this, claiming he was "happy" for her). Sherman says, "Becoming more successful than my friends became a guilt thing for me. I knew that they felt bad if I started to say, 'I'm in this show' or something, because they would just think, 'Gee, why isn't it me?' So I stopped telling them what I was involved in and had to totally play it down."

In their last days together Prince pressured Sherman into collaborating on a pair of portraits of each other in drag. And he exhibited and sold prints of the work without consulting Sherman or giving her any of the cash. Last year, when Prince became a successful artist in his own right, the two finally made amends. With his tail between his legs, he admits that "if one person is really making it and the other artist isn't, that stuff is like *People* magazine. They probably split or kill each other or beat each other up or something. I should have gotten out of the gallery because I also laid it on Helene – this thing about 'nothing's going on with me.'" About their breakup Sherman says, "I attribute it all to his not being able to deal with my success."

She replaced him – briefly – with someone who was already successful. While in Germany for the opening of Documenta, she met Joseph Kosuth, one of the founding fathers of Conceptual art. Now she dismisses the affair: "I was lonely, I had just broken up with Richard, and he had drugs." Kosuth denies having had drugs and, he says, "I was on the rebound, and she was blond and available. It ended when I wouldn't marry her. She had fantasies of us being king and queen of the art world." Yet Sherman's memories of Europe in the summer of '82 are anything but royal. "I was just kind of trailing after him," she says. "I felt like a groupie or something."

In demand everywhere by then, her portraits had become more inward-looking; one depicted a woman clinging tearfully to a blanket. At about the same time, her prices jumped to $1,000 per print. According to Winer, "They're photos and not paintings – you know, not individual, unique pieces – so her prices didn't go up dramatically. They just increased incrementally according to her reputation." Today, however, Sherman is one of the highest-earning woman artists. She receives about $10,000 a month in living expenses from the gallery and is paid the balance at another time. Moreover, she can afford to spend an additional $80,000 a year on materials and fabrication costs.

In the early eighties Sherman captured a wider audience and became a household name. But critical opinion was divided over her move into color, and Sherman's new works lost her some supporters. Of course, certain critics are entirely dismissive of all successful artists of this generation, claiming that they are star-struck and career-oriented. Yet given the enormous numbers of artists today, it is understandable that some try to stand out from the pack. Sherman's detractors are usually duped by how effortless her art looks. It's as though they believe that her work is just normal women's stuff.

Douglas Crimp, co-editor of *October* magazine and the first writer ever to tackle her art, says, "She is a very central artist.

I regard the early *Film Stills* as her most radical works – they had an almost throwaway quality and exist just as well in reproduction." Of her work since she moved into color and larger formats, he says, "Cindy's new pictures defy expectations. They continue to be shocking, which is not to say that they are not lovable." But photography critic Christopher Phillips is less impressed by her newer work. "The black-and-white *Film Stills* required a very intimate response," he says. "You had to admit the sometimes embarrassing appeal of these tawdry cinematic personae that she had dredged up from films of the fifties and sixties. Her new color work, on the contrary, tries so hard to deliver a big visual thrill that intimacy becomes impossible. The only position left for the viewer is that of voyeur, which is a much more traditional role in art."

Yet the appeal of Sherman's art hinges on the fact that she is being watched by an audience that is excluded from the action. She is at once totally visible and unfathomable. She is forever being consumed by the people who look at and buy her photographs, but she cannot be entirely possessed by them. This could be why she is so impenetrable in conversation and why she attracts so much attention.

Among her fan mail Sherman began to receive what she calls pseudo love letters inviting her to collaborate on a vague project with a French-born video artist named Michel Auder. She had already met him and, she says, "was flattered and thought it was neat, but I didn't know if I liked him. I also thought it was kind of creepy." But they did meet again, and Sherman discovered a package-deal relationship that included a compatible male artist who was older, already had a child and would let her be the star. Five months later, in 1983, they married. So far, that's all the collaboration they've managed.

"I've always sort of believed that as long as one part of my life was out of whack, I would like my work," she says. "So I was nervous that if I was happy in my love life I might lose my edge. Instead, it just made me look again at what I was doing." And so Sherman threw out the cute women in her art and opened the door to vengeance. Whereas in her early works she had portrayed herself as a "typical broad" – occasionally vampy, usually threatened – she now seems to have gained the confidence to turn all that on its head. Funny, but not without anger, her new works are big color prints that show the flip side of the feminine coin. Cindy the sex kitten became Sherman the tomcat.

Her characters mutated from the type of women that men want to date to being their ultimate turnoffs: wicked fairies, Medusas, bulimic people-eaters. The twin sets, the new boobs, the flattering angles disappeared and in their place came whiskers and lesions, toothy snarls, and a pair of artificial buttocks pointed at the camera. She invented, to say the least, a few more striking ways to address her audience.

Sherman's body barely appears at all in these photographs. And she no longer wears makeup, except in the studio. In one photograph dating from 1987, her eyes are reflected in a pair of sunglasses beside a pool of vomit. In another picture, her largest to date, she is absent altogether, and in her place is a distorted mask, gleaming with sweat and pus (she created the fleshy effects by carefully applying dog food to a commercially manufactured toy). Sherman says she wants to show that ugliness can be beautiful, and that beauty "is such a lie. That's what frustrates me about fashion magazines and beauty, because I've learned that it is just a matter of applying makeup in a certain way."

As "nice and polite" – and as self-conscious – as ever, Sherman has not been spoiled by her fairy tale's happy ending. She pokes fun at herself and calls herself a homebody (a condition she ascribes to being married). She is happy to spend all day in her TriBeCa loft or at her new summer house, where she hides behind her answering machine and doesn't go outside for days. She sees her art developing in two ways: "I'm continuing along with my idea of not using myself – just photographing landscapes and toys. And then, out of the Limoges project I did, where I made a photograph to put on a porcelain tureen, I'm making pictures of eighteenth-century figures, like Marie-Antoinette. I guess I feel freed up to do both things at once."

She has also become more outspoken. When, for instance, the Whitney Museum announced that it would be mounting an exhibition of her art in 1987, she was overjoyed. But then it was rescheduled for the summer, a time when the art world (and everyone else) is on vacation. Sherman was offended. "If I was a male painter with the same sort of recognition that I've received, my show wouldn't have been bumped," she says indignantly. But being pushy has never been Sherman's method. "I have never really felt like the toast of the town, and I haven't taken advantage of the luxury of being more well known than other people. Once I wanted to get into a club and finally got up the nerve to use my name and say, 'Well, I'm Cindy Sherman.' They just said, 'So what? Who are you?' "

She shrugs her shoulders and laughs. But it was a fair question. And one that she may never truly answer. ●

Yoko Ono

The New York Times FEBRUARY 1989

As well as being one of the world's most fabled widows, Yoko Ono is one of its wealthiest artists. Yet even stranger for one so famous is that her art is actually little known. A participant in New York's underground scene of the early 1960s and one of the very first members of the international Fluxus art movement – a loosely knit group of musicians, artists, poets, and film makers who tried to blur the boundaries between art and life, and in some ways were the first hippies – Yoko Ono became the personification of way-out, experimental art after she met John Lennon in 1966.

As an artist, Yoko Ono was a curiosity, and a bit of a shock. She was also an occasional whipping boy for the press through the late 1960s and the 1970s – blamed for splitting up the Beatles and denounced as an artistic opportunist. Once she published a sales list of her art's prices as a work of art. On another occasion, in 1965, she offered 200 shares in herself for sale at $250 each. As a joke on the newly invented label of Conceptual artist, she proudly dubbed herself a "con artist."

The Whitney Museum of American Art begs to differ, and beginning Wednesday (through April 16) will present "Yoko Ono: Objects, Films," an exhibition of her art from the early sixties on.

· · · · ·

"Yoko Ono was an artist who was part of a movement involved in exploring conceptual issues. Younger artists are again interested in these themes, so it seems a good time to bring them back into view," says Barbara Haskell, curator of painting and sculpture at the Whitney and co-curator of the exhibition. This show, comprising two dozen of the artist's sculptures and films – some of which are nominally familiar to avant-gardists and Beatles fans alike – will be held in the museum's lobby gallery and film and video theater. Financially and spatially, it is a modest project for the museum. But in terms of attendance, the Whitney expects a blockbuster.

Clearly, the life and work of Yoko Ono, who turns 56 this month, continues to inspire debate. The jury is still out on her art. Recollections of her work in the early 1960s vary wildly. Richard Bellamy, who directed the influential Green Gallery in New York, says, "I thought of her as a particularly severe case of 'suffering artist,' and was sympathetic. But there was little I could do about it practically except, for example, to ask Bob Scull to buy her *Sky Piece*, and later to send her $50 when she appealed from London. I wanted to help on a personal level, but couldn't get behind her art."

To David Bourdon, however, former art critic at *The Village Voice* and *Vogue*, Yoko Ono's book of instructions for musical and artistic pieces, *Grapefruit*, is "one of the monuments of Conceptual art of the early 1960s.

"Yoko has a lyrical, poetic dimension that sets her apart from the other Conceptual artists," he says. "Her approach to art was only made acceptable when white men like Joseph Kosuth and Lawrence Weiner came in and did virtually the same things as Yoko, but made them respectable and collectible."

And the performance artist Charlotte Moorman, a friend of Yoko Ono's from the early 1960s, adds: "The Beatles were fantastic. They left their mark. But a hundred years from now, it's Yoko Ono the world's going to remember, and not John Lennon or the Beatles."

Yoko Ono started sowing the seeds of her return to the art scene two years ago, after an absence of almost twenty years. In 1987 she accepted an invitation from the Carl Solway Gallery in Cincinatti to participate in its tribute to John Cage on the occasion of his 75th birthday, and minted an edition of eight all-white enameled bronze chess sets, priced at $7,500 each. Soon afterwards, with the help of Arthur Solway, the son of the gallery owner, she quietly got to work on finding an outlet for the pieces in New York. She says that she started wandering into art galleries to "check them out."

· · · · ·

Arthur Solway suggested Nature Morte, an important, small East Village shorefront gallery (it closed last fall). Peter Nagy, director of the gallery, was keen to exhibit Yoko Ono's works in one of the gallery's last shows. "I think her early stuff was some of the best Fluxus stuff done," he says. But when they met and he showed her the work of other artists represented by the gallery, she remained silent. "She said almost nothing," he says. "She was stone-faced, just smoked cigarettes and didn't even take her sunglasses off. Six months later I got word that she wasn't interested. The bottom line I got was that she wasn't interested in being shown as an old sixties artist. She wanted to come back into the art world as a functioning, contemporary artist. She also wanted a big, splashy reentry."

A show was pitched to the New Museum of Contemporary Art in SoHo. But the museum was preparing its Malcolm McLaren show, and was slow to respond to a proposal involving another crossover figure from the art and music scenes. Unaware of her efforts to secure an exhibition, John G. Hanhardt, curator of film and video at the Whitney, and co-curator of the exhibition that opens this week, approached Yoko Ono through a common friend. Hanhardt says that he has long wanted to screen Yoko Ono's films, and when the artist made her sculptures available too, Barbara Haskell, curator of painting and sculpture, and the rest of the museum swung behind him. Within weeks the dates were set, but the final selection of objects was made only last month.

For the Whitney retrospective, Yoko Ono decided to exhibit some of the surviving art works from her early days alongside new versions of the same pieces. Her crystal ball from 1964, *Pointedness*, which is displayed with the caption "This sphere will be a sharp point when it gets to the far side of the room in your mind," will stand beside a bronze cast of the same ball, made in 1988. There is also the white chessboard, as well as new casts of a selection of the artist's earlier objects. These new works, which have been cast in editions of nine, are being offered for sale by the Carl Solway Gallery for between $7,500 and $12,000.

Simultaneously, the museum's film and video department is exhibiting her films, many of which were made in collaboration with John Lennon. They include *Rape* and *Up Your Legs Forever* – which features the legs of, among others, John Cage, Jasper Johns, Robert Rauschenberg, *Rolling Stone* magazine publisher Jann Wenner, and the film maker Jonas Mekas – as well as *Bottoms* and *Fly*, the latter starring a representative of the insect kingdom who washes and struts across the landscape of a naked human body. It is accompanied by Yoko Ono's shrill vocal soundtrack – sounds that were typical of the music she recorded with Lennon and the band they formed after the demise of the Beatles, the Plastic Ono Band.

· · · · ·

Yoko Ono lives surrounded by art in the apartments she shared with the former Beatle in New York's odd Dakota building. Her plush environment is the antithesis of the downtown loft where she took some of her first steps as an artist in New York's

experimental scene. For a six-month period in 1960 and 1961, her home on Chambers Street was an important meeting place and concert venue for composers, performance artists, poets, and others. This sparsely furnished loft in an industrial area of lower Manhattan – housing nothing but a knocked-about grand piano and chairs made from old orange crates, which the artist would rearrange into a bed at nighttime – was a lonely outpost in the art world of the time.

Thanks to these concerts, says the composer John Cage, "Yoko became an important person in the New York avant-garde. People came from long distances to attend the performances. They were the most interesting things going on." Among the audiences were Cage, who was the group's spiritual leader; George Maciunas, who soon became its impresario; Max Ernst and Peggy Guggenheim, and Marcel and Teeny Duchamp.

"I was definitely part of that fringe scene," Yoko Ono says, "but I don't think that anybody was doing work like mine. My sources were in everything."

In 1961 Maciunas opened the AG Gallery on Madison Avenue and offered Yoko Ono a show, her first. She exhibited paintings with little burn-holes and a piece of canvas on the floor titled *Painting To Be Stepped On*. The "painting" was an irregular piece of canvas. "I didn't have the money to buy a canvas," she says, "so I was given a piece from the Army disposal store downstairs, and just used that."

· · · · ·

Yoko Ono virtually dropped out of the art scene in 1972, after a retrospective at the Everson Museum in Syracuse. Last summer, when the Whitney provided her with a means of reentry, the only problem was what to exhibit.

Then one day, over spaghetti at Da Silvano restaurant in Greenwich Village, Yoko Ono's live-in companion, Sam Havadtoy, an interior decorator, suggested to the artist that she recast her old pieces in bronze. "I got very upset," she says, "because I thought that this person just didn't understand anything about my work. My work was about a representation of ideas, and ideas are just like water or air. The work had an ethereal quality."

Soon, however, she came to appreciate the suggestion. "I realized that for something to move me so much that I would cry, there's something there. There seemed like a shimmering air in the sixties when I made these pieces, and now the air is bronzified. Now it's the eighties, and bronze is very eighties in a way – solidity, commodity, all of that. For someone who went through the sixties revolution, there has of course been an incredible change. I call the pieces petrified bronze. That freedom, all the hope and wishes are in some ways petrified."

What were once slight, papery, and translucent glass sculptures and see-through mesh paintings are now being presented in cold, impenetrable, permanent versions. A reflection, perhaps, of Yoko Ono's own story over the last thirty years, ever since she first appeared in New York as an eccentric and ambitious new arrival? ●

Susan Rothenberg

MANHATTAN, INC. MAY 1987

In recent months, the art world and the *New York Post* have been watching artists drop their handkerchiefs outside major galleries and wait for the best offer. On February 18, "Page Six" of the *Post* described Barbara Kruger's "bolt" from Annina Nosei Gallery to Mary Boone: Boone "has come to ride herd on some of the prize stock of the art world," "Page Six" aptly observed, but then mistakenly said that certain talents of a rival gallery — Sperone Westwater — were "currently corralled on the Boone farm." Angela Westwater, Sperone Westwater's managing director, pointed out the error to "Page Six" immediately, but it took her three days to get well and truly even.

Enter Susan Rothenberg, horse painter. Rothenberg, age 42, is a respected painter who rose to prominence in the mid-seventies. Her art is considered pre-Neo-Expressionistic with ties to post-Minimalism — which translates, in 1987 jargon, as school of big bucks. Rothenberg had been represented since 1976 by the 50-year-old Willard Gallery, directed by Miani Johnson, who inherited the gallery from her mother. Rothenberg's works initially sold for a mere few thousand dollars, and she quietly went about the business of being an artist, evolving over the years from painting horses to, in Johnson's words, "abstracted heads, hands, figures, sailboats, swans." Though media-shy, Rothenberg was never ignored by critics, museum curators, or collectors, and she quickly enough became Willard's show pony.

Then, last fall, Johnson decided that she would close shop at the end of this season. Rothenberg was not immediately alarmed — she could take her time to find a new gallery. But in February, Larry Gagosian, the bicoastal art dealer, made several spectacular sales that turned up the heat. Exhibiting eight of Rothenberg's early horse paintings from the collections of Edward Broida and others (although only three were ostensibly for sale), Gagosian fetched prices that shocked even Rothenberg — they stretched from $300,000 to the half-million mark. And since they were resales, nothing went to the artist.

As a result, Rothenberg became the hottest artist in the world for the duration of February. The dealers spotted a winner; Leo Castelli, for instance, says that "Gagosian's show brought Rothenberg back to mind ... so I contacted her." And he was not the first or last. Some of the biggest and wealthiest galleries in New York — including Knoedler & Co., BlumHelman, and Hirschl & Adler — chased Rothenberg, competing singly or, as with the Washburn and James Goodman galleries, joining forces for greater effect.

It was a race that made more highly publicized deals between artists and galleries look easy. In addition to the usual inducements offered an artist to join a gallery — catalogues, cash advances, and assistance toward production costs — the dealers tried to tempt Rothenberg with promises of increased percentages of her sales and, more importantly and pertinently, participation in the profits accruing from resales.

Rothenberg was in a quandary. On February 14, she sent a handwritten note to one bidder, Douglas Walla of Kent, that pleaded, "It's all still a big '?' I have met with some dealers and have gotten more confused. I need time." In particular, Mary Boone was jockeying into position. Her offers were "very seductive," Rothenberg confided to Paula Cooper (who, despite widespread expectations, did not bid for the artist). In addition to Kruger, Boone had recently taken on Sherrie Levine and was bidding for Malcolm Morley, who had just been released from Xavier Fourcade Gallery. She offered Morley six figures to join her stable; he agreed; they signed; the deal was celebrated — but then Morley changed his mind and went to Pace Gallery. And, on February 21, in a photo finish, Boone learned she also missed out on Rothenberg, who went to a surprise late bidder — the Sperone Westwater Gallery.

Angela Westwater, a demure figure on the contemporary landscape, is also an important one. "I'm not interested in just shopping for merchandise," she says. "I'm interested in a long-term arrangement with an artist, and Susan is interested in the same thing." Westwater says that she and Rothenberg reached a "well-talked-out oral agreement," according to which there is nothing paid up front and the artist receives 60 per cent of the price of each work sold. Rothenberg's first show at Sperone Westwater, scheduled for the fall, will comprise ten works priced between $55,000 and $100,000.

But the real benefits to Susan Rothenberg at Sperone Westwater will be less tangible. Westwater, with her partner, Gian Enzo Sperone, in Italy, can offer her a higher European profile as well as a stable of mostly European artists in which Rothenberg will be almost the only American — and the sole female — star. Rothenberg also says she likes Westwater's other artists.

Once the artist and her new dealer had shaken hands, all that was left was the announcement. Rothenberg telephoned and thanked everybody who had shown interest. "It was the least I could do," she says. And Westwater simply "walked out and told the first person I saw. That's how we went public," she beams. "It all happens fast enough — I mean, you don't really need 'Page Six.' " ●

BRICE MARDEN 1986

Brice Marden

Connoisseur OCTOBER 1991

In the eighth century A.D., during the Tang dynasty, the anonymous Chinese poet known as Cold Mountain turned his back on the imperial court and retreated to the mountains. Cold Mountain was a Buddhist ascetic, a vegetarian, and a skeptic who wrote three hundred songs denouncing "the world of dust." Living beside streams and behind waterfalls, alongside small communities of Buddhist monks, Taoist hermits, and the beasts of the wild, he peacefully practiced the Way to Enlightenment. His poems, four couplets to a page, are the inspirations for Brice Marden's new paintings at the Dia Center for the Arts in New York City.

In late-twentieth-century New York, in the eleventh year of the Reagan-Bush regime, Marden, unlike the poet who inspired him, is reaping the rewards of extraordinary good fortune. At the peak of the 1980s art boom, his work spearheaded the newsmaking resale market for Minimalist and Conceptual art. A Marden painting from 1977 that originally sold for around $40,000 went for $880,000 last year at Sotheby's, and New York art dealer Larry Gagosian claims to have privately sold one of Marden's paintings from the 1960s to collectors Linda and Harry Macklowe for more than $2 million. In 1989, two drawings were auctioned at Christie's for more than $500,000 each. Six years ago, Marden was given a $1 million advance by Mary Boone to join her gallery. And this year, Swiss dealer Thomas Ammann purchased three or four paintings Marden has yet to make for almost double that amount.

At 53, Brice Marden is handsome, with a high forehead, bushy eyebrows, long hair, and graying sideburns. He's most comfortable in black jeans and black, long-sleeved T-shirts and has a tendency to mumble. Fellow artist Chuck Close remembers that in the sixties Marden's "image of himself was as a James Dean type." But nowadays, the millionaire ex-Minimalist has cast aside the muses of sex, drugs, and rock 'n' roll and turned into a solid family man. He's in control of a mushrooming art, finance, and real estate empire called Plane Image, which was incorporated in the 1970s for taxation, medical-insurance, and profit-sharing purposes. And in very 1990s fashion, he has also been suing his former accountant for allegedly misappropriating funds. Asked to describe his lifestyle, Marden quips, "Bohemia ... Upper Bohemia."

His studio is in the heart of the squalor of the Bowery, down with the bums, but he taxis home every afternoon to a Greenwich Village brownstone lined with works of art by Henri Michaux, Franz Kline, Andy Warhol, and Marden's wife Helen and pottery, trinkets, and souvenirs (including a painting by a Haitian artist called Saint Brice) picked up by the Mardens on their travels.

By night, he and Helen are social animals (in the good old days, he was a fixture at Max's Kansas City) and regulars at the now-you-see-them-now-you-don't restaurants run by their friend Brian McNally. On weekends, they drive with their daughters, Mirabelle, 12, and Melia, 11, to their eighteenth-century farmhouse in Buck's County, Pennsylvania. Then there are Christmas time jaunts to St. Barts, in the Caribbean, where they kill time with Gagosian or the art collector and advertising magnate Charles Saatchi or Jann Wenner, the publisher of *Rolling Stone*. And most summers they escape to the cosmopolitan Greek island of Hydra, where they own a house and studio complex on a very warm mountain overlooking both town and sea. Such is Brice Marden's existence in the world of dust. "You mean I should be walking around in rags?" he asks sarcastically. (Yet this is possibly a question he also asks himself.)

More than any painter his generation, Marden is the bridge between the art-for-art's-sake ethos of the late 1950s and today's capitalist orgy. Typical of his generation, he is also questing for the New Age and expressing transcendental yearnings. And he has long talked about art as a "trampoline into spirituality," that "painters are amongst the priests." Now his paintings embody his interest in Asian religions, especially Zen Buddhism and Taoism.

. . . . .

Marden developed his Minimalist style during the 1960s, when he was in his twenties. At that time in American art, less was definitely more. The Minimalists, mostly sculptors, were reducing art to its essentials – shape, color, and form – and artistic extremists were insisting that painting was dead.

Then, in the mid-1980s, a decade after a new generation had revived figurative painting, Marden finally abandoned his uninflected rectangles of muted color, and a cobweb of dark lines was spun across the pale surfaces of his paintings. "In terms of my career," he told *Flash Art* magazine in 1990, "I got to a point where I could go on making 'Brice Marden paintings' and suffer that silent creative death. I also happened to be in a mid-life crisis. You get to this point where you just have to make a decision to change things." He added later that "you get stuck in an economic bind. You think you're being very independent and that you're not locked into some market. Then, twenty years later, you find that you can't change the way you paint."

If the buildup to his new style was gradual, the release was sudden. Most surprising was that when the new paintings were first exhibited at the Mary Boone Gallery in New York City in 1987, they looked, well, old-fashioned — like a cross between avant-garde painting and graphic illustration from the 1950s. "They're very modern, but not very contemporary," says *New York Times* art critic Roberta Smith. "But Brice's work doesn't have to be cutting edge. Instead, he's made paintings to which he's very connected. It took him years to learn how to make a mark on canvas because he was so identified, in his own mind and in everyone else's mind, with the idea that each color had its own surface and shape. Now he's going back to his roots, which are basically Abstract Expressionist." According to Robert Pincus-Witten, a critic and writer on Marden's paintings who now works at the Gagosian Gallery, "The problem with the recent paintings is not the paintings. It's with a new generation that is not able to read abstraction."

In an exhibition he curated at Boston's Museum of Fine Arts in March, Marden linked his own paintings to the work of the Spanish masters Zurbarán and Goya, as well as to Chinese landscapes, calligraphic scrolls, and jade pots. But the roots of both his Minimalist and his calligraphic styles are more readily found in postwar American art — the paintings of Kline and Jackson Pollock, Mark Rothko, Jasper Johns, and the scribbled slate-gray surfaces of Cy Twombly. (The French *tachiste* and *art informel* movements of the 1950s were also taken with chinoiserie.)

Marden's own roots are suburban. The son of a banker, Marden was raised in middle-class Briarcliff Manor in New York's Westchester County and studied at Florida Southern College in Lakeland, Boston University's School of Fine and Applied Arts (ex-classmate Pat Steir recalls that "he was handsome and the best painter in our class"), Yale Summer School of Music and Art in Norfolk, Connecticut, and finally, Yale University, where he got his master's in fine arts. At Yale, Marden looked for an alternative to the Pop art route out of

Abstract Expressionism — by wallowing in gray paint and making gridded-up abstractions.

In 1960, when he was a 22-year-old undergraduate at B.U., Marden met and married Pauline Baez, sister of the folk singer Joan, and a son, Nicholas, was born the following year. The Baezes were Quakers and involved in antiwar activities with such organizations as SANE (Stop All Nuclear Explosions), and Marden was drawn into their world — the Newport Folk Festival and the circle around Bob Dylan. He also did the sound on the film *Monterey Pop*. "It was a joke," he says, "because I'd never even run a tape recorder in my life."

In the summer of 1963, the little Marden family moved to New York and squeezed, with Brice's paintings, into a railroad flat on Avenue C on the Lower East Side. Since they needed money, Marden worked part-time as a uniformed guard at the Jewish Museum on Fifth Avenue.

His wife's parents were "horrified," he says, at reports of their daughter's living conditions. So his father-in-law, who worked for UNESCO, invited the Mardens to stay with them in Paris. They stayed four months, but then Marden and his wife split up (and later divorced), so he went back to New York, and she and their son moved to Carmel Valley, California. (Nicholas Marden returned to New York when he was 16. Now 30, he is the bass guitarist for the hard-core cult rock bands Deans of Discipline and False Prophets.)

· · · · ·

In 1964, the Jewish Museum mounted a Johns retrospective while Marden was working there, which gave him the opportunity to just stand, stare, and study. (In 1970, he painted *Three Deliberate Grays for Jasper Johns*.) Though Johns's visual puns left Marden unmoved, two things stuck in his mind: Johns's use of grays and his method of mixing paint with wax to yield a brittle, matte surface. Like Johns, Marden combined paint, beeswax, oil, and turpentine on a hot plate in his studio, applied it to the canvas with a brush, and then scraped it off over and over with a spatula until the desired opacity was achieved. The result was blank-looking paintings, with a lot to see. Their patinated surfaces transmit the warmth of old stone walls, and look like they would crack if tapped with the back of a spoon. It was these surfaces, rather than any brushstrokes, that he used to convey his emotional intent. This way, in 1965, he made his first monochrome painting.

Meanwhile, Johns was organizing a benefit exhibition at the Leo Castelli Gallery to raise funds for the Foundation for Contemporary Performance Arts. "[Painter] Alex Katz called me," Johns remembers, "and said that an ex-student of his would like to give a drawing to this exhibition and would I look at this kid's work. And Brice came up with a portfolio of works, and I accepted one for the exhibition, and I acquired it and I still have it." It was Marden's first important sale; his first solo show came the same year.

While on duty at the 1966 opening of the "Primary Structures" exhibition at the Jewish Museum, he met Klaus Kertess, who was preparing to open a gallery. Kertess made an appointment to visit Marden. "I went to his studio," he recalls, "and knew right away that I wanted to show his work. I loved the mystery and implacability and the beauty of how it was painted."

Kertess's gallery, the Bykert Gallery — named for Kertess and his backer, Jeff Byers (who was married to Hilary Paley Byers, the daughter of William Paley) — turned into one of the most innovative of the era. Marden's first exhibition was in November, but Kertess managed to sell only one work (collectors Barbara and Eugene Schwartz bought a drawing and hung it in their bathroom). Marden was just as broke after his show as before it. He says he had to use the last 15 cents of his advance from Kertess for the subway ride to a gallery opening uptown, where he asked Robert Rauschenberg's secretary, the painter Dorothea Rockburne, for a job in the Rauschenberg studio. He worked there through the 1960s.

"Bob was wonderful," says Marden. "He's very generous, and is probably the most naturally brilliant person I've ever met in my life. I loved watching him work with images, to see him choose images. But his real art was done when I wasn't around. I washed all the windows – you know." (In 1968, when Rauschenberg couldn't put his hands on the originals of his legendary 1951 all-white paintings for a show at the Leo Castelli Gallery, he had Marden repaint them.) But most of the time Marden was around, they drank. Rauschenberg recalls that the good-looking young painter was "very huggable." "Everybody's huggable to Bob" is Marden's reply.

When he wasn't drinking, Marden was smoking. "I always liked grass, though acid was my favorite thing," he says. "But I found that when you took acid, I mean every time you came back from a trip, there was a little bit less up there, so I didn't want to become an acidhead. But I smoked a lot of pot. With a constant use of it, there's this level of awareness that you're drawn into, this shamanistic aspect."

His evenings were spent at Max's Kansas City, where Mickey Ruskin, the proprietor, operated an attractively lax accounting system for artists. Max's, a hole in the wall near Union Square,

opened in December 1965 and quickly became the most famous artists' salon of the post-Pop era. In the front, the straight male painters drunkenly argued about the big issues of the day – whether a painting is an object or an image, whether it is permissible to create illusions in paintings and sculptures, and whether an artistic idea is more important than its artistic end product. In the middle, Ruskin served steak. And in Max's famous backroom, the fragile luminaries and exhibitionists in Warhol's crowd entertained and shocked one another and any of the stars and stargazers who happened by. Here, objecthood, process art, and the desirable thickness of stretchers for paintings were not hot topics. But everyone in the back was as high as everyone in the front, and until it changed ownership in 1974, Max's was hopping.

Through Bobby Neuwirth, an old Boston friend who was now his neighbor as well as Dylan's road manager, Marden renewed his acquaintance with Dylan and various members of his gang, by now including Edie Sedgwick. He met Jimi Hendrix at Max's and remembers the nights Dylan and Cary Grant walked into the throbbing scene. "Those were the only times anything ever really stopped the place," says Marden. "Ten minutes after Dylan arrived, Mick Jagger and Brian Jones came in and nobody noticed." (Though Marden's Minimalist style was unchanged, his titles indicate who his friends and influences were: works were named for artists David Novros and Carl Andre, and for Dylan, Janis Joplin, Otis Redding, and Nico, the vampy vocalist in the Velvet Underground.)

At Max's, he also met a young unknown painter named Julian Schnabel, one of the innovators in painting after modernism. But back then, he was, Marden says, "basically a pain in the ass. He kind of forced himself on the situation, and I resented the fact that this guy was coming on as though he'd been around forever." Schnabel remembers that the night he and Marden went to painter David Diao's studio after Max's closed, Marden "took a drunken swing" at him. "I thought I tried to strangle him," Marden admits.

Also at Max's, he met Patti Smith. In 1971, "she was a kid out of New Jersey who was always spouting off about Arthur Rimbaud," Marden recalls. His stark painting *Star (for Patti Smith)* took its dimensions from the poet's height and shoulder width and its colors from what he calls her "real pale skin and this jet black hair which was very impressive."

· · · · ·

Helen Harrington was a painter working at Max's as a waitress. She and Marden married in 1968. But soon after, there were problems, which Marden painted into his work. He complained to a friend that "my wife turned her back on me in bed for six months." She also left him, but no sooner was she gone than she came back. So Marden named his new series of works the *Back* series. The nine paintings are 69 inches high, Helen's height. The invitation to his second Bykert exhibition in 1968 showed her standing naked, back to the camera, in front of his paintings.

Evidently, theirs was (and remains) a deeply romantic relationship, and Marden taps it for links between his emotions and his art. In both his *Back* series and the two-panel painting *For Helen* (1967), he creates the sense of another presence, his wife's, and perhaps his own as well, as though he wanted to breathe life into raw matter. According to the critic Roberta Smith, his paintings have "a skinlike surface and a density which is almost that of another body. The kinetic response is mixed with the optical."

By the end of the decade, he had became Bykert Gallery's star artist and attracted a cult following of sorts. Among his devotees was Mary Boone, an intense young artist who was Kertess's assistant. "She was ambitious and driven," recalls Kertess, "good at selling, and she really liked Brice's work." Chuck Close, another painter at Bykert, says that the baby Boone took her job "extremely seriously. In fact, she claimed to be older then than she claims to be now." (She turns 40 this month.) Boone listened and learned, and now says with a chuckle that "when you worked in a gallery in those days, you mostly just sat around and talked." In 1978, she opened her own in SoHo.

Kertess claims that "for Brice, things had become quite financial by 1971." He visited the new Rothko Chapel in Houston, Texas, and Helen began exploring the world (travel and cooking are still her main pastimes). In 1971, she discovered the Greek island of Hydra, where they started summering; they bought their first house there in 1973. Marden's surroundings and personal life continued to find their way into his work. In 1972, he embarked on his *Hydra* paintings, inspired by the sere landscape. In 1974, he published *Suicide Notes*, a book of drawings (he says many of them started as stoned doodles). In 1978, he painted his *Annunciation* series while Helen was pregnant with their first child. And his 1978-79 *Mirabelle* drawings (named for the newborn) were made with his daughter in his arms after her 2A.M. feedings.

. . . . .

When the Solomon R. Guggenheim Museum in New York City mounted a retrospective of Marden's paintings in 1975, he was only 36. That year, Kertess gave up being an art dealer to become a writer (his book on Marden, *Plane Image*, will be published next year), and Byers, his partner, killed himself. Marden shopped around for another gallery.

He had been exhibiting in Italy and Germany since 1971 with Gian Enzo Sperone and Konrad Fischer; as a result, he had a connection with their gallery in New York, Sperone Westwater Fischer, and in 1976, he had a show there. But Arnold Glimcher of Pace Gallery (who had been a painting major at Boston University with Marden) was keen to show him. And Marden was also flirting unsuccessfully with Leo Castelli. "I can't remember exactly what I told him," says Castelli. "I must have said that it wasn't possible at the moment because there was an objection on the part of Kelly."

Ellsworth Kelly, already a member of the Castelli Gallery, painted monochromes and multipanel pictures that looked superficially like Marden's — especially the black-and-white and red, yellow, and blue paintings — although most of their work is worlds apart in design, surface treatment, and mood. Castelli says that Kelly called Marden "a vile imitator" and threatened to leave the gallery if Castelli took Marden on. "My panel paintings had never been written about," Kelly explains, "and when everybody started talking about Brice Marden inventing panel pictures, I got upset. He was a young gung-ho artist, but I had done all these things before without selling much."

As far as Marden was concerned, he "always thought it was flattering that Kelly should get so upset about it. He probably thinks he's the only person allowed to do panel paintings." In deference to Kelly, Castelli refused Marden, and Marden went to Pace. Not long afterward, Kelly went to Blum Helman Gallery.

Marden stayed at Pace for six years. In 1981, he was given a prestigious exhibition at the Stedelijk Museum in Amsterdam which toured to the Whitechapel Gallery in London. His wife left him again, he succumbed to the charms of cocaine as well as other sensual pleasures. He told Kertess that he sought the help of a substance-abuse psychologist at that time and was thinking about studying in a Buddhist monastery.

And he was unhappy at Pace. He says, "All the time I showed there, I felt I had to protect myself. I had seen so many artists go there and just sort of go to sleep. Arnie's really okay, but it's a business. There's a lot of art there, but business is the thing. It really made me nervous."

From 1977 to 1986, he worked on a commission to design stained glass windows for the cathedral in Basel, Switzerland, which played into his interest in religious geometric abstraction. For the commission, he consulted an alchemical treatise on the Holy Trinity and, about 1983, designed a set of windows in which the lead lines crisscross the tinted glass at irregular angles. This use of diagonal lines and the asymmetric internal shapes that resulted were Marden's first attempts to go beyond the limitations of the rectangle. Although the windows were never built, Marden subsequently felt loosened up enough to use diagonals in his paintings.

Meanwhile his work was being eclipsed by the new trend in figurative painting. His career emerged from the shadows only when neo-Minimalism aced Neo-Expressionism, a new development that set Marden up as an old master. But Pace wasn't treating him as a superstar; according to Boone, his earnings – a mere $250,000 – were half that of Jean-Michel Basquiat's, who was half his age. So in 1985, a year after Julian Schnabel ditched Boone and went to Pace, Marden accepted Boone's million-dollar advance and ditched Pace.

According to Close, who had also gone to Pace from Bykert, joining Boone's SoHo stable was an understandable move for Marden: it took him out of the blue-chip uptown atmosphere and obliged him to produce new work under pressure. Close also dismisses Marden's objections to Glimcher. "Brice always has trouble whatever dealer he's with. He sometimes feels uncomfortable with financial success. And rather than take responsibility for that, he tends to blame his dealer."

Boone's glamorous advance cemented the changes Marden's life was undergoing. Helen returned, and he cleaned up his act. "When you're going to make some sort of positive commitment about working," he says, "why mess yourself up with drugs and alcohol? I stopped drinking, I stopped coke, I stopped grass."

Helen turned him on to Asian art, and its influence could be seen in his drawings until they became a mix of gesture, graffiti, and calligraphic marks. Eventually, he had the confidence to work these shapes into his paintings. Their featherweight, jade-colored background looked like tissue paper, and the leaden lines in the foreground showed a decomposing grid. They were the biggest turnabout in his career but looked like visitations from the past.

Seven of the new works debuted at Boone's in 1987, and according to Marden, Boone was unsure about them. "I probably offered them to thirty collectors before they were sold," she says. They weren't the Minimalism that was back in demand. "We kept the prices down," Marden says. Most of them went for less than $100,000.

Two years later, they were priced at $125,000, and they moved faster. Boone says she "inspired" the slow-working Marden to speed up and make more and reveals her strategy for getting artists to produce: "Get them into debt. What you always want to do as an art dealer is to get the artist to have expensive tastes. Get them to buy lots of houses, get them to get expensive habits and expensive girlfriends and expensive wives. That's what I love. I highly encourage it. That's what really drives them to produce."

Marden splurged and bought his country house in Pennsylvania as well as extra property in Hydra for a studio and quarters for the kids. And the market for the new works picked up dramatically as his older works started being resold in the six- and seven-figure range. This year, Boone sold a new work, *Picasso's Skull*, for $650,000.

As soon as he had earned back his million-dollar advance, Marden took control of various areas of his work. "I didn't see any reason to move anyplace else," he explains, "but I don't like exclusivity. I don't like it in country clubs, and I don't like it in art dealers. What I wanted to do was bring it all under my control. I don't want Mary Boone controlling what happens to my work. *I* want control."

• • • • •

The last two years have been a maelstrom of highly-publicized maneuvers and bids, with an acclaimed show of Marden's *Grove* paintings from the 1970s at the Gagosian Gallery (it was the first time anyone, including the artist, had seen the works all in one place), a much-gossiped-about attempt by Gagosian to get Marden to leave Boone and join his gallery, and some sensational action at the auctions. To concentrate on his new paintings, Marden canceled plans for a touring retrospective exhibition that he was organizing with an American museum. And he invited the dealer Matthew Marks, a newcomer, to represent his drawings.

Marks met Marden when they were both at Pace. "He was my favorite artist there, but I was just a little kid upstairs in the print department," Marks says with a big smile. "At that point I was sort of in awe of all artists, but I *loved* Brice's work."

In 1986, after Marden had gone to Boone, Marks quit Pace and moved to London to work at the Anthony d'Offay Gallery. "Anthony hadn't done anything with Brice, but he was very interested," Marks says, "so we went to his studio, and then we started going all the time. And the first time Brice ever sent any work to London was for a show I worked on there – an exhibition of drawings by gallery artists. I went to the studio and picked out eleven of Brice's drawings, and that's really how it all started." D'Offay began representing Marden in Europe, and their arrangement continued until early this year, when Marden asked d'Offay for a large advance and was refused. Marden subsequently cut his seven-figure deal with Zurich-based Thomas Ammann.

Marks moved back to New York in the summer of 1989 with no definite plans. But as soon as the Mardens returned from Hydra, they asked him to lunch at Da Silvano's, a restaurant in Greenwich Village, and offered him the business in Marden's drawings. Of course, Marks was delighted to accept.

With Marden's works on paper as his inventory, the 28-year-old dealer was able to open the Matthew Marks Gallery on Madison Avenue this year. In May, he mounted a show of Brice Marden drawings and etchings, with prices ranging from $35,000 to $110,000. They sold out at the opening. The upcoming retrospective of Marden's graphic works slated for the Tate Gallery in London, the Musée d'art moderne de la Ville de Paris, and the Baltimore Museum of Art will be another feather in Marks's cap. According to Marden, when Boone learned that she had lost the drawings to a newcomer, "she wasn't elegant about it."

Her loss was compounded two months later by the outrageous prices Marden's drawings fetched when Robert Mapplethorpe's collection was auctioned at Christie's. Mapplethorpe had photographed the Mardens' daughters shortly before he died in 1989. In exchange, Marden agreed to give the photographer one of his drawings and sent him two so he could choose. But Mapplethorpe, who was suffering from AIDS, wanted both and never got around to making a deal. So after his death, his lawyer, Michael Ward Stout, asked Marden if the Mapplethorpe estate could buy the second drawing. Marden set the price at $30,000, was paid, and the matter was closed until Mapplethorpe's collection went up for sale in October and November 1989. Spectacularly, the drawings were sold to Shigeki Kameyama of the Mountain Tortoise Company in Japan for $572,000 and $528,000 — a world record for the artist's drawings.

Just prior to this, Larry Gagosian, one of the ringmasters of the resale market for postwar art, had stepped in and made a play for Marden. (If the rumor mill is to believed, one of Gagosian's chief amusements is bidding for Boone's artists.) "It was a real overture," says Marden. Gagosian worked through their mutual friend, the restaurateur Brian McNally, who offered a host of reasons as to why the painter should change dealers. Soon afterward, when Marden and

Gagosian came face-to-face over fish at a restaurant in Paris, Marden asked him frankly, "Well, what's the deal?" Gagosian replied by asking Marden to evaluate his own worth — "a standard businessman's ploy," says Marden. Marden's lawyer suggested that he jot down a "wish list," but Marden couldn't think of anything he wanted, so he dropped out of the game. Why become a "slave to Larry?" he asks.

. . . . .

According to the Mardens' friends, Helen's influence on her husband's business decisions cannot be underestimated. She is called Brice's muse and lightning rod, as well as a large piece of his conscience, and he speaks of her impact on him reverently. "I look at things she looks at," he says. "She was more interested in the East than I was, and she had to drag me to Thailand, which was a revelation. She also turned me on to this show of calligraphy at the Japan House. When I saw it, it just hit me."

"We never thought we'd have anything," Helen once exclaimed with delight on a tour of one of their three homes. "Isn't the art market wonderful?" And she makes an effort to share what they have. She has taken in two girls whose parents have either died or become unable to care for them. And with Julian Schnabel's ex, Jacqueline, and Paola Igliori, the ex-wife of painter Sandro Chia, she has also taken the down-and-out poet René Ricard under her wing.

While his wife and their daughters traveled in India and Indonesia, Marden spent the summer of 1991 locked in his studio racing to meet his deadline. All six of his *Cold Mountain* paintings go on display in New York City this month and will then tour to the Walker Art Center in Minneapolis, the Menil Collection in Houston, Texas, and the Centro de Arte Reina Sofia in Madrid. Thereafter, their tour of Europe may extend indefinitely. Marden knows more people will see these paintings than any he has ever done. Large and mysterious, they are like signs written in a runic alphabet and assert to the world of dust that Brice Marden has found his own Way. ●

Richard Prince

THE NEW YORK TIMES MAY 1992

Five years ago, Richard Prince made three paintings in disappearing ink. He kept one and sold the others through galleries in New York and Los Angeles, although the dealers who sold them and the collectors who bought them were unaware of the gag. When the imagery on the canvas started disappearing, the Californian collector called his gallery and complained. Both buyer and gallery director were furious.

"The funny thing," says Prince, perched on a paint-splattered chair in his TriBeCa studio, "was that when I explained that the invisible painting was more or less unique and offered to give back the $15,000 or replace the painting, the collector wanted to keep it." The second buyer, according to the artist, has stored his painting and has not yet realized that the image is gone.

Richard Prince, like Jeff Koons and Mike Kelley, is one of the bad boys of the art world. Long a player of games, he has made works under pseudonyms, like John Dogg, and once opened a fake art gallery, which few could find and even fewer could gain entry to (it was rarely open). In 1977, Prince destroyed his existing works — early figurative paintings, collages, and staged photographs — and turned exclusively to photographing photographs from magazines. This ultra-Minimalist way of making pictures — high concept, low labor — became wildly popular in American art during the early 1980s and now goes by the names re-photography and appropriation art.

These days the 43-year-old artist is concentrating on what he calls joke paintings — silkscreens of old cartoons, often from *The New Yorker*, often monochrome, often with captions he considers tragic. "A lot of the jokes I use are about death, alcoholism and madness," Prince says. Often the butts of the jokes are women. He gives an example: " 'My brother married a two-headed woman.' 'Is she pretty?' 'Well, yes and no.' "

"Jokes are a way of saying two things at once," he says. "I like the ambivalence, the black and white, the fence-sitting."

But Prince, whose devilish grin is bolstered by a sharp intelligence, is becoming at least partly respectable. He now has an exhibition in which all the works of art are plainly visible; all are certified as being by him; and all are in a place that is easy to find and admits everybody. The retrospective,

at the Whitney Museum of American Art, includes more than 80 examples of Prince's work from the last fifteen years. Even worse for his cherished outsider status, once the show closes, on July 12, it will travel to Germany, San Francisco, and the Netherlands. "I've been working on this project since 1987," said Lisa Phillips, a curator at the museum who organized the exhibition.

. . . . .

On the strength of his photographs of photographs, beginning with a set of four pictures of living rooms in 1977, Prince is frequently touted as the inventor of appropriation art — despite interesting photographic predecessors in the fifties and sixties and, of course, a centuries-old tradition of painters copying the works of others.

Nevertheless, in the late 1970s, Prince was onto what a younger generation of artists embraced as a hot new idea, one that became a major trend in the 1980s. Photographic appropriation became a blunt and effective challenge to the popular idea of art — much of it, like Prince's, favoring an impersonal, Warholian quality over the creator's own touch.

While working part time in the tearsheets department of Time Inc., Prince observed certain repetitions of images and poses in magazine photographs, whether advertising or editorial — the way women held their hands, for example. By enlarging details — a gloved hand, say — and exhibiting almost identical images side by side, he raised questions about originality and the identity of the artist. The shots of fashion models and living rooms also revealed something deadly about the representation of private spaces and private selves in the media. In those photographs (as in the joke paintings that came later), he presents a lifeless world of stereotypes.

Other artists were not far behind. After seeing his work in an exhibition in 1979, according to Prince, the intense young artist Sherrie Levine called him and asked how he had done his photographs and whether she could use the idea. Nonchalantly, he said he wouldn't mind. Years later, after Levine had stolen the appropriation spotlight and amassed greater critical acclaim, he is less cool about her call.

RICHARD PRINCE 1988

"People associate artists with doing things original," he says. "Here's someone who calls you up and says, 'I want to do your work.' I thought, 'Jeez, I haven't heard that one before.' " Levine, for her part, says, "I know that Richard thinks I get all my ideas from him."

In the early 1980s, a little New York school of re-photographers emerged, including Sarah Charlesworth, Sylvia Kolbowski and Barbara Kruger, as well as Laurie Simmons and Cindy Sherman, both of whom practiced set-up photography rather than appropriation in the strictest sense. Prince says he felt like the only man in this predominantly female group, whose immediate supporters among dealers and critics also tended to be women.

Prince was associated with other 1980s figures as well, among them Jenny Holzer and Robert Longo. Yet as the art stars of the early eighties became established, he saw most of his colleagues streak ahead of him. His comparatively quiet photographs were barely selling.

Most annoying of all was that Cindy Sherman, with whom he was romantically involved, was invited to take part in countless exhibitions, including the Documenta show in Germany, the major international exhibition of 1982, while he was not. (He now says that he refused to "audition" for the exhibition.) And because both artists showed at Metro Pictures, a SoHo gallery, he was constantly reminded of her success. As a result, Sherman says, he became "jealous and destructive." He, in turn, says he "ruined everything." After a year and a half they separated, and he was out of the gallery a year or so later. By 1983 he was ready to pull one of the biggest stunts of his career.

There had surfaced a previously unknown photograph of the prepubescent Brooke Shields, who at 17 was starting to become famous. Prince describes the picture as "an extremely complicated photo of a naked girl who looks like a boy made up to look like a woman. For me, she had the perfect body." He re-photographed the picture, named it *Spiritual America* and exhibited it by itself in a fake gallery on the Lower East Side below Houston Street – hardly a district for galleries.

· · · · ·

Some supporters were enraged that he would give prominence to such a plainly exploitative image. Meanwhile, according to Prince, the original photographer, Gary Gross, and his lawyer, A. Richard Golub, tried to stop the exhibition but couldn't find the gallery. (Golub's recollection is that they did find it and served papers. In any case, after a month the show was history.)

Nevertheless, trouble was brewing. Says Kate Linker, an art critic who was an early admirer of Prince's work: "Richard's absence of any political perspective about the images he so acutely selects poses a problem. He wants to almost wallow in the cultural loadedness of these images, and that makes one uncomfortable when faced with what those images actually do."

Soon after the Brooke Shields episode, Linker and the artist parted ways. "I got kicked out of the women's club," Prince says.

After 1983, Prince launched into less sensational series of re-photographs – of sunsets ("pictures that look like they were sent away for," he says); cowboys, lifted from Marlboro ads and shot through color lenses to accentuate their artificiality; and women, his favorite subject, as beauty and porno queens and gang molls. He often adjusted the color and exaggerated the grain of the page, obscuring the images and making them look more seductive than advertising.

A few years later, he started applying slick coats of paint to fiberglass car hoods and exhibiting them vertically on a wall. Then there were the jokes. "When I drew the cartoons," he says, "they were already drawn. When I photographed photographs, they had already been photographed. When I painted car hoods, they had already been painted. But the joke paintings really look like art." (Of the ones now at the Whitney, the *Times* art critic Roberta Smith wrote: "He stirs the found images of popular culture into a semi-legible stew that mimics the stream-of-consciousness automatism of Abstract Expressionism. In the process, he is progressively making his obsession with popular culture more personal and accessible, and also more beautiful.")

Ten years of neglect ended in 1987. Perhaps the change was due to his joke paintings, perfectly timed for the newly cynical art world. Perhaps it was that paintings sell for more than photographs, and Prince was ready to make the shift. Perhaps it was the fact that he was approached by Barbara Gladstone, a smart operator with a stylish gallery in SoHo. Whatever the reason, everything improved for him.

· · · · ·

Barbara Gladstone says she made "a big pitch" for the artist: "No gallery had ever invested a lot in him, and I wanted to do the whole ball of wax and have my hands on everything. The first thing we did was print earlier photographs." They now sell for up to $30,000. Even in this depressed market, Gladstone can command $35,000 to $70,000 for the joke paintings.

For fifteen years, Prince has worked in a wide variety of media and styles. He is comfortable with uncertainty, for even though the jury is out on his joke paintings, twelve are included this summer in Documenta. He has a luxurious new beachhouse in Bridgehampton, on Long Island, and an Acura NSX racing car. He is cavalier about his celebrity, and finds having money "humorous."

He's also uncommitted in his private life, and lives alone. There have been a couple of major love affairs since Cindy Sherman, but nothing since his brief marriage to Lisa Spellman, the director of the 303 Gallery, in 1990. "It sounds terrible," he says, "but I went from an artist to an art director to an art gallery owner."

Now, he jokes, "I'm dating this pair of twins."

Are they pretty?

"Well, yes and no." ●

Part Three

Business-Art

Frank Stella and
the Museum of Modern Art

FAME NOVEMBER 1988

Speculation has been mounting about alleged lurid goings-on between New York's Museum of Modern Art and the painter Frank Stella. In the opinion of the art world, the museum has always fawned over Stella, initially a precocious superstar, now a burned-out supernova. His desperately extreme abstract paintings fail to do justice to his brilliant debut. That much is widely held. The extent of the museum's minuet with Stella is more of a secret to which, until now, only the museum's staff and benefactors have been privy.

The best thing that Stella has going for him is MoMA. His retrospective there last year, his *second*, was accompanied by a hike in his prices at auction and in galleries: one mediocre work fetched $385,000. Some might call Stella's newfound bonanza the fruit of an epistemic shift. I call it a cozy coincidence.

Nowadays, Stella is busy making paintings for clients like Paine Webber, the corporation that funded last year's show at MoMA. (Stella has just finished decorating the 38th floor of Paine Webber's headquarters.) During that show, rumors were flying fast and furious about the precise ownership of the art on display. The curator of the retrospective, William Rubin, as well as the Rubin family, Paine Webber's chief executive officer, Donald B. Marron (who is also president of the museum's board of trustees), *and* other trustees of MoMA, are all proud owners of Stella's works.

Given this state of affairs, the fallout of which is radiating from the museum, is it any wonder that the relationship of art works to their viewers is changing? As one art student, when asked recently what her work was about, quipped, "It's about the relationship of the art object to the buyer."

. . . . .

Frank Stella, now 52, is most famous for his early paintings. In the 1960s, he was the beneficiary of massive changes in the art world, from "hot" Abstract Expressionist painting to "cool" Pop and Minimal art. (In the early eighties, he was lucky again when the scene switched back to "hot" for a while.) All of 23, the Princetonian was an instant hit at his first commercial show, in 1959. It was from this show of black paintings that William Rubin bought a picture for his personal collection, the first of many. Through the early sixties Stella's popularity endured, partly

because the snobs who couldn't take to Pop found his abstracts palatable, and partly because by the time Minimal art arrived Stella's nearly blank canvases were already there.

"What you see is what you see," Stella said dumbly. His art, said critics, was about the relationship of the object to the viewer. The muteness of his black surfaces interrupted only by thin white pinstripes, the unconventional shapes of his canvases, the contemplative stare that they induced in their spectators – Stella had all this down to a T. But last year at the Museum of Modern Art was something else altogether, something that left this viewer cold. His "paintings" now are three-dimensional gewgaws; they look like wrought-iron brushstrokes styled and permed and hung in money-scented air.

Many will dispute Stella's importance 29 years after his initial appearance. But no one will dispute that MoMA's promotion of his art is unending. The museum has awarded major retrospective exhibitions to only two artists twice. The other is Picasso. What about Matisse, Monet, Mondrian? According to Leo Castelli, one of Stella's dealers, "The Modern may have overshot the mark a bit, but in my opinion Stella deserves this distinction." In addition to Stella's two retrospectives – in 1970, when he was 34, and 1987 – MoMA exhibited his "Indian Bird" maquettes in 1979. It's enough to make us think he's the new Picasso.

. . . . .

I viewed last year's retrospective on a Wednesday, when the museum was closed. There was supposed to be no one else in the gallery. Suddenly there was a noise and my escort said, "Get over here, quick, behind this painting." Just as the painter Ad Reinhardt considered sculpture something one bumps into when looking at a painting, I discovered that Stella's misshapen reliefs are good for hiding behind.

We could hear a couple of voices discussing Stella's art with a proprietorial air and liberal use of possessive pronouns. Then, through the twisted metal on the walls, two steely wheelchairs slipped into view. These are the vehicles that MoMA staff have taken to calling "mobile curatorial thrones" because exhibition curators like to glide around in them when their shows are being installed. Here enthroned were William Rubin, the director of painting and sculpture at the museum, who effectively retired in August and is now director emeritus, and Larry Rubin, director of the Knoedler Gallery, who, with Castelli, is Stella's dealer. The brothers were privately fingering their bounty.

Although his peer painter Gerhard Richter has criticized Stella's early work as "too commercial," there were periods in the sixties and seventies when Stella brought in little cash. But immediately before his show at MoMA last year, in his most recent commercial gallery exhibition at Knoedler, one of his new works hit the $300,000 mark. In 1976, Larry Rubin was asking $25,000 for a large Stella, which was surprisingly low considering Stella's historic reputation. It is also known that he sold one work that year for as low as $16,000. Things improved from there, and Stella's new painted reliefs started to become something of a controversy. They were included in London's "A New Spirit in Painting" and Berlin's "Zeitgeist" exhibitions in 1981 and 1982 respectively. At auction, paintings sold for twice what comparable Stellas fetched at the gallery. Christie's sold one in 1980 for $93,500 and another in 1981 for $198,000. Larry Rubin says that a 1958 black canvas that previously sold for $450,000 would bring upwards of $1 million today.

Stella's prices soared last year with the news of his second retrospective at the museum – Christie's moved one of his "Circuit" series of 1981-82 for $385,000. Still, when one considers the prices lassoed by Stella's contemporary Jasper Johns, or even younger artists like Anselm Kiefer, Eric Fischl, and Susan Rothenberg, Stella's art is not such a huge money-spinner.

. . . . .

Though it is known that William Rubin himself is a collector of Stella, the museum is mute about this side of affairs. Eight works were listed in the checklist to the Stella show as belonging to "private collections," and at the end of the catalogue, William Rubin thanked the "several collectors who wish to remain anonymous" as well as his brother. But in fact he was thanking his brother twice, because Larry was one of the anonymous lenders. So was William Rubin's other brother, Richard, a professor of political science at Swarthmore and Larry Rubin's original backer. Still other works were loaned by trustees of the museum – architect Philip Johnson and art lover Barbara Jakobson – as well as by Robert E. Meyerhoff, who sits on the museum's painting and sculpture committee and its International Council.

Then there is the matter of Paine Webber, the corporation that funded the Stella show. Donald B. Marron is Paine Webber's chairman and CEO, as well as the president of MoMA's board of trustees. Marron's involvement with the museum is endless:

he is chairman of the museum's executive committee, and a member of its International Council, its committees on painting and sculpture, prints and illustrated books, and its nominating, finance, investment, business, and pension committees. As for Mrs. Donald B. Marron, she sits on the Committee for Special Events, otherwise known as the women's committee. (Marron told The New York Times, "My wife, Catie, is frequently impressed by what we do at the museum. But when I told her that Audrey Hepburn was going to be here, she was really impressed.")

Marron is a personal collector of Stella's work and donated to the museum one of the Stellas in the recent show. Paine Webber's corporate art holdings also include a quantity of Stellas (contrary to what The New Yorker reported in Calvin Tompkins's glowing roundup of corporate art-buying). And only this year the company commissioned four new pieces from Stella (via Larry Rubin) to adorn its headquarters on Sixth Avenue. Though one assumes that Marron knows more about the business of art than about art, the museum stands at attention when he speaks; the very tall Marron can push his weight around.

For example, just before Stella's show opened, Marron was perambulating around the museum. Not being a bona fide curator, he did not use a wheelchair. But when he spotted how small Paine Webber's acknowledgment appeared on the title wall, he threw a fit nevertheless. "He freaked out," says one of the show's designers who wishes to remain anonymous (anonymity not being the exclusive domain of the rich and influential). "Normal policy is to display the name of the funders as discreetly as possible. He said he wanted Frank Stella's name and Paine Webber's to be the same size, or at least for his credit to be half the size of Stella's. He just stood there and made a stink. Then, the deputy director, James Snyder, told us all to stop what we were doing. The next step was to contact Bill Rubin, and we all had a meeting in front of the title wall. In the end, Paine Webber's name was five inches high, below Stella's, which was about ten inches. Normally we don't bend on things like that, and if it hadn't been Marron, MoMA wouldn't have capitulated."

Paine Webber's name hit everyone who entered the exhibition, poking people in the eye, just as Stella's art would if they got too close. Had the name appeared the same size as Stella's, the exhibition could have been interpreted as a show of works by an artist called Paine Webber, financially supported by Frank Stella. Everything considered, the art student was right: the best spectators, today, are the speculators. ●

An interview with Hans Haacke

FLASH ART MARCH 1986

PAUL TAYLOR **Are you happy to be part of the Conceptual and political art revival?** HANS HAACKE I never quite understood what my work has to do with "Conceptual art," unless this label is applied to all those things that Duchamp associated with the "gray matter," rather than the retina. In the late sixties, I became politicized, like a lot of people. As I had been dealing with what I considered, at the time, to be physical and biological "systems," it appeared to be only logical, from the point of view of general systems theory, and particularly in view of what was happening in the social arena, also to address social issues. That seemed to require a shift in medium. I felt objects or physical "process" works could not accommodate the involvement with social matters. That led me to the incorporation of words. Our social relations are structured and are largely intelligible through verbal constructs. This development in my work coincided with the influx of words into the art scene of the period. **In *Hommage à Marcel Broodthaers*, a curious image of Ronald Reagan suggests that there is a perverse relationship between the political figure and the masses. Are you implying that politics has become spectacularized?** No, that wasn't on my mind. Mass demonstrations are not a new phenomenon. However, politics, as mediated by the press, has indeed become a spectacle. Clever politicians exploit that. Hitler was a master at it, and so is the actor Ronald Reagan. **Would art play a different role in such a context where even the political seems unreal?** Let's not be fooled. Behind the spectacle, politics continues, as hard-nosed and real as ever. And if a policy is built on fiction, its results are nevertheless felt in the world of reality. Blacks rebelling in South Africa are shot down with real bullets! They don't have the luxury to revel in fiction. What is really frightening, though, is the degree to which fiction is taken for reality at the Reagan White House. Reagan's "star wars" defense concept comes straight from the dream factory. If global policy is developed along the lines of a Hollywood script, we may very well blow up the world. What a spectacle! Reagan as a disciple of Marinetti. **The painting of Ronald Reagan and the one of Margaret Thatcher in *Taking Stock (unfinished)* are ironic. What do you think of the widespread use of irony in art today?** I like it a lot, as long as it isn't just glib and flirtatious. Irony leaves things in abeyance and invites the viewer to fill in the gaps. In other words, it is an appeal to the viewer's intelligence. I want to have some fun, and so should the audience have fun—by using their heads. **People sometimes say that irony is a way of anaesthetizing social injustice and is a form of smug complicity with the status quo.** That depends on which audience you are dealing with. **Again, are we talking about the homeless and the blacks in South Africa or the educated middle class?** Of course, irony would be totally out of place in Soweto. My sympathies with the victims of apartheid should not be mistaken to mean that they are my audience. I wish, though, that they should benefit from my work. People who visit art galleries, museums, and so forth obviously come from a different culture. The same is true for those who learn about what's in the galleries through the mediation of the press. A good number of them are, in fact, working in the consciousness industry, where opinions are made and promoted. That is the arena where my stuff could perhaps be of use. As I don't like to be lectured to, so I don't want to preach with a raised finger. Bertold Brecht said it quite well: that the task is to "make interests interesting." He was a master of irony. **Why is political art flourishing more than it was ten years ago?** I don't have a single or conclusive answer. One reason, I'm sure, is the arrival of the Reagan Administration. That served as a reminder that politics didn't go away, once the Vietnam war was over and the dust of the Watergate scandal had settled. The vacuum left by the political dropouts was soon filled by the resurgent New Right. In the art world, it ranges from an art critic like Hilton Kramer to the Saatchi whiz kids. But there is perhaps another reason: among younger artists, there seems to be a tremendous sense of alienation. Those who have not joined the yuppies and cynically play the game are thoroughly disgusted with the all-pervasive marketing mentality of the contemporary art scene. As a result they get politicized. The ideological polarization in this country has given such attitudes new legitimacy. They don't look ridiculous anymore. The "me" generation seems to be on its way out, as the nostalgia for the fifties is fading. You may even look at it in marketing terms. The art world, like the world at large, has been so saturated by the products of a phony individualism and coy rebellion that for no better reason than out of boredom the audience wants something different. Let me add, the type of art I just alluded to with contempt, has had as much an ideological and, by implication, a political effect, as so-called political art does. It is naive to assume that art works made without a political intent lack a political dimension. This is something Marcel Broodthaers knew very well.   **Then there are others, like Sue Coe, who think they are making political art by doing expressionistic illustrations of social injustice. Is that kind of artist a political one in your book?**   Like a number of other artists, Sue Coe makes political testimonies. She uses exhortation, and she appeals to the viewer's compassion for the victims of injustice, a bit like Käthe Kollwitz and artists of that generation.   **It is denotatively political.**   I believe the means with which I work are as political as the subject matter, that is to say, they play an equally signifying and interventionist role.   **If, indeed, such things can be equivalent. Are the media you use – painting, photo-text, sculpture – totally instrumental to your purposes?**   I don't engage in formal exploration for its own sake. I choose the medium that appears to be most useful for a particular occasion or purpose—and on the way I discover things. It is really more explorative and playful than it sounds.   **Could you, in the case of _Taking Stock (unfinished)_, have used photography and collage?**   No, because photography doesn't have the aura of painting.   **So it is not regressive to appeal to painting's auratic status these days?**   If you were to embrace the aura, I would be wary. I don't believe in halo-painting. I use the aura ironically. It glows within quotation marks, like the gold frames around my portrait paintings.   **You once commented to me that magazines like _Manhattan, inc._, which have a corporate culture section, are doing what you've done over the years, that is, are linking the interests of corporations with what we see as culture. Why are such critiques becoming widespread?**   The de facto mergers of the Whitney Museum with various companies, the remodeling of the Chase Manhattan Bank's SoHo branch into an art gallery, and particularly the way art is strategically employed to attract tenants for the new Equitable Life Insurance Building in New York – all these events seem to have served as signals that something is afoot. Also the letter Philip Morris sent to museums who had been recipients of the company's "largesse," buttonholing them to lobby against pending restrictions on smoking in public places, did not sit well with a lot of people. Nor did the Metropolitan Museum gain in scholarly reputation by mounting a show with the sublime title "Man and the Horse" to promote Ralph Lauren. But these are only the more spectacular and silly aspects of the corporate invasion of the art world. They make flashy copy. While the more fundamental problems are not ignored, they are often balanced against the argument that art was always supported by special interest groups like the church, the princes, etc., and that it would be unreasonable to expect that corporations don't want something in return for their money. This argument is often made in terms that reveal a tacit admiration for the cynicism of the scheme, not unlike the fascination with the entrepreneurial spirit of certain artists. I believe one doesn't realize what price we have paid for inviting business to take over.   **With the return of painting in the so-called advanced art scene, has the concept of art been commodified?**   Art works have always played a multiple role; one of them is that of a commodity. Paintings lend themselves better to performing this function than many of the things that came on the scene in the late sixties and early seventies. Much of that was burdened with the additional mortgage of being rather austere and dry. It is therefore not surprising that there was a backlash. One wanted to see colors again, something sensuous, have some fun, and believe again in geniuses and castles. No doubt, there are many other reasons for the "hunger for painting." The most remarkable phenomenon is, however, that the astuteness of an artist in developing a marketing strategy, to "position" himself – they are mostly males – is valued as an artistic accomplishment in its own right.   **Speaking as one who wasn't around in that era, I have nevertheless thought that the feelings about nonobject art ran deeper than that. I thought people believed art had really changed. The concept of art was meant to have been freed from the commodity and to be more ethereally artistic. Is that how artists felt?**   Yes, there was a heady sense that making art had nothing to do with making money. Of course, one still had to pay the rent. As always there were people with big egos, but fame was not measured in terms of sales. I am not the only one who feels the clock has been turned back.   **Is the idea of historical progress being discarded?**   This gets very philosophical. It may sound pretty trivial and also pompous: I would like to believe in a utopia, a more humane society, at peace with the environment. But I confess I'm not very confident. We are getting drained already by the struggle not to let things slip further into barbarism.   **Would a revival of Conceptual art be ironic?**   Rather than truly ironic it would be sad, like all revivals. ●

JOHN WEBER AND JOYCE NEREAUX 1993

The Marketing of Aboriginal Art

THE NEW YORK TIMES MAY 1989

"The natives are extremely fond of painting," wrote Thomas Watling, an Australian convict, almost 200 years ago. The Aborigines, who have inhabited the Australian continent for an estimated 50,000 years, have been painting on sand, bark, and their own bodies for the last 30,000. Suddenly their fondness for painting, now in acrylics on canvas, is landing them squarely in the lap of the international art world, for which they are adapting their grand creation myths, maps of the land, and ceremonial symbols to the West's easel-painting tradition. Once, the rectangular format of Western painting was totally foreign to the Aborigines. Today they are earning small fortunes by converting their traditional imagery into a commodity.

. . . . .

This new genre has been described as both the newest and the oldest art form in the world. And having proved highly salable in Australia, the craze is reaching Europe and the United States. "Dreamings," an exhibition of Aboriginal art at the Asia Society in New York last fall, broke attendance records. "We had a very strong word of mouth," says Andrew Pekarik, director of the society, who attributes the show's success to the general American enthusiasm for Australia. "Australia has a friendly image. Australia means koala bears, barbecues, Paul Hogan — all those nice things."

Although the paintings are a new fad in a jaded art market, their eye-catching patterns and decorations mask a thorny history of cultural convergence. This unlikely art boom has made overnight stars out of shy, impoverished men and women with little grasp of English and even less idea of how to handle sudden influxes of cash. Australian art dealers, previously unacquainted with the international market, are frantically improvising new trading policies, and collectors are rushing in to sell their holdings.

A new episode in the story of Aboriginal art occurs on Saturday, with the opening of an exhibition of paintings at the John Weber Gallery in Manhattans's SoHo district. John Weber, who handles the Conceptual and Earth art of Hans Haacke, Sol LeWitt and Robert Smithson, has priced the Aborigines' works up to $23,000. Aboriginal art already has a tenuous footing outside Australia — in the collections of Michael Jackson, Mick Jagger, the Queen of Denmark, Wim Wenders, John Kluge, Yoko Ono, the Vatican and others. In Paris, the Pompidou Center's ambitious exhibition of contemporary world art, "Magicians of the Earth," which opened last Wednesday, features a large installation of Aboriginal paintings, and the center plans an extensive Aboriginal exhibition for 1991. And in Hollywood last November, a star-studded party launched Caz Gallery, which is devoted entirely to Aboriginal art.

The sudden fashionableness of Aboriginal art is prompting the artists to organize and develop a business strategy. Many Aboriginal communities have employed "art advisers," whose job it is to supply painting materials and make sales.

According to Gabrielle Pizzi, who runs a gallery of Aboriginal art in Melbourne, "There is a lot of bad art and a little good art, but the art advisers are bound by contract to supply painting materials to everybody, and to try to sell everybody's work. The market is literally being flooded."

In place of a written language and a notion of art separate from the rest of life, the Aborigines — who number 225,000, or 1.5 per cent of the Australian population — have traditionally woven elaborate "songlines" across the continent, which constitute an invisible network of lore and learning, and portrayed their heritage in carvings and impermanent "paintings." Two centuries after white settlement, however, the civilization of these former nomads is in ruins. They suffer from high infant mortality rates, tuberculosis, alcoholism, malnutrition and a variety of other afflictions, including AIDS.

The meanings of their art are kept secret from whites, and the artists decline to discuss many of the symbols, which ultimately limits the ways that Westerners can respond to their art. Certainly, the new acrylic paintings can be appreciated as decorative objects dashed off for suburban living rooms and Western museums. They can also simply appreciate — financially. When asked why she made one particular work, for instance, a Central Desert painter replied matter-of-factly that she "did it to buy a Toyota."

. . . . .

In a way inconceivable to anyone but Andy Warhol and his followers, for the Aborigines painting has become a license to print money. In the city of Alice Springs, Aboriginal painters roam around with canvases under their arms for sale to tourists, and taxi drivers have been known to accept paintings instead of cash because they know they can unload them in the big southern cities for as much as $2,000 each. Many Aborigines spend money as quickly as they get it. If they have just made a sale, they may pay up to $500 for a cab ride home, sometimes hundreds of miles away.

Even if they can't drive, the Aborigines like to own cars. The sandy red road to Papunya, 175 miles north-west of Alice Springs, is flanked by abandoned cars in various stages of decay. Rusty metal and dusty windscreens reflect the sun and flicker for hundreds of miles, some of the shells doubling as halfway houses for sleepy artists on their way home from a heavy night in Alice.

Papunya is a government-run settlement of 400 people where the Aborigines first transferred their tribal images to canvas. The big events are playing cards and poking at slow-cooking steaks on the barbie. (Sacred ceremonies take place outside the settlement.)

A husband-and-wife team might be at work covering a paint-ing with the signature Aboriginal dot patterns. To observe them lethargically transposing their inherited stories and images is to discover an art-world proletariat that – to all outward ap-pearances – is being bred to paint. The men are perfectly cast black imitations of 1950s New York School types – hard-drink-ing, verbally inarticulate, paint-splattered heroes. The Lee Krasners and Elaine de Koonings of the Central Desert are mute in the presence of strangers, always playing second fid-dle to their husbands. The best-known artists, and the most collected across the world, are men like Clifford Possum Japaljarri, Michael Nelson Jakamarra, Maxie Jampijimpa, and Uta Uta Jangala.

The Papunya painting movement started in 1971, when Geoff Barden, a young art teacher, invited the settlement's schoolchildren to paint Aboriginal motifs. The town's elders, observing the efforts of the children who had not been initiated into the meaning of their art, joined in. Soon the Aboriginal fondness for painting had found a new sponsor. Barden began supplying paints and canvases to the men and supervising their painting sessions. His instructions were plain: "Nothing whitefella. No whitefella color, no whitefella per-spective, no whitefella images." He also told the artists when he considered their work finished, at which point he would take the paintings out of the settlement to sell them. They fetched about $75 each. As many as 600 were produced during his

18-month stay in Papunya. (He kept 62 of them – stacked and rolled against a wall of his parents' damp suburban garage.)

. . . . .

What happened to these paintings reveals the contours of the Aboriginal art boom. In 1986, Margaret Carnegie, a prominent Melbourne collector, bought them from Barden for roughly $80,000. Two years later she offered them to Melbourne's National Gallery of Victoria for the unheard-of figure of $1.5 million. In a confidential memo, the museum director said that he was "ethically concerned" and "politically cautious" about the escalation in price. He turned Mrs. Carnegie down.

Subsequently, she offered the museum just one work of the 62 – a 23-by-7-foot painting (the Aborigines refer to these as "truck size") by Tim Leura Japaljarri, a Papunya artist who died in 1984. With the assistance of the museum's Felton Bequest – headed by Sir Andrew Grimwade, Mrs. Carnegie's nephew – the museum purchased the work for $200,000. This set a widely publicized new standard for Aboriginal art. (The previous high paid by a museum for an Aboriginal painting – $7,800 – had been set only a year earlier.) The boom was suddenly official. Margaret Carnegie muses that she was "just terribly lucky with these paintings that they turned into money."

Of her bounty, she was obliged to pay $15,000 to the paint-er's widow, who works collecting garbage in Papunya. The widow immediately bought a car for her son. It was abandoned three weeks later – another shiny bauble in the Central Australian Desert.

. . . . .

John Weber and Joyce Nereaux, his wife and business part-ner, arrived in Melbourne in March 1988, after a trip to Alice Springs, which seems to have been more like a journey to Damascus. They had first set eyes on Aboriginal art at the Aust-ralian National Gallery. As Weber recalls, "We walked into the room and it was like, 'Oh, my goodness!' Wow, this is something else!' I mean, these people really know how to deal with com-position issues, color issues, and yet are very different from any mind set that I'd seen before!"

He immediately started negotiations with the dealer Gabrielle Pizzi and persuaded her and her supplier – the artist-owned Papunya Tula Company in Alice Springs – to give him works for sale on consignment, "which they haven't done for anybody before," he says. According to their terms, the John Weber gall-ery will take 40 per cent of any sale, Gabriella Pizzi 10 per cent, the Papunya company 5 per cent and the artist 45 per cent.

Weber asked the Australians to promise not to undercut his prices by offering similar works for sale for less in Australia, which means that his artists would instantly command higher prices for their works in Australian galleries.

. . . . .

The benefits to the artists are hotly debated. Here in the United States, Aborigines are a novelty; in Australia, they face an ongoing struggle. When a group of painters visited New York for the Asia Society show, they said they were made to feel like kings — hotel accommodations, trips to buy clothes, the lot. But when they touched down in Sydney and went into a bank to cash their honorariums — official Australian Reserve Bank checks — they were refused. "You could have found these checks and passports on the street," an untrusting bank manager told them, and turned them away.

The artists had checks, but no money. It is no wonder they want to print their own. ●

PAT HEARN 1987

Pat Hearn

MANHATTAN, INC. MARCH 1986

Pat Hearn is a rare commodity in the East Village – a snob. What's more, she's a New England-born-and-bred post-punk East Village art-dealer snob who at 30 owns the hippest young gallery in New York. As another dealer jealously put it, "Gracie Mansion is passé and Pat Hearn is where it's at. It reflects a change of direction in the East Village – at least a qualitative shift from kitsch to groovy." The Pat Hearn Gallery, on Ninth Street between Avenues C and D, is the easternmost as well as most uptown in style of any space on the Lower East Side. It's a veritable rash of contradictions, particularly the nourishing art-world mix of the rather good and the pretty bad.

Even during her student days at the School of the Museum of Fine Arts in Boston, Pat Hearn was regarded as a snob, which is a backhanded way of paying her the highest art-school compliment – of individuality. Amid the hordes of hippies and troubled young artists, Hearn's leather outfits and provocative video art works stood out; one of the video pieces, which included a short segment on bondage, was a winner in the museum's Boit Competition in 1983. For several years Hearn sang in a jazz band called Wild and Wonderful. Like another well-known art-world snob, Mary Boone, she was a gifted and intelligent artist before she turned to money-making. And like Boone's, her gallery is a premier showcase for the artists many now consider to be the most gifted and intelligent.

They are also the most recherché. Crossing the threshold into the Pat Hearn Gallery isn't simply a change of environment, from the decrepit to the savvy, it's also a change of era – like stepping into a London gallery in the sixties. Although she's blending European Op art and eighties American neo-Op, it's a measure of Hearn's superiority that she won't ever break down and giggle over the whole gag. Instead she will tell you pokerfacedly, "Great art doesn't go away and come back – it's *always* there and artists are *always* taking from it and making it part of their work." Moreover, she could tell you this wearing a twin-set and a beehive hairdo, and a demure smile you can't fault.

Among Hearn's artists, Philip Taaffe, certainly, makes bold, elegant, and ambitious paintings. He is one of the rare few who have put meaning back into Op art. Concomitantly, prices for his works have been hiked over a fifteen-month period from the low thousands to an official price of $15,000 for the major piece in his January show – which was also his largest piece to date. Peter Schuyff is selling better and better, but his paintings are looking more and more like gift wrapping (Hearn smartly booked his latest exhibition for immediately before Christmas).

With both of these artists, her gallery was on top of the anticipated return to geometric abstraction. Similarly, her current exhibition – a group show of sculptures by four Europeans – coincides with all the chat about mannerist sculpture's comeback. But Hearn is no opportunist; she's hip, with barely a wrinkle of irony in her demeanor. Her kind of drag is normally reserved for the very camp, yet Hearn assures us that she's absolutely on the level.

Three and a half years ago she married Thierry Cheverney, who around that time was exhibiting his paintings at the Pyramid Lounge. Eighteen months later she showed him at her first space, on Avenue B and Sixth Street, along with three others who have gone on to bigger and better things: George Condo, Hearn's first star, who has since left her for the Barbara Gladstone Gallery in SoHo; Milan Kunc, who was swapped with the Monika Sprüth gallery in Cologne (a move indicative of Hearn's international aspirations from the outset); and David Bowes, who has moved to the Tony Shafrazi Gallery.

Was Hearn angry at losing an artist as hot as Condo to Barbara Gladstone? And what about the resemblances of their stables, right down to details like reviving trade in the fifties Italian painter Lucio Fontana? "Well, I was sad to see George go," she says plausibly, but adds that "coincidences of sensibility are not uncommon. In any case, I thought of showing Fontana first. She got the idea after seeing my show."

"Nonsense," says Gladstone. "When Pat told me at her party in Newport last summer that she was showing Fontana, I remarked to her then that I had been arranging the same – with Rudolph Zwirner, a fellow dealer and Fontana collector who's collaborating on an exhibition with me in March. I had been trying to get good Fontanas for months. Besides, anyone knows you can't organize an exhibition like this in four weeks."

By the time Hearn had added the geometricists Taaffe and Schuyff to her stable, she had a dazzling and coherent group of artists that instantly became as well known in Europe as it was in America, aided by heavy exposure on the front covers of international magazines like *Flash Art*. Her artists sell in German galleries, with "adjusted" European prices, and she now owns her new gallery space in Manhattan, a huge ground-floor loft with a vast basement storeroom (the storeroom in the first gallery was a garage with access from the street only). The entire space totals 3,600 square feet and sits like a pristine jewel among the trash and urban decay of Alphabet City.

Hearn says she's improving the neighborhood, contrary to the objections of local tenants and others to precisely her kind of gentrification. "My space helps the street," she says earnestly. "It is the residents who have let it get run-down." But when it comes to the East Village art scene, she is reluctant to join in and assist in any way. Hearn refuses to pose for photographs or submit information about her gallery to what she calls "other people's money-making ventures." Hers is the only gallery that has been so, um, *aloof*.

Pat Hearn doesn't think she's all that outrageous. Her parties are quiet (no music, muffled conversation, a gracious smorgasbord). Her wit and charm can be glimpsed when she holds a conversation with her ever-shivering Chihuahua, Chi-Chi. Otherwise it's straight all the way. Geometrically, you could call Pat Hearn a square. In the East Village her gallery is a beacon. But in terms of image, locale, and success, she's far out. ●

The Hot Four

New York OCTOBER 1986

"**M**y two characteristics," says Ileana Sonnabend, "are greed and curiosity. When I see a cake, I want to eat it. My whole idea of a gallery is to develop artists, so I take them when they are young and cheap and I make them famous and expensive."

For nine months, Sonnabend, age 71, has been getting ready to bring forth a new brood. The art dealer who used to be called the "Mom of Pop" – and who now might be called the matriarch of American art – has just opened a controversial group show at her Sonnabend Gallery, at 420 West Broadway. As she has done many times in the last three decades, she is giving a few relatively unknown artists international exposure. The difference this time is that, to a large and perhaps alarming extent, her four newcomers have already taken care of business.

Only two years ago, Ashley Bickerton, 27, Peter Halley, 33, Jeff Koons, 31, and Meyer Vaisman, 26, were scarcely collected, little-exhibited artists. Bickerton and Vaisman had barely made any paintings at all. Halley had something of an art-world reputation as a writer – he had published on everything from sixties Minimalist art to *The Road Warrior* in small-circulation art magazines. The four artists were being shown at an obscure East Village gallery called International With Monument, which Vaisman and two friends opened in 1983. (Vaisman, to avoid a conflict of interest, was represented by the nearby Jay Gorney Modern Art gallery.)

Over the past two years, as the group members have begun attracting attention, their paintings and sculptures have come to be called neo-Pop, neo-Minimalist, and neo-Conceptualist. Whether the four are genuine inheritors of sixties-style radical art, self-proclaimed heirs to the true American art trad-ition, or brazen careerists has been the talk of the art world. More often than any other group of emerging artists – more even than instant art stars Keith Haring and Julian Schnabel – they have been accused of being cynical and manipulative. But whatever the reservations of critics, the International With Monument group, with the imprimatur of Ileana Sonnabend and, eventually, of Leo Castelli, has already made art history of sorts.

Oddly enough, Sonnabend is one of the less sensationalist dealers in New York. She has kept a low profile and high standards throughout the tumultuous upheavals and voracious deal-making of the art world in the eighties. Early this year, the four artists made a bid, after considerable maneuvering, to show with Sonnabend, and she accepted. Along the way, they turned down the prestigious Marlborough Gallery and the fashionable Mary Boone Gallery – or so they say. Some people are appalled by the way their business was conducted. Even Mary Boone has been heard to joke that their tactics are "like a cliché of my worst publicity."

The artists wanted to show with Sonnabend because she made her name during the heyday of postwar American art. "There were numerous meetings," says Elizabeth Koury, one of the directors of International With Monument gallery. "Every gallery you can name wanted to put on a group show like this. We had to hold meetings to decide on the right gallery. After all, this is a business."

. . . . .

The four young men who are about to become famous are friends who have knocked around together in the East Village for several years. Halley is the only native New Yorker. Bickerton, who entered the scene as assistant to painter Jack Goldstein, has lived in such places as Guyana, Hawaii, and England. Vaisman, born in Venezuela, came to New York when he was 20 and supported himself by working in an art-supply store while saving money that went toward opening up International With Monument. But Jeff Koons has had the most experience in the scene. He has been in and out of a number of SoHo galleries, including, for a while, the Mary Boone Gallery. He left Boone for the Annina Nosei Gallery when it looked as if Nosei would pay more attention to him. Later, he worked as a commodities broker, and he still dresses like a yuppie.

The four artists sculpt and paint; the younger pair, Bickerton and Vaisman, make "wall sculptures," thick paintings that jut out from the wall and can be viewed from three sides. Their hybrid art objects look completely different from those paintings full of comic angst that the East Village was associated with only a few years ago. The art that dominated the international surveys and magazines of the early eighties was spontaneous and gestural, but the International With Monument work

JEFF KOONS 1986

PETER HALLEY 1986

ASHLEY BICKERTON 1987

MEYER VAISMAN 1987

is distant and calculated. Neo-Expressionism is individualistic and heavily crafted, but this new style is anonymous and thinky and often strives for the look of industrial manufacture. What's more, the images are not appropriated from existing paintings. Rather, as Ashley Bickerton says, his bulky painted wall sculptures "can be seen as 'hyperrealizations' or caricatures of the conventional art object. These are paradigms of paintings."

Just before the frenzied East Village art boom peaked in 1984, Vaisman and two fellow students at Parsons School of Design opened their own East Village gallery with their savings. They had, says Vaisman, been "looking at art, downtown mainly, and didn't like much of what was being shown – a lot of Neo-Expressionism and stuff." The gallery's first-year budget was "nothing – $17,000 for rent and publicity – no salaries. The sales were $11,000. This year, sales are way over $500,000 – closer to three quarters of a million."

The gallery's artists, some of whom had established downtown reputations, were attracted to International With Monument for its critical edge. Halley, says Vaisman, was the only one who brought in slides – in January 1984. His first show was held fifteen months later. "A lot of people hated Peter's work in the beginning," Vaisman says. "Now they love it and claim that they've always loved it. Some people feel they have to love it or else they're going to be seen as fools." At Halley's first show, "the paintings cost between $1,500 and $2,500," says Vaisman. "Now they are from $6,000 to $12,000 for a painting that's about twelve feet long." Within three years, the gallery on East 7th Street has not only succeeded in living up to its ironically bombastic name, but its small group of artists are also becoming international figures.

The artists owe a great deal of their success to collectors and their agents, who buy and sell art by word of mouth. It is a network that they have been successful at infiltrating and stimulating – at times playing one agent or collector off another. Sonnabend is benevolent about their tactics. "The artists are children of their time, and manipulation is not excluded," she says. There are "more and more collectors. There are more and more galleries and there are more and more artists. The public is huge ... When Neo-Expressionism came in, it was easier for the collectors, and the public increased because the art was more accessible. Now I find that the public has increased but is also interested in ideas. That is surprising."

The public also wants to spend. The four artists were selling their work before they announced their deal with Sonnabend. International With Monument and the storefront gallery of Jay Gorney were placing their pictures and sculptures with such

well-known collectors as Charles and Doris Saatchi (who have their own contemporary art museum in London) and Robert and Adrian Mnuchin. (Both the Saatchis and Mnuchins recently paid an estimated $75,000 for identical Jeff Koons trains, each car of which is a stainless-steel cast of an original porcelain Jim Beam liquor decanter.) S.I. Newhouse, Jr., Barbara and Eugene Schwartz and their son Michael, Jerry and Emily Spiegel, Suzanne and Howard Feldman, Phoebe Chason, James and Pamela Heller, and Philip Geier of the Interpublic Group have also invested.

. . . . .

Jeff Koons is the ultimate entrepreneur of the new art market. He is said to have threatened an art magazine editor who did not publish his work. (He denies this.) He also understands the complicity between artist and market better than most. His stainless-steel casts of consumer baubles (the Sonnabend show features stainless-steel casts of "the whole gamut of statuary," he says) and billboard-size liquor advertisements are a send-up of sorts of the notion of arty collectibles and addictive consumerism.

Koons takes great pride in his extreme creative gesture: to make a Koons painting, the selection of the suitable advertisement is just the beginning. "I had to go through a lot of lawyers," he says. "I had to speak to every company to get permission. First of all, I had to know how to present my idea to them, and then to work with their lawyers and to work with the printers. These paintings aren't appropriated, they are reprinted, but they had to be reprinted off the original plates. The original full-size negatives were sent out from every company. The only thing that was transformed was the image from paper onto canvas, and then onto stretchers. So they're intellectual paintings. They're not handmade. They were made by a machine, and presented as paintings." But as far as avant-garde postures go, Koons's are not new – they derive from Marcel Duchamp and even Jasper Johns, who cast two beer cans in bronze. What's new is the scale of his operations and the fact that they are now so well absorbed into the art system. (Koons's sense of commerce, too, is a breakthrough: he has framed $6 Nike posters and sold them for $900.)

Peter Halley believes that culture and the art system "have become too circular to be subverted." Appropriately, his abstract paintings are stark diagrams of prison cells and computer conduits. Graphically, Halley's main theme is the similarity among social, architectural, and "informational" space, a similarity that he renders in circuitous Day-Glo patterns against a monochromatic background. The paintings, he says, "are addressing the validity of truths about science and architecture, and maybe even the rational underpinnings of the social order as a whole."

Ashley Bickerton, who also likes to intellectualize about his imagery, is less articulate. Compared with Halley's paintings, Bickerton's are cryptic jumbles of mathematical illustrations and oversize renderings of golf balls; they look like painted surfboards, which makes Bickerton the funkiest of the neoists.

Meyer Vaisman's abstract paintings, like Bickerton's, are stacked almost a foot off the wall, and the surfaces are often so highly glazed that it's unclear if any paint was used at all. Although they're abstract, they do contain traces of the human figure that run across a printed canvas weave.

Jay Gorney says Vaisman's work is "about the relationship between human, biological reproduction and photomechanical reproduction." Vaisman adds that the newest work is also about "shitting and laughing. I asked myself why I thought so much about shit," he said, "and I realized that it's because shit is a fertilizer."

Is all of this self-justification pompous nonsense? Some critics are adamant that it is. "They're hypocrits," says Kay Larson, *New York*'s art critic, "because they assume an ironic, distanced position and use it for financial and career advantage — to get a lot of money and fame. No art could ever do what they claim for it. They replicate not so much images as attitude. The defense of their work is a fairly exhausted one. It brings back all the unresolved questions of modernism — like originality."

· · · · ·

Many of the early enthusiasts for this work were introduced to it by Estelle Schwartz, an art adviser who provided entry into the homes of many art collectors. In and out of the galleries of SoHo, 57th Street, and the East Village, bemused gallery visitors often see Schwartz lecturing her classes on how to collect art. She makes at least 10 per cent on all sales for which she is responsible, and she has been especially supportive of Koons and Halley. By late 1985, art collectors had become keen about the new group, and sizable waiting lists — something previously reserved for big-name Neo-Expressionists and established artists — began to form.

Schwartz, a former writer for the old *Cue* magazine, rhapsodizes about the last few months as if they were Paris in the early part of the century. "The most exciting thing was that I had time to think about the work," she says. "I could get to learn about the work. I could get to know about the work of

Peter Halley and then Jeff Koons — the extraordinary, remarkable, brilliant work of Jeff Koons. I could talk to the artists. We could slowly acquire it. There was nobody there. Meyer Vaisman had a handful of young collectors who were busy in and out of the East Village and responded to that work. But international collectors and dealers were swarming all over the Village. They were zooming all over Europe. They were flying all over the place. And the best work in years was in a little gallery called International With Monument, between First and A."

With an eye on their dealers and agents, the artists began to figure out how to sell themselves. By passing the word that Charles Saatchi had just bought a work, they propelled themselves into the glorified realm of other artists in his vast collection. When Mary Boone and other galleries became interested — at the prompting, some say, of their own collectors — everyone heard about it within days. Estelle Schwartz says that by emphasizing the strengths of Sonnabend and Castelli, she influenced the artists to stay away from other galleries. The artists say that Boone wanted to show their work, but Boone denies this.

"She denies it?" Schwartz asks incredulously. "Well, she was late, I must say. She was totally unaware of it — until it became very hot."

· · · · ·

By the beginning of 1986, the news of an emerging clique in American art had become so hot that it was melting the conventional distinctions between artist, agent, collector, and critic. A collector's opinion had begun to count for more than a critic's; artists were doubling as critics and dealers, and because of the market's momentum, art criticism became powerless. Deal-making had firmly locked the immediate future into place. For instance, the dealer-turned-artist Vaisman is already represented by newcomer Gorney, along with Sonnabend. In 1987, Vaisman says, he will show with Leo Castelli as well.

Gorney believes that Vaisman will cooperate with Sonnabend in very much the way Mary Boone cooperated with Leo Castelli in showing the work of Julian Schnabel and David Salle. This kind of work has really swept the market.

"The phenomenal success of these artists is one thing, but then you notice it reverberating in other ways," he says. "It's going to be hot news for several years. Museum and gallery exhibitions are being organized for next season and the following season. I think that the interest of collectors is worldwide, as is the interest of curators. At this point, we're speaking to various dealers in Paris and London and Cologne. You know, L.A. just fell – a show at Margo Leavin Gallery, Jeff Koons, and soon, Meyer Vaisman at the Daniel Weinberg Gallery. I think Rhona Hoffman in Chicago will show Halley. Donald Young has shown Bickerton and Koons. Boston's Institute of Contemporary Art is doing a sculpture and painting show. There's one in Spain." He comes up for air. "We'll see who's in the Whitney Biennial."

• • • • •

Certainly, Ileana Sonnabend has found artists when they were "young and cheap," and in most cases, she has succeeded in making them famous and expensive. She established her record slowly and quietly, starting 45 years ago, when, at 27, she immigrated to the United States. She had left behind an elegant and well-connected life in Paris. Her husband, Leo Castelli, had just opened an art gallery with another dealer, but the war came and destroyed their plans. The couple were not typical refugees; Ileana's father, a wealthy Romanian industrialist, bought them a townhouse at 4 East 77th Street. In 1941, they arrived with their daughter, their daughter's nurse, a little dog, and 22 suitcases – many of them full of books they feared they could not find in America.

Over the next twenty years, their influence in the art world took hold, and they became powers with the breakthroughs of Robert Rauschenberg and Jasper Johns – the pair whose art provided the transition from Abstract Expressionism to Pop art and the movements of the sixties. In 1959, after a divorce that left room for future business collaborations, Ileana Castelli married Michael Sonnabend. And when the Sonnabends opened their gallery in Paris on Christmas Eve two years later, the Castelli-Sonnabend team grew stronger. The two became the most influential dealers in the world of contemporary art.

Rauschenberg, who joined the Leo Castelli Gallery in 1958, says his career really took off with the Castellis. As a husband-and-wife team, they had been "a historic blend. Whatever Leo couldn't see, she encouraged." Yet since the sixties, it has been Castelli who has got the praise for picking up new trends early.

Once divorced, Sonnabend, on the other hand, modestly went about her business – first with her Paris gallery, where she exhibited such American artists as Johns, Andy Warhol, and Rauschenberg, and then, in 1970, when she and Michael Sonnabend opened a gallery on Madison Avenue (it soon joined Castelli's gallery in a building on West Broadway). When they were married, the Castellis had basked in the glory of their postwar art discoveries, but Castelli's name was always the better-known. Now, in both the United States and Europe,

"Ileana" is a one-word résumé. Her name is spoken by young and old with equal familiarity, yet her reputation is different on each continent: here she is often seen as a promoter of European artists; in Europe, she has been seen as an agent of Americanization (she and Castelli were accused of trying to influence the outcome of the Venice Biennale of 1964, in which Rauschenberg became the first American to be awarded the international grand prize for painting).

• • • • •

This summer, in their Venice apartment, Ileana and Michael Sonnabend and their gallery director, Antonio Homem, who shares their lower Fifth Avenue apartment, idly rehearsed a conversation they must know by heart. "Americans don't understand Europe," she began. "That's why they're over there in the Hamptons instead of being here at the Biennale. They resent things that they shouldn't, and are afraid of things that don't exist. But in Europe in the sixties, I found the same closed situation for Americans. The Europeans had their artists. They didn't think that a nation that they still called 'new' could have art, so I thought it would be a good thing to show them that art is universal. Returning to New York, I tried to interest galleries in showing European artists. That's when I decided that we were going to show Europeans as well as Americans, and I have followed that policy ever since."

Once, the pace of the New York scene quickened with the virtually simultaneous success of Rauschenberg and Johns, and then the Pop artists, followed by the Minimalists, post-Minimalists, performance artists, Conceptualists, art photographers, Neo-Expressionists. Now, with the rise of these hybrid Pop-Minimal-Conceptualists, the Sonnabend Gallery has proved the cyclical view of history, remaining one of the few constants in the art world's mutating spectacle and Oedipal rites of succession.

• • • • •

This month's group show is a bridge across generations. To her artists, Ileana Sonnabend is a symbolic connection to the past. And in today's art, as in politics, religion, and family life, links to tradition are seen as a cure for social estrangement. Naturally, as art becomes increasingly businesslike, the imprimatur of great names from the past helps to gloss over its opportunistic newness, and Sonnabend was sufficiently impressed by these artists to lend them her name.

"Obviously, the art is Conceptual, and I have been involved with Conceptual art all along," she says. "It's very strong, fresh new work, and exactly significant for our time. It deals with issues that are present now. I can't pinpoint them, but they have to do with the new way of looking at things, advertising and television. The problem is going to be duration. Now they are very fashionable. I hope that this will continue and that their work will be enduring.

"Meyer Vaisman came to see me first and proposed the show," Sonnabend continues, "and I said yes, but I wanted to know more about the artists, because I'm slow. When I went back to International With Monument, I was very impressed with the gallery. So what we, both Leo and I, wanted to do was to keep the galleries that were working with the artists – the original galleries – and work in collaboration with them. We don't have to do it, but we will, out of a sense of fair play."

"What we were looking for," says Vaisman innocently, "is the kind of light Ileana Sonnabend can throw on our art. The work that we're all doing has to do with those early beginnings of the Castelli and Sonnabend galleries."

"The opportunity that has been given to us to have this show in that arena is just amazing – because of who she has shown in the past," adds Jeff Koons. "It's the excitement. It's the real thing." And Peter Halley, who is regarded as the intellectual of the group, says, "She's like history. I recently read a catalogue of her collection. I mean, it was just like the history of twentieth-century art – you know, like Europe and fleeing from the Nazis, and then the fifties."

Ileana Sonnabend admits that art dealers have recently changed young artists' expectations.

"Now artists think that everything should be sold before it's made," she says. "I don't know if it's decadent or if it's natural, but it is, and it's new ... I'm a little conservative and slow, and I'm a little afraid of all this. But if I show these people, it's because I think they are good and that I can consolidate their success. If they are able to survive, it is only because they are able to survive their present success."

Michael Sonnabend, who is now 85, refers to the radical years of American art. "There was a time," he says, "when the artists thought you shouldn't sell any work, because if you did, you were commercial, and if you were commercial, you were a capitalist, and if you were a capitalist, you were an enemy." Antonio Homem compares this attitude with that of Bickerton and Koons. "I think their work plays with the idea of consumer objects," he says. "Koons is transfiguring them, whereas Bickerton is making objects in which the idea of being bought and consumed and installed is part of them. And that is actually a new development, although it's true that Andy Warhol was also working with the idea of consumerism, too."

Warhol states the case more bluntly. "The dealers are becoming art directors," he says. "They tell you everything ... The dealers tell me what to do."

. . . . .

Although their intentions can be dismissed in the market frenzy and gossip about their work, these four artists are deadly serious about their challenge to the clichés of artistic creation. Like Sonnabend, they think their work is penetrating an unexplored area. "We're deconstructing the complex structures of the entertainment industry and the advertising industry," says Halley. "We're saying that the humanistic machinery by which art is evaluated is no longer valid. I do see our work as a return to the line of inquiry that began with Pop and Minimalist art – even going back to Johns and Rauschenberg." These are consoling words to American art dealers, for while Neo-Expressionism was chiefly European, this art is market savvy and all-American.

But Rauschenberg, for one, isn't impressed. "I'm afraid that America is losing – has lost, even – the grip on being the center," he says. "The people who might be to blame for it are the dealers who aren't really dealers. Nouveau American dealers have destroyed the market and the integrity of the artists. There are only about ten people who run galleries in Manhattan who are dealers with integrity and style."

Rauschenberg counts Sonnabend among them. "She and I have always been good friends," he says. "A lot of my friends complain that she does such – how do you say it? – 'international bookkeeping.' I never know what she owes me or what I owe her, and neither one of us has ever made a problem about it because I know that she is not interested in being rich. She could have been rich a long time ago, but she always reinvests all of her earnings into new art, new discoveries."

"I have a responsibility toward my collectors," says Sonnabend, "and I have a responsibility toward myself, which is even more important."

. . . . .

Sonnabend also has a responsibility toward her artists, about whom she speaks maternally. "My idea of art-dealing is to serve the interests of the artists," she says. "I don't mean only materially. What I do for artists, if they let me do it, is to give them love, understanding, to try to help them make the right decisions for their careers. I like to protect them and to serve them."

Without prompting, Sonnabend raises the subject of retirement. When she eventually calls it quits, she intends for Antonio Homem to assume all responsibilities in the gallery. "He's really myself," she says. "He understands me very well. It's just like being myself. It's wonderful."

By the time Sonnabend retires, her legacy will be an art scene that has been irrevocably changed. Many of the developments since the heyday of the New York School are the work of Castelli and Sonnabend and the dealers who followed them.

As it happens, these dealers usually outlast their artists. And Ileana Sonnabend stands a good chance of outlasting the reputation of the four artists who will burst into prominence this week at her gallery. Still, one can never discount her record for finding talent — and making it world-famous. ●

JAY GORNEY 1987

GRACIE MANSION 1984

KENNY SCHARF 1985

KEITH HARING 1985

The Decline of East Village Art

Vogue may 1989

High up in Christadora House, a landmark building that overlooks Tompkins Square Park in New York City's East Village, SoHo art dealer Christine Burgin was hosting a dinner party when somebody looked out the window and saw flames. A nearby building was being consumed by fire; indeed, scorching red light electrified the hull of the tenement and illuminated the sky. To the guests, all of us from the art world, the image was just another apocalyptic East Village scene – the stuff of a thousand Neo-Expressionist canvases. But to Burgin's 30-year-old husband, Amos Harris, the stepson of Ann Clark Rockefeller and an owner of the Christadora and other neighborhood properties, the fire spelled danger. It might have been one of his own buildings down there burning.

Harris ran off to check while the eating continued with gusto. On his return, the young landlord was all smiles: his holdings were safe. Nothing substantial had been harmed – except for a couple of junkies who, apparently, had made their home in the slum. "Do you mean they burned to death?" I asked. "Yeah, but those people are lower than cockroaches," came the reply.

That was a year ago, shortly before the Christadora became the target in last summer's Tompkins Square riots. The demonstrators turned the luxury condominium complex into a symbol of the gentrification of the area.

A few years ago, their targets might have been the art galleries. The rapid rise and decline of "East Village Art" – embodied by the sudden appearance and disappearance of little storefront galleries that sprang up between the Bowery and the East River, Houston and 14th Streets – created one of the most startling developments of the contemporary art scene. The galleries showcased all the varieties of 1980s neo-Pop, but they also served as the avant-garde of gentrification on the Lower East Side.

By 1987, the galleries themselves had fallen prey to the inflated real estate values they had helped create. As they attracted new residents and businesses to the area, they priced themselves out of the market. One by one, the East Village art dealers have closed down or shifted their wares farther downtown – particularly to SoHo.

"Architecturally, the East Village was unsatisfactory," says Mera Rubell, a prominent art collector whose company, Rubell & Miller, rents out new gallery spaces in SoHo – especially in the large gallery malls on Lower Broadway. "It's sad that it all came to an end in the East Village. It was a wonderful community and opportunity for young artists and galleries. But the artists need other, larger spaces. And galleries feed off one another – they want to be near other successful galleries. And at $16 to $25 per square foot, SoHo today is cheaper than the East Village storefronts."

"It was the landlords," agrees dealer Jay Gorney, who moved from the East Village to SoHo in 1987. "They became incredibly greedy."

Of course, the East Village wasn't always Real Estate Hell. In the 1960s – the era of Love-Ins, Be-Ins, and Smoke-Ins – the neighborhood was a haven for alternative activity, an East Coast Haight-Ashbury. In those days, the Dom on St. Mark's Place (now a community center) was home to Andy Warhol's Velvet Underground. Bill Graham's Fillmore East on Second Avenue (which eventually became the Saint, a gay disco, and is now slated to become a cinema complex) showcased Jimi Hendrix, The Who, and Janis Joplin. The neighborhood was also the site of sore conflicts among local Hispanics, hippies from all over, and the Ninth Precinct police force.

The area's clubs have always monitored the changes. When New Wave music hit in the mid-seventies, CBGB'S, an old bikers' bar on the Bowery, became the East Village headquarters of the sleazier side of the New Wave scene. It was followed by the brighter and more juvenile Club 57, which opened in the basement of a Polish church on St. Mark's. "Club 57 was like a clubhouse," says Keith Haring. "The best thing about those days was that they were so unselfconscious and unpretentious. And there was so much talent. Everyone was supporting everyone else."

An art-music-fashion scene emerged out of Club 57 crossed with the hip-hop music scene from uptown and the Bronx, exemplified by such musicians as Grandmaster Flash and Afrika Bambaataa. Jean Michel Basquiat was still a pseudonymous graffitist, the Collaborative Projects group was gathering a swath of aggressive erotica, punk graphics, graffiti art, and political manifestos for its historic Times Square Show, and new alliances were being made between film makers, designers, writers, and artists to whom the SoHo scene seemed hopelessly out of touch. In those days, the neighborhood was inexpensive and its novelty an untapped resource. Soon enough, the idea of selling the East Village image in commodity form hit home, and a movement was born.

Bill Stelling, a 29-year-old small-time East Village landlord, opened the Fun gallery in 1981 in a rented studio with Patti Astor, an underground movie actress he employed at his roommate referral service. Their little gallery showcased the first wave of the new East Village scene – the graffiti, hip-hop, and psycho-pop painters. The art was dirt-cheap (at Kenny Scharf's first show, the most expensive painting cost $900), and the dealers naively took a mere 30 per cent on sales rather than the usual 50. Stelling owned a building on Third Street that housed Quentin Crisp in the attic and a young artist named Peter Nagy in the basement.

Within a year, Nagy joined forces with his friend Alan Belcher and opened another of the new wave of art galleries. Nature Morte occupied a small storefront on Tenth Street, a stone's throw from Fun and close to other pioneering spaces – Group Material, Gracie Mansion, and Civilian Warfare. "Fun wanted more galleries in the area," says Nagy, "and for a while, there was a real sense of camaraderie."

"When Alan and I opened the gallery," says Nagy, "we were really naive. We weren't that serious. We just thought, 'Let's do a show,' like Mickey Rooney and Judy Garland. But it was a watershed period. So many people from our generation wanted to be artists. We were all raised on art rock, pop fashion, low culture, so the art world had to split right open. It had to accommodate three new aesthetics: the appropriation thing, the graffiti thing, and the kitsch-punk thing."

Then came the boom. At its height, magazines like *Flash Art* and *Art in America* were publishing splashy supplements on the East Village scene, and there were no fewer than seventy new little galleries. The influx was on, with fledglings from all over the country descending on the neighborhood in a bid to be the next Madonnas and Kenny Scharfs. The whole mood changed. Deborah Sharpe, whose gallery opened in 1983, just ahead of Michael Kohn, PPOW, and Pat Hearn, remembers, "When I moved my gallery in, there wasn't exactly a friendly welcome. We weren't part of the clique. We were considered the young professionals."

Patti Astor is more explicit. "The point was lost when people like Pat Hearn took grungy 5,000-square-foot tenements and renovated them with all this money," she complains. "I thought there was something sick about it – the adventure

had gone out of things. The whole scene had become a real money factory." Soon, Fun Gallery closed. Bill Stelling moved his share of the business to 56 Bleecker Gallery, and Astor moved to Hollywood, where she has worked in a deli while awaiting her big break as a movie producer, screenwriter, and actress.

The most revealing East Village art success story belongs to International With Monument, which was opened in 1984 by artist Meyer Vaisman and two friends from art school. Within two years, however, Vaisman and his artists made the symbolic leap to the big SoHo galleries, a sign that bigger money was finally in the offing. "The East Village was great for a couple of years," Vaisman claims, "and it was initially important to me to have a friendship with artists. Soon the museums got involved, too, and the gallery got out of the red. But the East Village scene died from a lack of adequate spaces and from artists' ambitions to show in bigger galleries. As more and more shitty galleries opened every day, with more cheap versions of SoHo art and Neo-Expressionism, the situation became less interesting. I wanted to get out."

Vaisman and one of his partners sold back their shares in the gallery, which were purchased by Ealan Wingate, who had worked for the Sonnabend Gallery. But within months, the gallery's stellar lights – Richard Prince, Sarah Charlesworth, Jeff Koons, and Peter Halley – were grabbed by SoHo dealers. (Vaisman landed at three galleries – Gorney, Sonnabend, and Castelli.)

The other galleries saw the writing on the wall and began to follow suit. By now a hit as both a dealer and a painter, Nagy was exhibiting his own art at International With Monument, and he too jumped ship. He also closed Nature Morte, in 1987. "I could tell the whole scene was falling apart," he says.

Among the last of the fashionable galleries to abandon the district was Pat Hearn's. But her gallery has been stylishly out of synch all along. "When Pat Hearn first opened," recalls dealer Michael Kohn, who reopened his East Village gallery in Los Angeles in 1985, "everyone thought it was the most ridiculous thing they'd ever seen. She had this big beehive hairdo, and her gallery had a sort of sixties fake rock garden in the interior and ceramic tile floors. It was like a B-52s album come to life."

But Hearn's artists transcended her image. One of them, Philip Taaffe, is arguably the most successful of the new generation of neo-Pop, -Op, and -Conceptual artists to come out of the East Village. When Hearn sold his paintings at her first space, they went for a few thousand dollars; last year one sold at auction for $95,000. And this month, Hearn is showing Taaffe in a two-gallery show, at her new three-story SoHo gallery and at Mary Boone's $100-per-square-foot West Broadway gallery. Gore Vidal is writing the introduction to the show's catalogue. Says Boone, "To Pat, I guess I represent the older generation."

There are hardly any galleries left in the old neighborhood, and the storefronts are again for rent, while the galleries get better per square foot on Broadway, but the spaces are bigger, the overheads higher. "There is no question that this is going to be a tough new time for young artists," says Mera Rubell. "In the East Village, works could sell for $500 to $1,500. Now SoHo commands $5,000 to $6,000 for an artist's first show."

According to Patti Astor, "The SoHo dealers are real happy to have the East Village scene over in SoHo now. They don't have to worry about having black people running around. Everything's safe. I think art should be dangerous and they think art should be safe. Safe makes money. Dangerous makes history."

But who makes history in a scene inflated by money and media attention. In the East Village, as in the art world at large, fashion and marketing maneuvers have taken the place of real change. When last year's Tompkins Square riots erupted, a few survivors from the East Village of the 1960s remarked to me that at last the people were asserting their power against the trendy young landlords. But conflict in the East Village has become ritualized posing, and change purely illusory. Those were no ordinary riots – they were designer riots. I saw the neo-political protesters and the new gentry, and there was no visible difference between them. In the East Village these days, both sides are wearing Gaultier. ●

Part Four

Acting Up

Guerrilla Girls

MANHATTAN, INC. APRIL 1987

Their identities may remain concealed, but the Guerrilla Girls are for New Yorkers a new fact of life. Since the spring of 1985, when they achieved instant notoriety with their unceremoniously worded attacks on the male-dominated art world, they have published twelve posters. Featuring statistics on discrimination against women artists — in galleries, museums, art magazines — their bulletins spread fresh dissent along the hallowed walls of SoHo and the East Village. But this month their target is uptown — specifically, the Whitney Museum of American Art.

On April 16 at the Clocktower Gallery on Leonard Street, a new polemic is being launched. Tentatively entitled "Guerrilla Girls Speak Back to the Whitney," the show will be, they say, "everything that you wanted to see in the Whitney Biennial. We expect that it will eclipse the biennial." A series of large statements set against the blackened walls of the gallery, the show is designed to give vent to the women's gripes about the art world's money business. This counter-biennial also marks the biennial of the Guerrilla Girls as an organization and occasions some reflections on their history, their tactics, and their impact.

"We've made feminism fashionable again," asserts one Girl, "and what comes of that depends on people in powerful places. Certain galleries have already realized that their locker-room atmospheres won't cut the mustard. We've also helped women realize that they are treated as a separate class in the art world and that collective action is more effective than private deals." And the action is snowballing. In January, *ARTS Magazine* donated one and a quarter pages of advertising to the Girls, who used the space to outline the exacerbated conditions for black women artists. In February, Miriam Friedlander awarded them the National Organization for Women's Susan B. Anthony Award. And, on the heels of their Clocktower exhibition, a retrospective of their posters will open in June in the Brooklyn Bridge Anchorage.

But the streets remain their prime site — one with a grand pedigree in twentieth-century art. Avant-garde, agitprop artists and billboard advertisers alike have long recognized the humble thoroughfare of modern life as the collision site of culture and consumption, the axis of information dissemination.

Ever since Martin Luther graffitied the doors of his neighborhood cathedral, posting notices has been history. It's a little illegal, but it's also free.

The Guerrilla Girls call themselves "the conscience of the art world"; but while earlier feminists asked why there are no great women artists, these women ask why there are no rich and famous ones. Their activities stand out against the art world's recent fascination with dry, theoretical feminism. In contrast to women's liberation at the stage of its third Ph.D., there is nothing highfalutin about the Guerrilla Girls. As one little voice explained over the telephone, they only want to change the world.

Expectedly, some noses have been put out of joint by their shenanigans. Posting notices is a hit-and-run form of attack that doesn't allow the victims to answer back. When a series of their posters announced that certain institutions were under "surveillance" for their treatment of female talent, sympathizers were offended. One of the posters' targets was the curator of the New Museum of Contemporary Art, William Olander, who strives to be kosher when it comes to the sexes. "The word 'surveillance' coalesces so easily with government policies and the invasion of one's private life," he objects. "The Guerrilla Girls are plainly not sensitive to the power of language. Instead of calling names in the art world, why don't they infiltrate it?"

For one thing, much of the Guerrilla Girls' strength derives from their secrecy. Their ploy is an inversion of Rumpelstiltskin; that fairy-tale extortionist literally came apart when his female victim discovered his name, and these women are not taking any chances. Even the coordinator of the Clocktower, Tom Finkelpearl, only negotiates with them over the telephone, although he says he has been noticing suspicious women sussing out the space. As propagandists, their methods recall everything from Radio Free America to the Red Brigade, and they try to give the impression, like Big Brother himself, that they are everywhere — with spies in high and mighty places like art magazines. In fact, the organization is small, nonhierarchically structured, and susceptible to discovery by the average downtown investigative reporter. They're unknowns. Punchiest as a collective, they are also buoyantly unfettered by egoism.

The Guerrilla Girls do not escape certain female arche-types. Mysterious women's sects span the ages, from the Sapphists of Lesbos to medieval witches to rad-fem separa-tists (although this time around there's the *de rigueur* dose of irony). Yet, as one Girl testifies, "Publishing our names would destroy our anonymity, and therefore both our effectivity and our careers as artists would be gone, be dead." So, as suits the heroines of this art-world fairy tale, I'm not telling. ●

JENNY HOLZER 1986

Jenny Holzer

VOGUE NOVEMBER 1988

For years now, Jenny Holzer's art has been like a bug in the system. Holzer makes outdoor posters and electronic billboards with brief, punchy messages about life and death ranging, like life and death, from the banal to the brilliant. Her ephemeral admonitions about abiding social ills have made thousands of unsuspecting men and women in the street think twice. One, spelled across a vast electronic sign in Times Square, asserted, "Money Creates Taste." Another, mounted on the skyscraper-high sign at Caesars Palace implored, "Protect me from what I want." Indeed, Holzer's public announcements have learned a good deal from Las Vegas. She knows that a message's appearance — and the way it is addressed to the reader — can be as important as what it says. She has also discovered that big, electronic, commercial signs are things of beauty.

On the surface, Holzer's embrace of commercial techniques is post-Pop. The billboard scale of James Rosenquist's paintings of the sixties was derived from his experience as a sign painter and Andy Warhol ingeniously applied mass-production printing techniques in his depictions of mass-produced objects. But Holzer is not about to celebrate consumerism. As a former poster paster in the business of direct action, this left-wing feminist uses big business's dazzling, almost magical billboards with a twist. "It was interesting to change from the underground connotations that posters have to Big Brother overtones, because the big signs make things seem official," she says. "It was like having the voice of authority say something different from what it would normally say."

Once or twice she has had run-ins, as in 1982 when the Marine Midland Bank unceremoniously removed her posters from a lobby art show because one line read, "It's not good to live on credit." "I limped over and retrieved the work from the janitor's closet," Holzer said later.

Now the bank wouldn't dare, for Holzer has become the Official American Artist with the recent announcement that her art will represent the United States in the 1990 Venice Biennale. And just before that announcement, while a portrait of Holzer was adorning the cover of *ARTnews* magazine, the art world learned of two other big solo shows for which most artists would give their right arms — at the Solomon R. Guggenheim Museum and the Dia Art Foundation, both in New York City.

Almost overnight, the 38-year-old Midwesterner has gone from social subversive to artistic ambassador. "I'd like to think that the change is because people are interested in harder subject matter now," she explains. "And maybe they are more tolerant of different ways of expression and different media."

Despite the ultra-urban nature of her public art, the plainly dressed, no-nonsense Holzer lives tucked away in a farmhouse in upstate New York. In addition to her public art projects, she exhibits in galleries in New York City, Chicago, Los Angeles, Paris, and Cologne. Her work is in greater demand than even her mechanically reproducible art can accommodate, and is at the center of a torrent of publicity. In 1983, she married artist Mike Glier, and in 1986 they settled on their farm with cats, dog, and a horse. Six months ago, Lili Holzer-Glier was born.

Holzer has meticulously paved her own way. With her eye on the future, she has made some canny business decisions that have cushioned what otherwise might have been a struggle. Seven years ago, she was offered ten thousand dollars for the lease on her SoHo loft. "It seemed like a wonderful deal just for moving," she says. With the money, she bought an abandoned building on the Lower East Side. Today, it's worth more than a million dollars. Her generosity is also noteworthy. Holzer is known to have quietly given money to artists, and she frequently donates art and funds.

Artistic success took ten years of slogging and networking. Two years after moving to New York City in 1977, Holzer fell in with a group of artists known as Colab (short for Collaborative Projects). "They would have these shows in peculiar non-art places," she recalls, "and try to make art that would make sense to someone in the Bronx and to people who don't go to the Metropolitan Museum every day. I thought, 'Mmm, sounds like a good idea.' " She plastered New York City with her one-liners, and quickly discovered the power of hit-and-run tactics. "When my things are on the street or on electronic billboards and there's no attribution and people aren't thinking about art, they take content at face value," she says. "They simply read it and think about what it says — nothing more and nothing less."

Holzer's signature medium, since 1983, has been LED (light-emitting diode) machines, those anonymous black boxes across which flashing red letters (and recently green and yellow ones as well) dash and disappear. Without paint or canvas, pencils, or even a camera, her art is just dancing points of light which tease and taunt with statements like, "Go to where people sleep and see if they are safe," or, "With all the holes in you already there's no reason to define the outside environment as alien."

The Holzerisms don't preach. They are provocative, but aren't pushing any single point of view. "Rather than throwing out one line and saying 'This is the way to truth, beauty and righteousness,'" she explains, "I'd say, 'Here are all the possibilities, these are all fervently held beliefs.' I thought this might instill some sense of tolerance in the people who read them. There are, say, three hundred conflicting truisms, all equally true, all under one roof. That's when things get rich."

Concurrent with the old adage that everything is political, Holzer's mottoes are emblazoned everywhere, from football stadiums to baseball caps. Some are chiseled into stonebenches. Of course, the art world is as political as the rest of culture, and the choice by the American committee of Holzer as the next United States representative at Venice was partly strategic. "That people are more willing to entertain troublesome topics," Holzer says, "signals the end of the Reagan era."

Moreover, Holzer's name is already well known to European contemporary art audiences. It was in big group exhibitions in West Germany in 1981 and 1982 — rather than in the United States — that she won her substantial art-world support. "In terms of the official art world, I went to Europe and came back."

In the studio on her farm, Holzer holds up a little metallic block the size of a bullet. "This is where it all is," she explains. "The memory, and all the words and patterns are in here." On her desk are just a pad and pen used for thinking up her messages. Naturally, the more romantically inclined who view art as a ticket to freedom may be switched off by Holzer's self-imposed limitations. LED boxes are hardly befitting an unfettered imagination. But Holzer is resolutely cheerful about her computer-age progeny. "I have to say that I like the way they look," she says. "They move and flash and blink and go backwards. Movement makes up for a lot."

However, her work's limitations don't stem only from her materials. Holzer's art needs unprepared minds for its effect. When her signs and posters are installed inside art-world spaces — where boundary-breaking has been the rule for decades and where the ordinary bourgeois finds relaxation in surprises — the charge of her cheeky messages is dulled. In her often leaden installations, Holzer's posters, LED boxes, stone benches and,

now, coffins chiseled with rows of text (there will be thirteen such sarcophagi at Dia next spring) administer measured doses of affront and horror. Her writing, too, is anticlimactic: aphorism becomes platitude. Instead of igniting, her art frequently stalls.

Fortunately, Venice — half-city, half-museum — may be Holzer's perfect site. There, her audience will be unsuspecting tourists mixed with the international art crowd already wise to her game. And in that unpredictable setting, the artist might just manage to electrify everybody with the beauty and power of shock. ●

Tim Rollins + K.O.S.

Vogue JANUARY 1990

• • • • •

"When I first joined K.O.S.," says Annette Rosado, a junior in high school, "my girlfriends didn't know what had happened to me. They thought that maybe I was killed, maybe I got into drugs, or maybe my family moved away. The truth is, I just wasn't into partying anymore. I was doing art instead, and earning some money."

Rosado is a member of a group of Hispanic school kids from New York's South Bronx who call themselves the Kids of Survival, K.O.S. for short. They have exhibited paintings and prints in dozens of exhibitions, including the Venice Biennale in 1988, the Dia Art Foundation in New York, on view through June, and, opening this month, the Wadsworth Atheneum in Hartford, Connecticut. They've hit the front page of *The New York Times*, been splashed across the pages of art magazines, and had their paintings purchased by the Museum of Modern Art, the Whitney Museum of American Art, and the Philadelphia Museum of Art. Their works are featured in the prestigious Chase Manhattan Bank, First Bank of Minneapolis, and Saatchi collections. Indeed, these art brats are as skilled at holding a champagne flute and an art-world conversation as any artists. (Their proud parents, however, are considerably more shy.)

Compared to K.O.S., most of the shooting stars in modern art history have been as old — and as white — as Grandma Moses. Annette Rosado is 17, and the other long-term K.O.S. members, Richard Cruz, George Garces, Nelson Montes, Jose Parissi, Carlos Rivera, and Nelson Savinon, range in age from 17 to 21. In addition, younger kids have drifted in and out of the group over the last six years, and there is now a handful of new K.O.S. recruits. Many of them live in burned-out neighborhoods where the possibilities for self-destruction are within easy reach. Already, one member of K.O.S. was shot and killed for a gold chain in his possession, and four members of the kids' immediate families have suffered or died from AIDS. K.O.S. is an opportunity for these kids to express themselves, earn money, and cross over from the Bronx into the racy (and racist) Manhattan art scene. Rosado says with a giggle, "My girlfriends now know all about what I'm doing. They still think art is a bore but say I'm incredibly lucky to be hanging out with all these guys."

• • • • •

The Kids of Survival — if we are to believe their own version of events — are Marvel Comics' *X-Men* in the flesh, a group of outsiders who have united to fight evil under the guidance of a brilliant professor. Their "professor" is Tim Rollins, a 34-year-old artist who started teaching children in poor neighborhoods in 1980. Two years later, after intense frustration over conditions in the schools, he hit on the idea for Tim Rollins + K.O.S. and founded the Art and Knowledge Workshop in the South Bronx, which he and the kids use as their studio (they now have a second studio in Manhattan). Not only an inspiring organizer, Rollins is something of an artistic visionary. In the last eight years, Tim Rollins + K.O.S. have become a successful innovation in New York City's rotting school system — as well as the most colorful scene-makers in its blooming art world.

It started when Rollins, his nose still wet from art school and with an M.A. in education from New York University, landed a job in the Learning to Read Through the Arts Program at schools in the city's grimmest locales. "The schools are like prisons," Rollins says, and rather than play warden, he formed a special group out of the troubled, troublesome, dyslexic, and "learning disabled" pupils at Intermediate School 52 in the South Bronx.

Believing that education is a two-way process, Rollins invited the kids to collaborate with him on paintings, prints, and sculptures. "Tim became emotionally involved in all the day-to-day details of each kid's life," says Kate Pierson, singer and keyboard player in the popular rock group the B-52s and Rollins's girlfriend for the past nine years. "He's so intense — always rocking furiously in his rocking chair. If something goes wrong, for example if one of the kids drops out of school, he gets really upset."

• • • • •

Though born into a working-class family in rural Maine, Rollins's art education perfectly qualified him to become a dour, politically correct career artist in his own right. He is a graduate of the School of Visual Arts in Manhattan, where one of his teachers was Conceptual artist Joseph Kosuth and he went on to be-

TIM ROLLINS + K.O.S. 1992

come Kosuth's assistant. Rollins was also a silent fixture at the Artists for Social Change meetings that were a weekly event in SoHo during the 1970s. In 1979, he co-founded the political artists' collective called Group Material (which survives today without him), and he tripped off to China to visit educational and artistic communes.

Instead of churning out smart art for a jaded market, however, Rollins turned utopian. The young artist-teacher had been moved by educational reform texts such as Paulo Freire's *Cultural Action for Freedom* and the example of the German activist artist-teacher Joseph Beuys. Nevertheless, Rollins's Conceptual art training had alerted him to art's political dimension and emphasized that the finished object is not necessarily the most important part of the art experience. "I was also very interested," he adds, "in the gang atmosphere in Warhol's films, as well as the films of Pier Paolo Pasolini and the way Pasolini worked. He'd start with a grand theme such as the Gospel according to Saint Matthew and find these non-actors to play the parts. He even cast his mother as the Virgin Mary."

Conceptual art and cultural politics, however, are things about which most excitable, young kids can barely contain their indifference. As a teacher, Rollins had to find an inspiring way to impart information and interest the kids. He started by reading books to his pupils and asking them to visualize the stories. Eventually, the kids' sketches became the basis for collaborative works of art. They made prints and paintings on themes and incidents from Franz Kafka's *Amerika* and *Metamorphosis*, *The Autobiography of Malcolm X*, Orwell's *Animal Farm*, Carroll's *Alice's Adventures in Wonderland*, Defoe's *Journal of the Plague Year*, a book about the temptations of Saint Anthony, and inevitably, *The X-Men*. The stories in Schubert's romantic song cycle, *Die Winterreise*, also struck a chord, so the group made prints based on the sheet music. "The songs are morbid and death-obsessed, like the songs of Mötley Crüe," says Rollins. "And teenagers love that stuff. In fact, the romantic imagination of the nineteenth century is the teenage imagination of today."

Although a lot of hands have gone into the paintings, they have a look of uniformity. Ironically, they bear an unmistakable signature. All of them have mutant or cacophonous images (such as the head of Jesse Helms on a dog's body in the *Animal Farm* series and the panoply of trumpet forms in *Amerika*), and all are painted or printed on a grid of book pages glued to canvas. Rollins calls them the trophies of his collaboration with the kids, and many who admire the experiment agree that the finished products are secondary to the process.

Nevertheless, since 1985, some of the best galleries in the world have lined up to exhibit Tim Rollins + K.O.S. and have fetched prices for the group's work ranging from $500 for a drawing to $100,000 for a big canvas. Rollins says he pays the kids $7 to $10 an hour and hands over extra for themselves or their families as necessary. "The kids make a lot of money," says Rollins, "but not too much. I don't want them to get screwed up and start thinking they're rock stars." He did, however, take Carlos Rivera to see the Isenheim Altarpiece in France last year for the boy's 17th birthday. As Rivera told the *Times*, "I was in shock. It was like something that just hit me. I never thought in my lifetime I'd get to see it except in books. I was so happy I felt like crying."

Rollins refuses to play the martyr role usually associated with community work. He pays himself a salary of $30,000, which he says is set to rise to $50,000 this year following the group's successes (still peanuts for a successful artist). Two years ago, he stopped teaching in schools altogether and began work on the South Bronx Academy of Fine Arts. This projected high school will be based on an art curriculum and is being established with funds from the sales of paintings and from foundations and private donors.

"When did it happen," asks Rollins, "that working with kids became a saintly, do-gooder thing? It's a basic duty of society. The reason that kids are running wild is that no one is there for them. Like the elderly, they have been ghettoized. Their best friend is usually the TV. I think their best friend should be an adult." A best friend with a vision, we might add. ●

ACT UP

NEW YORK NOVEMBER 1990

Last year, on an airless August night, the singer Michael Callen rushed into a meeting in the Village and announced that a well-known friend had just died of AIDS. "I have always hated moments of silence," Callen said, and he invited the people in the room to make "some proud, gay assertion of our will to live – our will to fight ... Use your imagination." The room broke out in applause, cheers, and whistles – a strange symbol of mourning but also a gesture of defiance against the epidemic. Welcome to the upside-down world of ACT UP – the AIDS Coalition to Unleash Power.

This year, the hottest gay spot in town is the Great Hall at Cooper Union on Astor Place, where ACT UP holds its Monday-night general meetings. In summers past, gay scene-makers partied on Fire Island, oblivious to the devastation that lurked within. But their agenda has changed radically since the seventies: Sex, Drugs, and Disco Dancing have turned into Safer Sex, AIDS Drugs, and Demonstrating.

"It's tough being gay these days," said one ACT UP member whimsically. "You not only have to be hot-looking, you also have to be politically correct."

One Monday night in summer, TV cameras from Financial News Network are taping the proceedings. Here, in the room where Abraham Lincoln addressed New York, hundreds of pretty boys, muscled men, smart-talking lesbians, and a handful of committed straights are thrashing it out – reporting on new treatments for AIDS, preparing to send a team to Puerto Rico to promote AIDS awareness, raising funds to support Harvey Gantt in the race against Jesse Helms for his North Carolina Senate seat, and on and on for hours.

Though ACT UP's numbers have grown steadily since it was founded three and a half years ago, its ranks have also been decimated, month after month, by AIDS. Indeed, ACT UP grows bigger as it grows smaller. Many in ACT UP are sick from AIDS or are infected with HIV, the virus believed to cause it, and there are frequent Monday-night announcements about the hospitalization or death of yet another member. If it weren't for the group's breakthroughs, for its success in cutting through indifference and red tape and in getting AIDS treatments to people who need them, it might all seem hopeless.

Announcements are greeted with cheers as one speaker after another takes the microphone and works the room. "If Nelson Mandela was in New York today, he'd be here with us," says one, to thundering applause. Another, proposing a "sleep-in" on the grounds of Gracie Mansion – to protest Mayor Dinkins's policies on homeless men and women with AIDS – has the crowd egging him on.

"If David Dinkins is not willing to provide decent housing for people with HIV infection and HIV disease, then we're not going to let him sleep, either!" More clapping, whistling and cheering.

In the relative quiet of the back of the hall, near a 30-foot-long table stacked high with fact sheets and press clippings, ACT UP merchandise is on sale – T-shirts, tank tops, buttons, booklets, stickers, and posters that declare SILENCE = DEATH in Day-Glo colors, or ACT UP in unmistakable black-and-white headlines – as well as T-shirts, badges, stickers, and posters designed by Keith Haring, who was a member of the group and one of its major benefactors until his death, from AIDS, in February.

ACT UP is possibly the only activist organization ever to promote itself in fashion boutiques and art galleries around the world. Its merchandise has been crucial to its success: the T-shirts are both fashionable *and* militant-looking (they were intrinsic to last summer's "look" – cutoff denim shorts, thick belts, buzz cuts, bomber boots, and tattoos). Sales across the country will raise $200,000 this year (part of ACT UP's annual $1-million operating budget). Not since the days of punk rock has the humble T-shirt been such a politically charged fashion statement. And on December 2, ACT UP is holding an art auction in SoHo, hoping to raise the bulk of next year's funds.

"What distinguishes us from earlier protest movements," says ACT UP's David Barr, the assistant director of policy at Gay Men's Health Crisis, "is our ability to transform what we do into media events. Many of us are in graphic design, public relations and media, but instead of selling soap, we're selling ACT UP. This is not new when you're talking about selling a president, but it's new for an activist group."

In terms of public relations, ACT UP has its work cut out for it. On the group's hit list are homophobia and indifference to gay issues; tardy testing and approval of treatments for AIDS and its opportunistic infections; a chronic shortage of hospital beds; health-care inequities among women, intravenous-drug users, and the homeless; discrimination against people with AIDS by employers, insurance companies, landlords, immigration agencies, and religious groups; and profiteering by pharmaceutical companies.

An audacious mix of up-to-the-minute marketing skills, media savvy, and theatrical acts of civil disobedience quickly put ACT UP on the New York political map in a way unrivalled among activist groups – except, perhaps, by Operation Rescue, the anti-abortion lobby. Among activist groups, however, ACT UP is the most reviled. President Bush's Health and Human Services secretary, Louis Sullivan, vowed to never deal with ACT UP after a vocal delegation drowned out his address to the Sixth International AIDS conference in San Francisco in June. "The excesses of [ACT UP] do not help the cause," Bush said afterward.

Last December, 111 members of ACT UP and WHAM! (the Women's Health Action and Mobilization, a reproductive-rights group modeled on ACT UP) were arrested for storming St. Patrick's Cathedral and disrupting Mass. The next day, ACT UP was condemned in editorials in the city's major newspapers, and John Cardinal O'Connor declared that demonstrators would stop the Mass again "over my dead body."

In 1987, when he was mayor, Ed Koch called ACT UP a group of "fascists" when a delegation shouted him down at a gay-history exhibit. He also promised to arrest and penalize participants in any of ACT UP's illegal "actions," which were wreaking havoc in his public and private lives. What's more, in Italy this summer, the organizers of the Venice Biennale refused to install a commissioned work by the ACT UP artists' collective Gran Fury that attacked the Church's policy on condoms. The Italian press claimed that the Pope was behind the ban, and headlines screamed, POPE IN AIDS SCANDAL AT THE BIENNALE. (The other artists rallied behind Gran Fury, and the work went up.)

"While people in ACT UP want to express their opinions, they don't think anyone else should," says Stephen Joseph, New York's health commissioner under Koch. "For me, it was personally very distasteful and disruptive – they took over my office and even spray-painted slogans, cemented handbills and plastered stickers all over my house."

Even within the gay community, ACT UP can be unpopular. Darrell Yates Rist, a gay writer for The Nation, called the group "chic street protesters." Twisting the knife, he also dismissed much of the discussion about AIDS as "fashionable hysteria."

• • • • •

Yet the mood is anything but defeated. Since ACT UP was formed as "a diverse, nonpartisan group united in anger and committed to direct action to end the AIDS crisis," its general meetings have grown to attract up to 700 people every week, and the "phone tree" of people willing to participate in demonstrations now lists about 3,000 names. Their anger is directed at what they call "government inaction," and they describe their meetings and protests as "cathartic" and "empowering."

Though ACT UP has no leaders and every member is a spokesman or spokeswoman, the catalyst for its formation was the writer Larry Kramer, who gave an impassioned speech in March 1987 at the Lesbian and Gay Community Services Center in the Village to a crowd that had come to hear Nora Ephron (she canceled at the last minute, and he was asked to fill in). Kramer, described in The Nation as being "as mad as the Ayatollah," is a volatile man by turns wrathful and weepy. He excoriated his audience for its passivity in the face of the "gay holocaust." (Now, three and a half years later, Kramer's own immune system is weakening.) By the end of the evening, his audience was moved to take action and reconvene. Two days later, the group's numbers increased from 300 to 500.

The new group's members came from such organizations as Gay Men's Health Crisis, founded by Kramer and others in 1981 and still the largest AIDS organization; GLAAD, the Gay & Lesbian Alliance Against Defamation; the SILENCE = DEATH Project (a group of artists who designed and distributed the poster that has become ACT UP's logo); and the Lavender Hill Mob, a small brigade of rabble-rousers who surfaced in the wake of the gay militancy of the late sixties. Others soon followed – hundreds of them, some of them teenagers.

"I'd been waiting for an opportunity to kick ass for years," says one member. "But until 1987, the struggle against the epidemic had no focus."

In 1987, there were 27,000 cases of AIDS nationally. Since then, the number has multiplied to about 153,000. There are about one million more who have been exposed to HIV – this in the United States alone. But from the outset, Larry Kramer argues, press reaction to the epidemic was apathetic, and this helped AIDS get out of hand. In the early years of the epidemic, he says, when there were only 891 reported cases, The New York Times carried just seven articles about AIDS (none of them on the front page). Compare this with the incident in 1982 when seven people were poisoned by tainted Tylenol capsules: the Times ran 54 articles, he says, four of them on page one. His conclusion is that the mainstream world couldn't care less about homosexual men and others affected by AIDS, and that they had to take their fates into their own hands.

"What motivated me then," he says, "is what motivates me now. It's taking too long to get drugs into our bodies. The government is murderously slow. The research is uncoordinated. And the second president in a row doesn't give a damn."

Just two weeks after his original exhortation, ACT UP held its inaugural "action" on Wall Street. "We went after the FDA [Food and Drug Administration]," says Kramer, "because they weren't processing drugs fast enough." The prop department of the New York Shakespeare Festival crafted an effigy of then-FDA commissioner Dr. Frank Young, and the protesters hung it from stage gallows outside Trinity Church. "Dan Rather filmed it on the *CBS Evening News*, and within two days, the FDA said they were going to accelerate the whole drug-testing process," says Kramer. "So we were off and running."

. . . . .

News, posters, and word of mouth quickly helped pack ACT UP's meetings at the Lesbian & Gay Center on West 13th Street (ACT UP moved to the larger Cooper Union this summer), and the group has subsequently spawned more than twenty committees and forty aligned groups – also called ACT UP – in cities across the United States as well as in London, Paris, Berlin, Montreal, Melbourne, and Sydney. Hardly a week goes by without an ACT UP protest somewhere, and spin-offs, such as Queer Nation and the gay "citizen patrol" group Pink Panthers (all with their own designer T-shirts), are also proliferating.

"Political groups of all stripes are calling on us because they want the ACT UP endorsement," says ACT UP's Maxine Wolfe, a professor of environmental psychology at the City University of New York Graduate School. "Suddenly, we're the biggest game in town."

The reason for ACT UP's notoriety is that ACT UP plays dirty. Many of its members say they have nothing to lose and will get arrested to make their point, happily committing acts of civil disobedience everywhere from Albany to Atlanta, as well as engineering countless "zaps" – small, instantaneous protests done in response to an emergency or tipoff.

In a demonstration in March 1989, 5,000 people met at City Hall and blocked peak-hour traffic to protest the city's hospital crisis. In typical ACT UP fashion, the protest was groomed for the media – demonstrato.s were in cardboard boxes styled to resemble homeless shelters while others tended

to them in doctors' and nurses' uniforms. Pictures and reports of the action led the evening's news. (Not long beforehand, Dance Theater Workshop's Bessie committee, which gives awards for dance and performance, had presented ACT UP with a special award for street theater.) There are the "phone zaps" and "fax zaps," where the telephone and fax lines of ACT UP's targets – such as Northwest Airlines, which had refused to allow people with AIDS to fly on its planes – are jammed with complaints and nuisance calls.

And sometimes, ACT UP plays by the book. May 4, 1988, was earmarked as "National Women and AIDS Day" to alert heterosexual men and women to AIDS prevention. A delegation from ACT UP went to Shea Stadium to hand out condoms and fliers in English and Spanish that stated, "AIDS is no ball game," "No glove no love," and score sheets of facts on safer sex. They also bought blocks of seats, entitling them to a greeting on the giant electronic bulletin board, and unfurled banners at choice moments that read, AIDS KILLS WOMEN, STRIKE OUT AIDS, and SILENCE = DEATH. These messages were televised nationally.

"We're different from many progressive groups that never leave their neighborhood," says Wolfe, one of the people who thought up the action. "And the people at Shea loved us."

. . . . .

One of ACT UP's repeated targets has been Burroughs Wellcome, the manufacturer of the AIDS drug AZT. ACT UP charges the company with profiteering and has made it the brunt of its most outrageous demonstrations – which have won the group grudging credit as far afield as the London Stock Exchange and the *Wall Street Journal*.

When AZT was approved by the FDA, in 1987, the drug cost $10,000 for a year's supply. It was perhaps the most expensive drug ever marketed, and way beyond the reach of many people. In December 1987, after the cost drew widespread criticism, including protests by ACT UP, the price was reduced by 20 per cent. In April 1989, in an abortive bid to lower the price further, members of ACT UP infiltrated the company's headquarters in Research Triangle Park, North Carolina.

"We wanted to publicly embarrass Burroughs Wellcome," says Peter Staley, a former Wall Street broker who takes AZT. "Using Wall Street equity analysts, we determined that there was a profit margin on the drug of up to 80 per cent." The protesters bolted themselves inside one of the company's offices and convened a press conference by telephone.

Five months later, ACT UP staged one of its most daring and widely publicized coups. Staley and six other members of ACT UP put on business suits and forged identification badges, then slipped onto the trading floor of the New York Stock Exchange. They chained themselves to a banister, unraveled a banner that said SELL WELLCOME, set off miniature foghorns, and stopped trading on the floor for the first time in its history. A spy inside the exchange smuggled out photographs of the action, one of which appeared the next morning in *The Washington Post*. Five days later, Burroughs Wellcome announced a second 20 per cent reduction in the price of AZT.

"People were impressed when they discovered that we're not wimps and that we risk bodily harm to make a point," says Staley. Even ACT UP's detractors had to admit that the group had successfully assaulted a corporate Goliath.

ACT UP is also widely credited with devising and promoting "parallel track" drug testing, which will administer experimental drugs to terminally ill patients unable to get into regular clinical trials — a system with consequences for the treatment of diseases such as leukemia, other cancers, and Alzheimer's. (The Department of Health and Human Sciences has made other drugs available to people with AIDS, in a "compassionate use" program.) ACT UP has also protested the inhumanity of administering placebo treatments to dying patients.

What's more, the group is given credit for getting ddI and ddC — antiviral drugs related to AZT — into "expanded access," and has won approval for about a dozen drugs, including Ganciclovir (which has proved effective in fighting cytomegalovirus retinitis, an opportunistic infection that leads to blindness).

"We've revolutionized the drug-approval process," says Staley. "What used to be a ten-year process for getting a drug approved quickly became a thing of the past."

Slowly, ACT UP has won recognition in the scientific establishment. Dr. Anthony Fauci, director of the National Institute of Allergy and Infectious Diseases and the National Institute of Health's Office of AIDS Research, now regularly consults representatives from ACT UP's Treatment + Data committee.

"At first," Dr. Fauci says, "when ACT UP was just getting people's attention, they were very confrontational. I know — I was their target. But I now realize they have a perspective that's extremely valuable. They have some very important people who are informed and decisive and who have pointed out shortcomings in our approach that have led to the implementation of new ideas, most notably the parallel track."

Members of ACT UP have been asked to join numerous government AIDS-advisory committees, and have been credited in a new book, *Good Intentions: How Big Business and the Medical Establishment Are Corrupting the Fight Against AIDS* by Bruce Nussbaum (published last month by the Atlantic Monthly Press), with helping bring about "revolutionary changes in the biomedical research world" and forcing the Food and Drug Administration to increase access to experimental drug treatments.

"We're successful because we are able to get numbers behind what we do," says Jim Eigo, one of the leading researchers for ACT UP. "And now we are starting to be taken seriously." The last nine months, Eigo says, have almost been a dream.

. . . . .

Despite its medical and media triumphs, ACT UP is associated in the minds of most people with last year's debacle at St. Patrick's Cathedral. Its target was Cardinal O'Connor, an advocate of Operation Rescue and an opponent of education about condoms, not just in Roman Catholic *and* public schools but also in shelters for people with AIDS. His position on AIDS prevention is unshaken by the scope of the epidemic. "Good morality is good medicine," he says.

All hell broke loose in God's house on the morning of December 10, 1989. There were 43 arrests inside the cathedral, and 68 outside, among 5,000 protesters — members and supporters of ACT UP and WHAM! — who were there to assail and mock the cardinal. Demonstrators outside dressed as clowns and bishops and wielded a condom the size of a giant torpedo labeled CARDINAL O'CONDOM. One man dropped by dressed as the Flying Nun.

Within the sanctity of the cathedral, just as the cardinal began his sermon, the protesters staged a "die-in." Some lay down along the nave and chained themselves to the pews, blowing whistles and shouting slogans such as "Pro-choice is pro-life" and "Condoms save lives." Worshippers were aghast as uniformed police marched in with walkie-talkies and wire cutters and proceeded to handcuff the demonstrators and haul them out on stretchers.

Everything returned to normal for a while as the cardinal took to the microphone and asked his congregation to pray. But then came Communion, and the action by one man that captured the attention of the entire press. As ACT UP's Tom Keane, a lapsed Catholic, recalls it, he "scrunched" a consecrated Communion wafer in his hand, dropped it to the floor and mumbled, "Opposing safe-sex education is murder."

Horrified priests picked up the pieces, and cathedral security collared Keane. He was removed by police and charged with disrupting a religious service, disorderly conduct, and resisting arrest. (But the police and press missed John Wessel, a former Jesuit seminarian and regional director of the National Endowment for the Arts, who broke the Host and flung it over the heads of the congregation.)

After Mass, Keane was damned, along with the other desecrators. Ed Koch, who was present at the Mass, condemned the protesters who had entered the cathedral, and he was echoed by mayor-elect David Dinkins and vice-president Dan Quayle. The cardinal was featured on the front pages of the next day's tabloids (the *New York Post* showed him performing purification rites in the cathedral). Keane's sacrilege – unauthorized by ACT UP – totally eclipsed the issues that brought the protesters together.

Three days later, ACT UP and WHAM! called a press conference to explain their motives and do some last-minute damage control. "It's a sad day in hell," says Peter Staley, "when ACT UP gets beaten in the publicity game."

· · · · ·

Meanwhile, the dying goes on. So does the struggle. Among other things, the health crisis has inspired homosexuals to organize in a way that may have ramifications beyond AIDS. Nevertheless, Larry Kramer often feels driven to despair, maintaining that not enough people are responding to the crisis. In an article in *Outweek*, he even advocated rioting at the San Francisco conference. "There are 13 million gay men out there," he says, "which means that there are 26 million parents of gays who seem not to care that their sons are dying."

The rage continues, but it is often spiked with humor. "We are not just another protest group," says Jim Serafini, a psychologist who has tested HIV-positive. "Faced with the prospect of one's mortality, a lot of us have gained an ironic sense of humor. We've lived in a death-drenched community for ten years, and to keep our sanity we've had to joke – as well as raise hell. So what if people think we are going over the top? We can see the profound absurdity of our situation and laugh at it."

He hopes that, when looked at from the other side of the crisis, when AIDS has ceased its terrible gouging, the men and women of ACT UP will appear saintly, not sacrilegious – not as victims but as heroes. ●

The Activist Art Revival

NOVEMBER 1990

*Written around the same time as the preceding article on ACT UP, "The Activist Art Revival"
is published here in its entirety for the first time. An edited version titled "Activist Art" appeared in Melbourne's
OUTRAGE magazine in October 1992.*

Last summer, a band of eleven American AIDS activists and artists called Gran Fury scored the kind of media coup that money can't buy. The scene was Italy, at the world-renowned Biennale of Venice, and the action began when the Biennale's director of visual arts refused to mount Gran Fury's billboard. Consisting of a photograph of Pope John Paul II juxtaposed with a shot of an erect penis and a text attacking the Catholic Church's stand on condoms and AIDS prevention, the offending work became a lightning rod for publicity. Rumors — including charges that the Vatican was behind the ban — flew in every direction, and within the seconds it takes for activism to strike its target, Italian newspapers were on the trail of a story. The next day, headlines all over Italy proclaimed, POPE IN AIDS SCANDAL AT THE BIENNALE.

Even better for Gran Fury, many of the papers quoted the text of the billboard, thereby spreading their message about safer sex way beyond the relatively elite crowd that visits the Biennale. "The Catholic Church has long taught men and women to loathe their bodies and to fear their sexual natures," read thousands of Italians over their espressos. "This particular vision of good and evil continues to bring suffering and even death by holding medicine hostage to Catholic morality and withholding information which allows people to protect themselves and each other ..."

"We couldn't have orchestrated that kind of publicity even if we wanted to," says one of the Furies. Yet publicity is exactly what Gran Fury does want — and so do at least a dozen other new artistic groups who are using their creative skills to infiltrate the media and promote change. Every time their images are reproduced and quoted in newspapers and magazines, their message is communicated to more people than could ever be reached inside the art world.

. . . . .

At the end of a decade of instant careers, one group of artists after another has turned away from individual stardom and reclaimed art as a tool for social change. The trend started peaking just as auction prices for contemporary art reached their pinnacle. But when a handful of politicians, led by Senator Jesse Helms of North Carolina, targeted feminist, gay, and lesbian art as a cancer to be cut out of society, the artists' campaigns assumed a new urgency and ascended to the level of national news. Overnight, art was pushed to the front lines of the sexual revolution.

Today's "art attacks" are less likely to be seen on bleached and floodlit gallery walls than plastered onto the walls outside — in posters, stickers, billboards, and bus shelters. They are distinguishable from their often lackluster sixties predecessors by shrewd, eye-popping designs lifted from newspaper headlines, contemporary art, music videos, and advertising. What's more, they exhibit an ironic sense of humor, as is testified by the tongue-in-cheek names the collectives give themselves. The amazing rise and profusion of these groups is proof, once again, that the art world is the place where the unthinkable quickly becomes the ubiquitous.

The art world is the target of the Guerrilla Girls — the coven of feminist artists whose posters skewer art galleries, museums, and critics for their exclusion of women artists and artists of color. Other groups, such as Get Smart and Akimbo, from San Francisco, attack political figures, such as Helms, and government bodies, such as the National Endowment for the Arts. The Pinkies collective supplies WHAM! (the Women's Health Action and Mobilization) with posters, leaflets, and T-shirts to use at pro-choice rallies. And Group Material presents eclectic exhibitions and "town meetings" on issues such as homelessness and education.

The list goes on, including Gran Fury (named after the Plymouth cars used by undercover police), Bad Seed, from Los Angeles, and the video collectives Testing the Limits and Diva TV have all been galvanized by AIDS. Art Positive and Gang assert gay rights, but the AIDS and gay groups alike claim that the visibility accompanying AIDS has created an anti-gay back-

KAREN FINLEY 1991

DAVID WOJNAROWICZ 1984

lash comparable to the red-baiting of the McCarthy years. And then there are individuals – such as Karen Finley, the saucy performance artist, and David Wojnarowicz, a painter of apocalyptic scenes who happens to have AIDS – who have been singled out for attack by conservatives and swept into the tidal wave of arts activism by default.

. . . . .

Despite all their differences, the groups and individuals operate on the same slingshot principle: they believe that small, well-packed shocks to the system can knock out the Goliaths of sexism, censorship, and homophobia.

The shots fired by the Guerrilla Girls were first to get the attention of the art world, precisely because they are aimed at the art world. In 1985, seemingly out of nowhere, posters started appearing on the walls of SoHo – that dormitory of art in downtown Manhattan – and spread to other cities. The posters were noticeable because they were well-designed – in bold black-and-white headlines – and memorable because they were rude, ad hominem attacks on prominent figures in the art world. Signing themselves "Guerrilla Girls – the conscience of the art world," the authors maintain an intimidating anonymity and only pose for cameras and speak in public behind gorilla masks.

"How many women had one-person exhibitions at NYC museums last year?" asked one early poster. The answer: "1" at MoMA, and "0" at the Guggenheim, Whitney, and Metropolitan museums. Another poster named twenty prominent galleries including Leo Castelli, Mary Boone, and Pat Hearn that "show no more than 10 per cent women artists or none at all." According to one of the Girls, "we started out using statistics because we felt that the best way to bring the issue to people's minds was to present the facts – rather than just saying that women have been discriminated against."

Some of their tactics seem to have worked: while they deny that the Guerrilla Girls were the cause, galleries such as Boone's and Hearn's have significantly increased their representation of women artists.

. . . . .

Yet papering SoHo with liberal propaganda is like littering in a landfill. Accordingly, many activist-art groups are going further afield. General Idea, a three-man Canadian collective, has been working together since 1968, making witty, campy installations, videos, and paintings on a variety of issues and in an impressive array of locations – from the Toronto stock exchange to cable TV. In 1987 they hit on the idea of transforming Robert

Indiana's famed *LOVE* logo into one that read *AIDS*, and then they really began to assault the street. Suddenly, the gaily colored hieroglyph was painted on trams in Amsterdam, printed on lottery tickets in Germany, illuminated in the window of Manhattan's New Museum of Contemporary Art, and distributed on stamps virtually everywhere else. "The most familiar words in our culture are words that circulate through the media and through advertising," says General Idea's AA Bronson, "so that's the way we've chosen to work."

Gran Fury responded to General Idea's logo with a four-letter painting and stickers proclaiming *RIOT* – again in the stacked-letter design of Indiana's *LOVE*. And in so doing, there was no love lost between the two groups. According to Gran Fury's Avram Finkelstein, "To depict AIDS in the same way as *LOVE* is to imply that sexual freedom leads to death, and that's disempowering. So we did the *RIOT* painting, which is another reaction to sex and AIDS – one that promotes action." (AA Bronson replies: "We thought the *RIOT* painting was atrocious – just from the artistic point of view. We were nevertheless very flattered.")

Then came Marlene McCarty, a recent addition to Gran Fury and at one point a designer of graphics for WHAM! Unaware that Indiana had already done a schema for such a painting, she contributed to the debate with a painting called *FUCK*. "With *FUCK*," she says, "the lineage went a complete circle. After all, the whole concept of love is based on whom you can fuck and not fuck. I also wanted to say that the AIDS crisis doesn't mean you stop fucking. It just means you think about it differently. I wanted to bring it all back to the personal and say, well, FUCK."

. . . . .

Get Smart was started in the East Village by the performance artist Holly Hughes and a handful of her friends when the National Endowment for the Arts started faltering under pressure from politicians. Back then, the issue was the supposedly "obscene" photographs of Robert Mapplethorpe and Andres Serrano that were touring American museums with financial support from the NEA. But in July 1990, Holly Hughes and three other performance artists found themselves in hot water when the NEA withdrew grants awarded to them for fear of provoking further right-wing attacks.

The artists counter that their right to free expression is being violated and that they are being bullied and scapegoated. "We are being used as a diversionary tactic to distract the American public from the Savings and Loans scandal," claims

Hughes. "It's no accident that the artists under attack are primarily gays and lesbians. It's a real cynical exploitation of the panic caused by the AIDS crisis."

When the NEA's refusal of grants to the four artists hit the news, Get Smart's membership swelled to sixty "hard-core" participants, with two hundred more passing through the weekly meetings. In September, the group attracted its first serious press consideration with an "action" at the Bessie Awards – the New York awards for dance and performance art that are supported by the Philip Morris Company, which also makes massive contributions to Jesse Helms.

Twenty Get Smart members dressed as cigarette girls (and one Marlboro Man) and carried red-and-white cigarette trays labeled "Helmsboro." At the awards ceremony, they handed out leaflets rolled up as cigarettes that bore an incendiary anti-Philip Morris message. Articles followed in *The New York Times* and theater magazines across the country – an embarrassment to the tobacco company, and proof that novel tactics can garner publicity. (What's more, the conservative campaign is stimulating demand for work by the artists who are under attack. According to Harry Lunn, the photography dealer who published Mapplethorpe's now-famous sadomasochistic series, "the controversy is good for business. It's helping the market for this work.")

· · · · ·

Despite its air of urgency, arts activism is as old as modern art and has surfaced in various guises across the world since F.T. Marinetti, the Italian poet, announced the birth of the Futurist art movement in 1909 and followed it up with countless acts of propaganda and provocation. The sixties in the United States saw the heyday of groups such as the Black Emergency Cultural Coalition, Guerrilla Art Action Group, and Artists and Writers Protest the War in Vietnam. Political postering was a major impetus for the student-led riots in Paris in 1968. In the 1970s, the quality action was in England – in the punk graphics promoted by New Wave rock bands and art-minded promoters such as Malcolm McLaren that advocated an anarchic "revolt into style" on T-shirts, record covers, and in a handful of calculated newspaper and television hijinks.

Meanwhile in New York, politically correct artists attended the Artists Meeting for Cultural Change rallies and browbeated about the system. A few who were to become eighties art stars, such as Jenny Holzer, papered notices around town as part of Collaborative Projects, the art-in-public-places collective formed in 1978. On both coasts of the States, women's art collectives

such as Heresies were fanning the feminist flames and anticipated the arrival of Guerrilla Girls, while the antics of New York's graffiti artists in the early 1980s finally opened many eyes, minds, and art collectors' wallets to the artistic action on the streets.

But what really set the current scene ablaze was ACT UP – the AIDS Coalition to Unleash Power – formed in New York in 1987 to fight the AIDS epidemic through direct action. Although no kind of art movement, ACT UP has given rise to many of today's smaller activist collectives and a few notable individual artist-designers, such as Gran Fury, Don Moffat, and Vincent Gagliostro. "So many of ACT UP's graphics and actions are about seduction and selling," says Vincent Gagliostro, who always uses black-and-white press photographs with bold, generic headline type and red highlights in his handouts and posters for ACT UP. "In terms of propaganda," he says, "I'm a great admirer of the *New York Post*."

"Gran Fury," says the group's Michael Nesline, "uses the art world as a platform for our observations about the political nature of the AIDS crisis. From there, it isn't all that difficult to manipulate the media." Indeed, in addition to the scandal at Venice, Gran Fury has met with considerable success. The group's parody of a Benetton clothing ad, KISSING DOESN'T KILL – GREED AND INDIFFERENCE DO, has adorned the sides of buses in New York City and the entrance of the Whitney Museum of American Art, and in 1988 the group was awarded the Manhattan Borough President's Award for Excellence in the Arts (Visual Arts Division).

The best of the new activist graphics is exemplified by the poster HE KILLS ME designed by Don Moffat, a graphic artist and member of Gran Fury who has subsequently struck out and held a number of exhibitions as an individual artist. Originally created to be carried at ACT UP demonstrations, his poster's eye-catching design and perverse sense of humor set it apart from activist graphics of any other era – particularly in its wry appropriation of contemporary art: the Day-Glo orange is reminiscent of punk graphics and the paintings of Neo-Geo artist Peter Halley; its offbeat combination of eccentric abstract design and grainy black-and-white figure echo the paintings of David Salle; and the fit of photo and text is pure Barbara Kruger. Perhaps most memorable of all is its sarcastic tag line. HE KILLS ME is a gem of gallows humor.

Yet Moffat explains the work in terms of its message. "When I made it," he says, "I was embedded in the tragedy of losing a lover to AIDS, and I was feeling murderous toward Reagan. The bull's-eye is aggressively hostile, designed as a target moving in his direction. All the rest is about making a riotous image that will hold its own on the street."

By wedding style and substance, activists are breathing new life into contemporary art – imbuing it with new meanings and a long-lost sense of urgency. At its best, their art is not intended just for looking at and thinking about. It is also made to inspire the art audience to get up, and act. •

Part Five

Post-Pop

JASPER JOHNS 1989

Interview with Jasper Johns

INTERVIEW JULY 1990

PAUL TAYLOR **It has been said that the American flag in your paintings is a stand-in for yourself.** JASPER JOHNS Hm? **People have said that the flag, in your early paintings, represents you. Is that true? Is that how you used the flag?** I haven't said that. Is that what you're saying? **No, but it has been said about you.** Well, a lot of things have been said about me. **Nevertheless, I wonder if you think it's true.** Do we have to go through this about everything that's been said? Do you think something's true just because it's been said? **No, but I would wonder whether this thing is true even if it had never been said.** That the flag is a stand-in for me? **Yes.** Where? **In your paintings.** In my paintings? I don't believe so. The only thing I can think is that in Savannah, Georgia, in a park, there is a statue of Sergeant William Jasper. Once I was walking through this park with my father, and he said that we were named for him. Whether that is in fact true or not, I don't know. Sergeant Jasper lost his life raising the American flag over a fort. But according to this story, the flag could just as well be a stand-in for my father as for me.

. . . . .

What Vincent van Gogh is to the Japanese, Jasper Johns is to Americans. While van Gogh represents a fiercely individual expression of modernity that is proving irresistible to corporate Japan, 60-year-old Johns is a prophet of the stony-cold, inexpressive postmodernity that has influenced American artists from Pop and Minimal through today's appropriation and Neo-Geo art. Both artists are at the center of an incredible financial storm that is transforming the landscape of the art world. And more than once, both have shattered records at auction: the $17 million paid by publisher S.I. Newhouse for Johns's *False Start* is the highest amount ever paid at auction for the work of a living artist.
At the same time that Johns's prices went out the window, and just as he unveiled a painstaking and cryptic new series called *The Seasons*, which is saturated with backward glances at his life and work since the 1950s, Johns became the Official American Artist with his winning show at the 1988 Biennale of Venice and a spate of retrospectives of his work. The art world seemed to turn full circle, and Pop, once again, became the order of the day. All of this, as well as a retrospective of his drawings now at the National Gallery of Art in Washington, D.C., has thrown the shy and resolutely private artist back into the limelight.

. . . . .

Jasper, you're renowned as being an inaccessible, even secretive, person, and you give few interviews. Ever since we boarded the boat in Venice together two years ago I've been asking for this interview. Perhaps it's no coincidence that the ideas in your work are hidden and that many of your motifs, such as flags and targets, are interpreted as masks. While there are clues everywhere, you are playing a game of hide-and-seek with your viewers. Are you deliberately cagey? I don't think of myself in that way. In terms of work, it interests me to play with aspects of images that become more or less available as you look. I'm interested in how changing aspects of the images can affect your recognition and your response to them. **The catalogues of your work in the last few years, those produced for your shows at Venice, the Walker Art Center, and now in Washington, D.C., exhibit a great deal of effort on the part of the curators to decipher your images and to trace the passages of your motifs from work to work. Everybody who writes about your work seems to have to look for clues and to hunt around.** I think that people do that because then they can say that they see something that is difficult to see, and that gives them something interesting to write about. **But often the recurring motifs in your work are so hidden that they are unnoticed until someone points them out.** That's true, but that's true everywhere in your life, isn't it? **The hidden motifs in your work these days seem to be in marked**

contrast to your paintings of flags. No, they aren't. In all cases, the outline of particular forms are followed rather faithfully, but not entirely faithfully, and filled in with some variation in color and texture. **But the blatantness of your early imagery is gone. I mean, there's no mistaking a flag. It's a nice, big recognizable image.** In some of the paintings, but not in all. One of my largest paintings is a flag. It's painted in whites, and probably yellows by now, and I remember having it in my studio when somebody – I've forgotten who it was, I don't think it was someone involved with art, except perhaps a mover or someone like that who had come to move something – simply went up to my painting and leaned against it. He saw it as the wall – it was hanging on a white brick wall. The flag images exist at many different levels of recognizability. Some are in red, white, and blue and are easy to see. There's a gray one that I think is very difficult to determine as a flag. But once you know the flag is something that I'm involved with, then you have clues to let you know what it is. That interests me – the degree to which what we know affects what we see. I'm also interested in how the eye and the mind work, because as we look from painting to painting we see the next painting differently, according to what we've seen before, probably. **Do you think an artist has only a few ideas?** I think there are some limiting factors. It depends on what you consider an idea. An artist can have many ideas, but usually there's something that connects them, or limits how far apart they can fly. An artist probably has a particular energy that needs to be explored, some kind of central force. And anything he does connects to that in some way, so that many ideas somehow simplify into a larger idea, or a different idea, which means that you're able to connect different thoughts to one kind of thought. Then you realize that that's that artist. **In your case, do you think you have only a few ideas?** I often think that I have many ideas. But then, when I look at things, I'm able to make connections, and then I think, Well, I don't have many ideas at all. I went down to Washington yesterday to look at the drawing show, and I saw that it's been organized in a kind of thematic way. The connections that can be made among various images have been exaggerated. If there are two of this and two of that and two of that, then they put all the twos together so that you see the "two-ness" of these different things, which wasn't an idea of mine necessarily. But it's there. **Do you believe in genius?** Hm? **Do you believe in genius among artists?** Well, one uses it as a way to express one's delight and amazement about certain work. **Is genius in society rather than in individuals?** Well, that's a question that's interesting. It's about parts and wholes, and how they function. If genius is in the whole, then it's probably also in the part, don't you think? **You've said that you're not very good at drawing, that you "can't draw." So why are you so interested in drawing?** Why am I so interested in it? **In the current drawing retrospective, there are over a hundred works. Is the meaning of a drawing very different from a painting?** Yes, but I don't know exactly how much. Sometimes drawing can be a way to establish an idea. Sometimes it can be a way to quickly alter an idea, or to do something without giving it, say, the same weight that it would have in painting. Often it can be a question of speed or lightness or thinness, quickness. And it can be an entertainment, practice, relaxation. It can be all those things, whereas painting tends to be more weighty. **With the exception of a few works, including *Diver*, your drawings are made after your paintings of the same motifs are done.** *Diver* started as a way to figure out a diagram for the painting, and then it was finished later as a kind of drawing. **Of course, most artists draw motifs before they paint them.** That's one of the reasons I don't think I draw very well; drawing is not very natural to me. **Is this connected to the fact that you choose motifs, such as a flag, that have predetermined designs?** Perhaps. **How do you feel when you see your works in reproduction?** I often like them. **You've made black-and-white paintings too. Of course, black and white is not to be found in nature – it's an effect of photography and printing processes. Is painting in black and white a reference to these intermediary processes?** I wonder. I wonder if black and white comes about because of photography, or because of drawing. Obviously it preceded photography, but I'm trying to think whether it did in painting or not. I don't know. **Well, now it's incredibly common.** Yes, of course. **Is this connected to the spread of the media, particularly magazines, newspapers, movies, and television?** You may be right. **Given the range of color in painting, it seems an arch, ironic thing to make black-and-white paintings, as you have done. Were you aware of the degree to which other media were influencing painting as an art form?** I doubt that there was that awareness. I imagine it was something more subjective than that, but I don't really remember. **Did you imagine seeing those works in reproduction as you were making them?** No. **Do they lose anything in reproduction?** They probably lose and probably gain, both. **Does it ever inspire you to see one of your works in reproduction?** I don't really think so. I'm trying to remember. Certainly early on, when my work first appeared in reproduction, I was probably interested to see it represented in a different scale. And I know I made a couple of paintings on top of those reproductions. **Have you ever made works expressly for reproduction? I don't mean editions of prints, but works designed**

for endless reproduction. **No.** **What about photographs?** No. I've probably taken a dozen photographs in my life. **That's odd, isn't it?** I don't like looking through the thing. **The so-called "viewfinder"?** Yeah. I enjoy certain photographs but I don't keep up with photography. I have acquired a few photographs. I have that portfolio that Diane Arbus did. I have a couple of Walker Evans photographs, and photographs of Jackson Pollock by Hans Namuth. That's about it.

You have rarely quoted directly from photographs in your work. There is, of course, the photo of Leo Castelli that appeared in *Racing Thoughts*. **But I imagine that there are very few other quotations from photographs, if any at all.** Well, I've used a few silk-screened images of my own work, of objects. But they're not art photographs, if that's what you mean. There's also a lot of collage material in my paintings where you can see newspaper photographs. But they don't tend to register as separate images. **Who took that photo of Leo?** I think he did. I can't remember the story, but he told me that he had taken it. Apparently someone in the gallery came across it years ago, and I don't know whether he gave it to all the artists in the gallery, or whether the person only gave me this object. But he blew it up and had a jigsaw puzzle made out of it. And that's the way I used it. **Last year you painted another one of your early map paintings. Why?** I made another one, yes, because I was working on one that had been damaged. I don't know what had happened to it, but it had a lot of damage. It looked like it had been soaked in water for a long time. I was doing this restoration, and I said – just said casually – that it would be easier to repaint this than to restore it. Then I started thinking about that, and I wondered, Well, would it be? So I decided to try it, and made another one. Also, I remembered something that Ad Reinhardt once said about a painting of his that belonged to the Museum of Modern Art and had been damaged, I think, by someone cleaning the floor or something. Something had splashed on it. It was one of those very dark paintings with – **Black on black?** Yeah. Alfred Barr had asked him to repair the painting. And Ad said he had told Mr. Barr that it would be easier to repaint it. I don't know whether he kept his paints mixed or what, but you can see with that kind of surface that it would probably be very difficult to go in and do something without its being noticed. It might be easier to take a new canvas and repaint the forms. But Alfred Barr was insistent that he wanted the same painting back. He didn't want another painting. I thought that was an interesting idea. **Was it difficult to repaint it – I mean, to paint another one?** No, it wasn't difficult. It was rather easy. It has a different quality, of course, because the way I apply paint changes over time. **Have you ever repainted an image like this before?** Well, I've repeated many images over the years. Many people think that that's what I do all the time. **Were you posing a philosophical question to yourself by making that work again?** I think I was simply replying to my idea that it would be easier, and wondering whether it would be easier. **What do you think of the differences between the new finished work and the old finished work?** Well, I didn't get to compare the works, because I didn't have them together. **Do you think the new work, having been completed, changes the old work?** No, I don't see why it would. **It makes it more like two of a kind, rather than one of a kind.** Well, they're very different. Many people would think that all of my paintings are of one kind. It just depends on the way you see things, I guess. **What about Andy Warhol? Do you want to talk about him?** I don't know what I can say about Andy. **I believe there was some reciprocity between your works in the sixties. At that point he had obviously been influenced by you. But you also made a reference to him in a piece of yours. You used one of his screens.** I don't know what I had in mind. Andy gave me a screen which said – God, I've forgotten what it says – something like: "Fragile Glass." It must have been something that he used in his paintings that he had left over. And I used it in my painting *Arrive/Depart*. I think it was the first screen that I used. After that I had screens made of my own to use. I always meant to make Andy a present using his screen, and I began, but I never finished. **Why did you use his screen?** Because I knew he had them. I didn't know how you got them made or anything at that time, and I wanted to experiment with them. **Was it in any way a tribute to him or his way of making pictures?** Well, not deliberately a tribute, but he was the person who came to mind to ask. It's a tribute in that he's the source. It wasn't meant as a tribute. **His book** *POPism* **describes his initial meetings with you. He mentions a kind of chilliness toward him, and that you thought he was swish.** I haven't read the book, so I can't reply to that. **I think he said that both you and Rauschenberg thought he was "a swish."** I would like to see that, to see if he said it or if he said someone else said it. **Perhaps there was an intermediary person that reported it to him.** That's what I think. **Who do you think that was?** A mutual friend. Initially I met Andy in the Castelli Gallery during a show of my drawings and sculpture. He was with a friend of his whose name I can't remember. Either each of them had bought a drawing from this show, or they had bought the drawing together; I don't remember. We were introduced, and I said, "Oh, I know your work." And he looked at me in surprise, and said something – I don't remember what. I was talking about his commercial work, which is what I knew, because at that time I did display work. Bob Rauschenberg and I were working together, and one of the jobs that we had gotten was to interpret some of Andy's shoe drawings in a kind of three-dimensional window display. It was at I. Miller, I think. And so I told Andy this, and he said, "Why didn't they ask me to do it?" And that's all I knew about Andy at that time – that he did these shoe illustrations for I. Miller. **So you were interpreting his commercial work commercially at the same time that he was interpreting your art work artistically?** I don't know where he was with his own work at this point, because I didn't see his paintings until later. But at that time he had a kind of audience for his commercial work. It was considered very interesting by a lot of people. People would talk about him, and they would say that Andy would draw the lines and someone else would blot them, and then it all came out in the Sunday papers, in these ads. And certain people enjoyed them. I think the first person I heard talking about them was Cynthia Feldman, who was married to the composer Morton Feldman. At any rate, I don't remember when that show of mine was. Then at some point after that I was taken to Andy's studio, which was in his house on Lexington Avenue, where his mother lived. I went to look at his pictures. I don't think he had begun to use the screens at that point. There were things like the painting of the cosmetic operation on the nose. That's the time at which I first saw his paintings. Now, what am I coming to? **You were getting around to the "swish" word, I think.** No I'm not. I'm not getting around to that at all. **So what did you really think of him?** What I think is, I don't think that was a proper statement. And I don't believe it's Andy's. **You mean you don't think he actually believed it.** Well, I hope he didn't. I didn't care for the ... I don't know what you'd call it ... all of the entertainment-world aspect of Andy. I didn't really like that. I liked a lot of his work, and still do. But there was something exaggerated about the theatrical aspect. **What are your favorite works of his?** Oh, the ones I have are probably the ones I really like most. I have a Marilyn and a group of the sculptures. **Did he influence you?** Well, it depends on what you mean. Everything influences me. I don't know how to respond to that one. I can't say he influenced me in this way or that. I've looked at an awful lot of Andy Warhol, and usually you don't look at things if you're not getting something out of them. **Warhol in the last years of his life, and Roy Lichtenstein in his murals, and you in your recent series, _The Seasons_, have anthologized images that you have used in the previous thirty years of your work. There are quotations from your works from the fifties through to the eighties in these three different bodies of work, and I wonder what it means. It's interesting that the three of you have done it at roughly the same time, during the 1980s.** Well, those four paintings of mine, _The Seasons_, were concerned with places and properties, so that I see the use of my earlier motifs as having to do with the subject matter of the paintings. They contain numerous images that relate to things that are around me. So in a sense they represent, largely, possessions. Each painting relates to a studio where I was working. And I was moving. I had just moved into a studio in the Caribbean. And I had moved back into town from the country, and then I was moving another studio from downtown to uptown. I was doing a lot of shifting of things from place to place. So I had the idea to do the four paintings. It began with one painting, and it was just going to be one painting, _Summer_. And then I saw that I could do this other thing and made four paintings. Once you commission yourself to do something like that, then you have to execute it, and you have to draw on whatever you can find that's useful for accomplishing the work. **In these works you embarked on a narrative series for the first time. Up to that point your work seems distinctly anti-narrative.** There had to be four things that were related. **But this was a sequence, a temporal sequence, such as you find in narrative art, in fiction, and so forth. That's a change for you, because your earlier images were so emblematic.** Well, it's just the convention of that subject, isn't it? It's the seasons. **Why did you introduce autobiography into your paintings?** They're not particularly autobiographical. Where is the autobiography? **The different paintings pertain to particular stages of your life and artistic career.** That's just a kind of clichéd tradition of representing the seasons, isn't it? What would you do? **The incorporation of flags, _Mona Lisa_, cross-hatching, and other motifs from your earlier work all suggest that you're narrating a form of autobiography. I wonder if you're telling the story of your own development by incorporating these elements in your work.** But I don't see that it tells of any development. That's the point that I'm making. I don't really see that it's a narrative, in that I don't see what it narrates – unless you think that the representation of the seasons is in itself a narrative. I don't see it that way. In a sense none of it represents me. And, in a sense, all of it represents me. It's like any other painting in that respect. You can say it does, or you can say it doesn't. **In the sixties, Marcel Duchamp said that he thought art would go underground.** Having already done so himself. **But it didn't. Instead, it became incredibly public.** I wonder if there is the possibility that there is an underground art. I don't know. **Today there certainly seems to be the opposite.** As far as predictions go, Duchamp's certainly didn't work, did it? I have no feeling that there is anything that you would call underground art. **People used to talk about being outside of the system and about dropping out. But what is "outside" now? I don't know.** I don't know either. **But I would say that you may be becoming metaphysical.** I suppose it's a metaphysical question. Well, I can only say that I'm not aware that there is an outside or an underground. **On the practical side of this question of visibility, do the extraordinary prices fetched for your paintings at auction affect your painting now?** You mean my working? **Yes.** I don't know. I hope not. **What are your feelings about collections of art that once seemed destined for museums but that are now being split up and auctioned off? How do you feel about that when it involves your own art?** I think it's terrible. But that's just because one assumed that these things would go to some public place. Of course one had no right, I guess, to assume that. But one did. **Why is it terrible? Do you mean that it's a pity that these collections are not being kept together?** No, no. I don't think that's so bad. I just like the idea that art is publicly available. The first time I saw paintings they were in museums. I never knew anyone who had a painting. So that's how I think painting is available to people. But maybe that whole idea is ridiculous. I heard a radio program by accident the other day. I was in the country, and I was going mushrooming, and I turned the radio on. It was Sunday, I think. And Leo Castelli was hosting a lunch or breakfast at the Algonquin. And among all the art-market talk, this question came up. And Leo said, "It's not sad, because eventually they'll all be in the museums anyway." Which may be true. I hadn't thought like that. I think it's just that when one assumes something, one finds it upsetting to discover that one's assumptions have no real weight. **Is it important for you that your work be seen in museums?** It's not that it's important to me that my work be seen in museums. It's that I think that museums are where most people, most young people and poor people, contact art. And I think of art – maybe wrongly – as being identified with the young and the poor. I think that's where art comes from, from the young and the poor, and that their access to art is through museums. I mean, they're not generally going into the homes of rich people to look at pictures on the wall. **It's a liberal idea of yours, this one.** I don't know whether it is or not. I haven't thought it through. It may just be a description of my own background. **Your paintings were never inexpensive. They were never affordable for the young and the poor. The joke is that now they're not even affordable for the wealthy. They're priced for the super-rich. What do you think about this?** I think that when that becomes the case, it's even more important that paintings be publicly available. That's what I think. And I think that has been the pattern – usually as works became very costly, the owners died off and left them to public institutions. And that seems to me a reasonable state of affairs. Who knows how it will continue? **I suppose you're gratified by the knowledge that at least one collector might leave his collection to the Museum of Modern Art.** Are you talking about someone specific? **Newhouse, I believe, is going to leave –** I didn't know that. **Well, that's what I heard the other evening from somebody in his family.** Really? I hadn't heard that. Well, we'll see what he has in his collection then. It changes from time to time. I think the odd thing is to think that works in museums now have value, which of course they are thinking nowadays. That's really tragic. The earlier thought that they were priceless is certainly a much nicer thought. ●

ROBERT RAUSCHENBERG 1986

Interview with Robert Rauschenberg

INTERVIEW DECEMBER 1990

Robert Rauschenberg left town more than twenty years ago for remote Captiva Island in Florida, having put American art on the international map at the Venice Biennale, where he won the Grand Prix in 1964. By that time, the Pop, Process, Conceptual, and Performance art movements that followed in the footsteps of Rauschenberg and his contemporaries had transformed the New York artscape forever.   Captiva was the source of endless new series of paintings, sculptures, photographs, and prints – leading up to his recent *Gluts* and *Borealis* works – as well as a career in activism and artistic agitation. And there, from the midst of nowhere, Rauschenberg established his Change Foundation (to assist struggling artists), and became one of 26 artists to withdraw from a show of American prints at the 1970 Venice Biennale "as an act of dissociation from United States government sponsorship." His activism continues today, in efforts to defeat Senator Jesse Helms and in his quixotic ROCI (Rauschenberg Overseas Cultural Interchange).   Rauschenberg also keeps a studio (a former Catholic orphanage and chapel) in the NoHo section of Manhattan, where he is putting the final touches on his major exhibition of 1960s silk screens at the Whitney Museum of American Art (opening December 7) and preparing a spring retrospective at the National Gallery of Art in Washington. Here, with his trademark glass of whiskey held close to the mouth like a microphone, Rauschenberg is garrulous on many subjects and tight-lipped about others which could inspire entire books on their own.

Fortunately for Rauschenberg scholars and fans, there is a new biography – *Rauschenberg: Art and Life*, by Mary Lynn Kotz, out this month from Abrams – that might separate the grain from the chaff.

· · · · ·

PAUL TAYLOR **Apart from occasional visits here, you've left New York. How come?**   ROBERT RAUSCHENBERG It seemed to be a very changing time. All my friends were getting divorced; I was lonely. So I went to an astrologer. I didn't have time or patience for psychoanalysis, which doesn't interest me. I thought, I can find out what's going on in just one afternoon. So I went to Zoltan Mason, who was highly recommended by a number of people. You have to write down your profession, and I wrote "painter." He didn't know who I was. During the whole course of his analysis he assumed I was a housepainter. He said that whatever I do, I should stay out of the mountains. I have acrophobia, so that's a good idea. I feel fenced in when I see rocks that are too old, and that's what mountains are made out of – heights and rocks that are too old. He also said, "You should head for the water and the sun." I was born in the Gulf of Mexico, down in Port Arthur, Texas. And I had been going to Florida already. I'd just get in the car and drive. And every time I got to Captiva Island I felt a particular kind of spiritual affinity, almost a kind of magic, and so I started going there more frequently.   **Do you still see an astrologer?**   No.   **What star sign are you?**   Libra, on the cusp of Scorpio. I make the joke that I keep my success in Scorpio, and I work in Libra.   **Do you know anything interesting about your chart that bears on who you are?**   I don't do it that seriously or thoroughly. I know that I have a period of great restlessness and disaster every seven years. It started in the forties, and the astrologer could pinpoint almost every dramatic change and upset. He was just right on. So that's why I never felt I had to go back.   **When are you due for your next crisis?**   I don't know. I'll have to get some old calendars out and check. *(laughs)*   **A few years ago you told me that you don't really like to comment critically on your younger colleagues. Nevertheless, I wonder how the New York art world seems to you today.**   Pretty incestuous.   **You think so – despite the fact that the whole operation has grown so much bigger?**   It's hard to go to a gallery in New York and see something that doesn't look familiar. And I don't mean just like *my* things.   **It's cannibalistic?**   Yeah, right. I have quoted myself too often about this, but from early on I always wanted my works – whatever happened in the studio – to look more like what was going on outside the window. I still feel that way.   **What are the opportunities like here for new artists?**   Well, if they don't fall asleep with success, I don't see any reason that things couldn't be as exciting as, say, the fifties or sixties were for American artists. But I think it's almost to a fault that there are so many galleries. My friend Brice

Marden was teaching at the School of Visual Arts, and on the first day he noticed that the only curiosity young artists expressed was to say, "Tell me how to get a gallery," and "Tell me how to get a loft." So he said, "If you want that, I'll tell you the gallery you should go to, I'll tell you how you find a loft. But don't come back to school tomorrow if that's what you want." I think the focus on these things is premature, and it's eclipsed the curiosity about – and joy of – making art works.   **It means that art has a different meaning now, doesn't it?**   I think so. I think collectors are responsible, dealers are responsible, auctions are responsible. By the time you establish your priorities, there really isn't any fun or need to interest yourself in what you're doing. And this I find disastrous.   **Do you think there are particular artists who helped bring about this state of affairs?**   I think it was the success of American painting.   **So you might be one of the artists who helped bring this about – you and the generation of artists immediately after you who became successful at a young age?**   I think there was a misinterpretation of what we were doing.   **By whom?**   The general public and the investors.   **How did they misinterpret it?**   Well, let's take paintings that you had to *give* away – which is the way I started. *If* you were lucky (*laughs*), somebody would take one. But those things gained an exaggerated value so quickly. This appealed not only to artists but also to people who were not that serious about art, as well as collectors. And this fed back into: "Maybe I'll get this one – a painting by this person – because it also might be very valuable someday." People did not experience a painting on a one-to-one basis. That seems to have been lost in dollar signs and investment. Something else that's happened in the last fifteen years or so is that galleries have become art works in themselves. The artist is almost the cosmetic of the gallery rather than the *soul*, which is the way it used to be.   **If you had your way, what would be the role of art in the world?**   I think it's an exercise for the artist to enlarge his or her vision, as a way of proving that you are living.   **It's a heartbeat, in a sense.**   Yeah. I mean, if you have a very boring life, if you haven't earned your birthright, it doesn't matter whether you're here or there.   **Your association with Leo Castelli has quite a history. Why, after all those years at Castelli, did you start showing at another gallery?**   I felt that Castelli had a disinterest in my work. I didn't leave the gallery – I'm still in there – but I'm mostly showing at Knoedler Gallery.   **Did Knoedler show more interest?**   Well, I didn't move out of disloyalty. I signed a one-year contract with Knoedler, which does not exclude being in other galleries, like Castelli, Ileana Sonnabend, the Texas gallery, and my Swedish one.   **How do your works go in the auctions?**   Expensively.   **Are you happy about that?**   Not really, because of all the economic ramifications.   **How do you feel about the incredible Jasper Johns prices?**   Well, Jasper's always been, from his very first show, a quality painter. And I think people like the fact that after all these years his changes have not been radical. I'm not putting him down for that. But in my case, when I change drastically, as I often do, there's a lot of gamble and doubt. Otherwise, I'd fall asleep in the studio. I'm not against making money, because I use it quite rapidly. But my genuine focus is not on that, and I've been making an in-house joke that *I* can't even afford my works anymore. When I keep one, I think, Oh, my God! Can I afford this?   **That's funny.**   But I'm working on my foundation now. So the *special* works that I choose to keep will be part of that foundation.   **How do you want history to describe your association with Johns?**   (*chuckles*) Richly.   **How?**   Not talking about money now?   **No.**   We were the only people who were not intoxicated with the Abstract Expressionists. We weren't against them at all, but neither one of us was interested in taking that stance. I think both of us felt there was too much exaggerated emotionalism around their art. And, well, I was on the street, and Jasper was in his mind. My first break was that nobody took me seriously, even though I hung out at the Cedar Tavern, and drove Franz Kline home when he was too drunk. Jasper wasn't taken seriously either, and I was considered a clown. We were friendly, harmless critters, you know.   **We have previously talked about your relationship with Jasper. How much will you go on the record about this? I think that there are lots of reasons to talk, especially in the current climate of suppression of gay art and artists.**   Well, I wouldn't go into any of the sexuality. One of the reasons is that – is this off the record?   **Can't you say it in a way that's on the record?**   Well, I think I'd better just leave it alone. I'm not frightened of the affection that Jasper and I had, both personally and as working artists. I don't see any sin or conflict in those days when each of us was the most important person in the other's life.   **Can you tell me why you parted ways?**   Embarrassment about being well known.   **Embarrassment about being famous?**   Socially. What had been tender and sensitive became gossip. It was sort of new to the art world that the two most well-known, up-and-coming studs were affectionately involved.   **I wonder if things are different nowadays.**   I think it's different. The fifties were a particularly hostile, prudish time.   **Are things worsening again?**   I'm afraid they are, with Bush and Helms.   **In 1970, only six years after you represented this country at the Venice Biennale, you withdrew from the same show as an act of disassociation from United States government sponsorship. That was a period of** considerable arts activism. **Why do you suppose that now there is so much arts activism again?** It's self-defense. **Could it possibly indicate that artists are not out to make a buck exclusively, contrary to your story about the art students asking Brice Marden how to get a loft and a gallery? I'm sure that increasing numbers of artists see art as an agent for social change.** Well, that is a healthy thing right now. All kinds of activists are aggressive in spite of our present state of politics; it might tone up some of the muscles artists used to have. The Vietnam war seems so long ago. Still, I remember how passionately I was against it. Most of my life has been politically oriented. That's the reason that I had my big tax bust ... There were only two artists on the list then, Andy and myself. The IRS said, "Bust these guys, no matter what it takes." Warhol contributed to McGovern's campaign — And I'd given money to the Black Panthers. **What do you think about that now?** Oh, I'm *proud* of it. It cost me a fortune. I lost a lot of art and had only two months to come up with $150,000. An investigator insulted me, saying, "If you don't do this, I'm going to crack down on anyone who's ever been associated with you, just as thoroughly as I have on you. And, by God, if you don't agree to this, all your friends are going to be victimized, and I won't get my promotion." **Who bankrolls your activism?** Me. **How?** Out of my pocket. I had to sell my big Twombly. I had to sell my early Warhol and Jasper's first color painting. Then I add whatever I make from my exhibitions and sales. **How did you feel being part of the Russian pavilion at the Venice Biennale this year?** I loved it. I thought it was a great compliment. I think that the whole form of the Venice Biennale is going to have to denationalize. This year has seen some of the most sensational, surprising moves in terms of creating a worldly, generous, sophisticated democracy. Nationalistic competition, I think, is dead. ●

ROY LICHTENSTEIN 1992

Interview with Roy Lichtenstein

FLASH ART OCTOBER 1989

PAUL TAYLOR **How has the criticism of your work developed since the 1960s?** ROY LICHTENSTEIN Criticism was universally deprecating in the beginning, and it's often still snide. Not all of it. Some of it takes the work seriously. Critics didn't seem to make a lot of difference. **It would be wrong to say that your work was not at all critically appreciated in the beginning.** It's almost right. Robert Rosenblum and Leo Steinberg were for at least the idea of it. I don't think Leo Steinberg wrote specifically about me, but he allowed for the genre. There were people taking it seriously, and then collectors, avid but not many, who were interested. **Your work nevertheless became such a big and famous phenomenon – along with the work of your peers – that I can't imagine you thought it was unpopular.** It was strange. Maybe the established artists disliked it more than even the critics because it seemed to be changing the focus of the art world, which it did, of course. And it seemed to fly in the face of every belief. **Did you imagine in the beginning that this was what you were doing?** I thought it was entirely different, because I thought of myself as an Abstract Expressionist – before the comic strips. So I kind of had an idea of how my cartoon paintings would be viewed. I had no idea of the kind of influence they would have. **To what do you attribute that influence? How did it happen?** I think that Abstract Expressionism had deteriorated into a sort of mannerism, which I was certainly involved in – not that Pollock or de Kooning had deteriorated. But at that time, there were certain characteristics of art that everyone knew and everyone was doing – the calligraphic stroke and various textures. I tried to see art from another viewpoint and do away with anything that was considered beautiful and to subject art to other means was something I guess that art needed. Though I must say in retrospect that I didn't have this thought out entirely. **Were you looking at Dada art?** I don't really think of myself as Dada and non-art. I thought I was composing and doing things that other artists did. I just wasn't using the texture or the subjects that were being done. It's not really so far from Léger. I'm looking at that one over there (*points*) ... that's why I bring it up. Still, in Léger, you get a mark that looks a little mechanical but a little bit handmade – both at the same time. There were others – Schlemmer had used drafting instruments, El Lissitzky ... people who tried a way of making painting relate to the modern world. **As well as those who made paintings based on photography.** Sure. So we just needed that change apparently. **What do you call that change?** The change from the School of Paris, I guess, was to use frankly commercial art techniques. In Abstract Expressionist times, there was the idea that you could paint anything and everything was okay, but they didn't mean commercial art. There was a sense that everything is okay if it's new and organized, but they weren't thinking of something like commercial art. It was always disdained. They thought that I was actually only enlarging a cartoon, and bringing it into an art situation – a kind of Dada statement. You could look at it that way, and I realized it had Dada attitudes, but you could say that about any major change. Certainly Picasso – he wasn't Dada, but *Demoiselles d'Avignon* looked like a major, ridiculous anti-art statement when it was done. Now it looks like art. **Did the success of Jasper Johns in the late 1950s help to pave the way for this new attitude? Do you feel indebted to Johns's paintings?** Certainly it was an influence, but there were a lot of influences, and I wasn't particularly thinking of Johns. I didn't have him in mind, but I think he was an influence on everything that was an influence. Happenings were part of the influence, though I never did Happenings. Trying to get away from Cubism, and use American objects and differentiate it from Europe. I knew Allan Kaprow well. Oldenburg was involved, and that was an influence, I'm sure. He had done the bacon and eggs and things that look like merchandise. **But the differences between his work and yours are substantial.** The subjects were alike – associated with junk. They were in the history of the constant vulgarization of subject matter. (*laughs*) But his were expressionist. **Despite your claim that you were trying to get away from Cubism, Cubism remains part of your lexicon – apart from just the appropriation of Picasso in the later work. In your earlier work, such as the painting of the back of a canvas, the Cubist heritage is there, even though the subject is removed, second-degree.** There are certain single object things I did, maybe straight cartoons that get away from Cubism. But I think cartoons themselves were influenced by Cubism – the fact that it was okay to make a black line and fill it with a color is from Cubism – to paint one object, like a shirt or a hand, and not modulate it otherwise, is probably from Cubism in a way. **Is this** to say that in your opinion Cubism is the century's most important art movement?   I would think so. I was born long enough ago to be a product of World War II and art school was all about Cubism and Abstract Expressionism. So, in trying to rid myself of that, which I felt I did at certain points, certainly the mural here at Tel Aviv was Cubist-influenced in its composition. But I don't think my work has to be Cubist, and so I feel freed from it. Directly doing my own Picasso frees me from the influence of Picasso, whereas my early work looked like it was always trying to escape Picasso. By doing one, I felt freer.   **To get back to my earlier question, to what do you attribute Pop art's influence?**   Maybe there were no other avenues to go. I mean, I think there are always other ways to go. I don't know what they are yet, but they will occur. It always seems impossible. After Pollock on the one hand and Mondrian on the other, where would you go? I feel lucky that my work found somewhere to go, and someone else will find another way too. The new expressionism found a mythology that was new, but the method was still late Abstract Expressionism.   **Do you mean the painting method?**   Yes.   **But the eclecticism was very Pop, the idea of being able to quote, and that the world of art was readymade for pillaging. Although the movement was frequently hailed as a return to subjective painting, the opposite may have been true.**   Yes, that's right. I think that one of the real differences was that the models were two-dimensional rather than three-dimensional. Although the models always really were two-dimensional in a certain way. I mean, people would draw from the model, but they would draw like Michelangelo or someone. A person didn't come about that by himself. He'd be painting like a child probably, if he didn't have those two-dimensional models. So it was not really a three-dimensional model, and this gets to a sort of truth – Pop says this in a way. It was saying that the model always was art. It also further defines art by showing another way to be art, that all of these things could be art.   **If that was always the case, why did this point of view in general, and Pop art in particular, become academic in the late 1980s?**   There probably is a lot more art being done, and a lot more focus on art. I'm amazed at the difference between the audience in the sixties and the audience now – the numbers. Museums were relatively empty when I was a child.   **When you were painting your Abstract Expressionist work, were you operating in some state of innocence or oblivion?**   Yeah. I had the idea then, I think most people did, that you respond to your painting, which was simply a reaction between you and your work, and that if you're completely honest about the way that you're doing it, then it will be you. It really was de Kooning. (laughs) That naiveté allowed you to do a lot of work. Now, I don't know how anyone does anything. The mark down there you know isn't you, and you're aware of all these things. I don't see how you can get through art school. If you're not completely original you're wasting your time. That must be an awful pressure.   **Is there an irony in your belief that while there are more artists and a bigger audience for art, there might be less to do?**   Until someone finds a way.   **Do you think that it will be some individual who finds a way?**   Yes.   **What do you think about the cult of Warhol today, and the neo-Pop movement? Perhaps those are two separate questions.**   I think it's a remarkable thing he did. He built his own Hollywood. At first it was a fun idea to have superstars and direct his own movies. Then it actually became Hollywood, and was taken seriously – not the specifics of the movies but he's better known than most people in Hollywood. What started as an amusing idea became real.   **Why do you talk about his movies when I mention Warhol?**   I think it was the "cult" word. I think that if he had only painted, he wouldn't have created a cult. But his whole apolitical life seemed to fit in with postmodern thinking. That's hard for me to deal with. That is, he was apparently apolitical. I'm sure he wasn't. But it was the attitude, an acceptance of everything.   **When I mentioned Warhol, you responded with a thought about his films. Yet the Museum of Modern Art presented him almost exclusively as a painter.**   The paintings were wonderful there. They were very strong. But I think that his influence on most people had to do with his life, and the idea of his movies. I'm sure that most people haven't seen them. But I think his art was strong, and I think that his best work was early, though you could find very good work all through. I think he had a tremendous influence on Conceptual art. In fact, he may be the source of Conceptual art, because of concepts that seemed to come from him that weren't necessarily in the paintings he did, but in other things – even things like the balloons, and the idea that you didn't really do it yourself, that other people could do it. I'm sure that other people had a hand in it, but I'm sure that he was making the artistic decisions, no matter how removed he wanted to pretend he was.   **And what about neo-Pop?**   It's hard for me to see it. Some of it is criticized as though there were no earlier Pop art. (laughs) I saw Jeff Koons's show three times at Ileana's, and I don't know exactly what to make of it. Almost everything I can say about it, people said about me, that it's just kitsch blown up, you know. But it makes some sort of impression from looking at it. I really don't know what to say yet. Peter Halley – I think I like his work as well. But then it's more frankly abstract but it still has hints of objects – batteries or something.   **Tomorrow, your mural here at the Tel**

Aviv Museum is being unveiled to the public. Is this now your third mural in existence?   I did one in 1970 in Düsseldorf at the Medical College. It's brushstrokes – cartoon brushstrokes that go around the walls. It's ten feet high but it's maybe 300 feet of different brushstrokes on dots. It's a simple mural painted right on the wall. There was no effort to prepare the wall other than to paint it white. I didn't think of murals as any different from paintings, though sometimes you react to the architecture. I'd just as soon avoid the architecture, really. But you know it's different and you make a different kind of statement. In the Equitable building [mural of 1985-86 in New York], it was almost a take-off on grand religious work, with the sunset and the sky on top working its way down. It wasn't religious obviously, but I was trying to make it grand in that way. There I really took into account the architecture that was surrounding it – the windows, the things that went right into the thing actually influenced the design of it. Then that hand wiping off the mural appears to be revealing the windows. At Greene Street, there were a few architectural details – the niches. A Picasso head is in one, and an Art Deco strip covers the pillar.   **Why is the hand wiping the mural – is it to show that behind the painting there is a glass-box architectural construction?**   It's a mural and I appear to be wiping it off, but I'm actually painting it. It's both using the architecture and a play of using the architecture because people say that a mural should fit in with the architecture. I think that a mural can be anything on a wall; it doesn't make a bit of difference. But to take some of the architecture and bring it in and make reference to it gives me an idea for how to compose the mural. It's just part of the way you put it together. You could do it any way you want.   **Is this to introduce an element of site-specificity?**   Yes, but it's a kind of mock site-specificity.   **Why do you want to mock it?**   Because it's a cliché.   **How did it become a cliché?**   People just think that a mural should be "appropriate" and therefore would not "violate" the architecture and those things that you hear about in design and art school. To overuse it is something that interested me, if that's possible to do. There wasn't architecture around this Tel Aviv mural. It takes up the whole wall, though I did refer to the ramp.   **Why did you make a gift of this mural to the Tel Aviv Museum?**   Just because I wanted to do a big one, I wanted to give something to Israel. It's a good question. Mark Scheps [the museum director] is very persuasive. I've thought about it. I probably wouldn't do another one for nothing. It isn't that I did the mural for Israel and not the other indigenous people. It don't mean it that way at all. I mean it for anyone in the area. The museum needed assistance. Their budget is small. And not that many museums would ask you to do a mural that would take up a lot of room, because you're really preempting space in the museum. It was the first to ask. I'm sure it sets a very bad precedent for me.   **Weren't you a signatory to a petition about Israel? I thought I read your name among other signatories in the newspaper.**   You mean about giving a break to the Palestinians? My feeling is for compromise, that Israel should give up something. But I also understand that it's a tricky situation. I do see both sides of it. I don't believe Israel has any Biblical right, more than anyone else does, to the territory or some idea like that. But they are here. And yes, they should ideally share, but what is the Arabs' real intention? What is the PLO's real intention or Arafat's intention? But it will probably end with a compromise.   **When you do a mural here ...**   ... it looks like a big support for the state, I suppose. And, though not a Zionist, I support the state.   **And then to make a gift of it.**   I see the can of worms. For one thing, I kind of agreed before all of this happened. The situation was the same, but the *intifada* hadn't begun. I thought about it in this light. But the people who support my work in Israel are usually on the right end of things. Maybe I'm rationalizing that it has nothing to do with politics.   **This brings us back to what you called Warhol's apolitical stance. Where is the politics in your work?**   In the work? There isn't. I don't think my work is political.   **So if Warhol's apolitical, what are you?**   I know what you're saying. I think it's very hard. You read a lot into it. I read a lot into it when I say that about Warhol. Isn't irony political? In the beginning, I thought my work was partly political in that people thought it was a celebration of commercial art or something, which could be interpreted as a right-wing political statement.   **But it's also said that it's a left-wing statement because it opposes the elitism of art.**   That's a strange way to look at it, but it's just as valid because you're really reading into this Rorschach. It can mean anything you want it to. But I thought of it as depicting the culture in that these things were non-works of art. Cartoons did represent a low-art position, but then I was being ironic about my work being low-art, because I think of my work as reorganizing them completely, so even if they look the same, the whole purpose is different. So it shows up the culture but it also makes a work of art.   **How is that "political"?**   It shows the capitalist system in an ironic way. That's just an interpretation that I put on it. I realize that it may not say that and that it could be interpreted many ways. I always thought it was rather funny that the Minimalists were seen to take left-wing political positions – or some did, Morris or Andre – when there wouldn't be a working man in the world who would look at it as art. And our things were looked at as right-wing. I have no idea why. It doesn't make any sense at all.

It's a celebration of consumerism. But through the use of irony, your art distances the activity of consumerism. It highlights it and isolates it. Yes. In the beginning I certainly didn't think it would sell. I thought maybe that if Leo Castelli wouldn't take it on, nobody would. Maybe Green Gallery at the time. They were the two. So the idea that it would sell was not in my mind at all. I thought it meant something. I thought I had really done something important. I had that feeling. And I was happy whether they took it or they didn't, because for once I felt that I had done something. I didn't care if I had a gallery or if I didn't have a gallery. The insecurity of not being sure of your work makes you want the security of a gallery – not that you don't necessarily want them if you're successful. But I remember clearly not caring, for maybe the first time in my life, whether I had shows. So selling wasn't in my mind at the beginning. But the fact is that consumerism takes in everything finally, you find out. What about the Equitable Insurance Company having the [Thomas Hart] Benton mural – a clearly anticapitalist mural. It's just there as decoration, a quaint thirties idea. **Is abstinence from, and criticism of, the art system any kind of solution? You, on the other hand, really embraced the Equitable as ...** ... a bastion of capitalism. Yeah, I know. I hate that idea, but there I am. Maybe my idea was a very public mural. It can be seen by people. There aren't many good works of art that are public in New York. The building is connected with the Whitney, so it has a museum possibility. It was the Whitney that asked me to do it in the first place. I did think about those things, about aggrandizing the sale of space in the building or whatever else it was doing. And that's not exactly what I'd like to think this mural was doing. There are so many things connected to it. There are political questions connected with every kind of public work, it's amazing and they're so convoluted. It's like the one you asked me about this mural. It started before the *intifada*, but it doesn't mean that there weren't issues. **Did your use of irony in your early work arise from any particular branch of political or philosophical thought?** No, I was just a kind of liberal. But, even then, I realized that politics was very hard to read. **Have you changed as an artist since the sixties?** I'm basically doing the same thing. In fact I think I was doing the same thing before the sixties. But I do think I've explored other things and brought other ideas into it. I think my further exploration of brushstrokes is important. I'm not against ideas because I'm not particularly for completely conceptual work, because I think the idea of conceptual work came mostly from Andy and partly from Pop in general. Basically, I haven't changed at all, but I hope that I've gone into other ideas. **Did success change you?** I don't think it changed me. I think it allowed me to do more than I may have done otherwise. **Someone told me once that success is the end.** Well, you try not to have it affect you, but it has to in a certain way. I don't go around all day thinking I'm successful. I don't see people a lot. I have a routine of work which I do. There's always the fear that it will take the edge away. I'm sure the edge I have isn't the same as the edge I had at the beginning. You can't keep up that kind of energy. I'm not sure it would make any difference if I were ignored. It's very hard to tell. Success must have an effect, but you can't predict the effect, and for me to try to judge my own work is difficult. Does my judgment mean any more than my work, or other people's judgments? **What about Jasper Johns, and the incredible prices his work is fetching now?** Does it make any difference if his work gets $50,000 or $1 million? They're all astronomical amounts. I've made enough for a long time, so does making ridiculous quantities change anything? **What does it do for the art market? Is it destructive?** I think it's a very strange situation. I feel very uneasy. That a living person's work should be worth so much seems to fly in the face of everything I believe in – more equitable distribution of things. Once you're not really struggling, it doesn't make much difference to you what your work gets. But people now see money when they see art, and I don't think that's a good situation. ●

Robert Indiana's Love Story

CONNOISSEUR AUGUST 1991

"Love is central to my life," says Robert Indiana. "I am dedicated to the proposition, like all Christians." Indiana's paean to love – the stacked-letter design with the cat's-eye *O* – was created for a Museum of Modern Art Christmas card in 1964. For the next ten years it appeared everywhere, especially after the U.S. Postal Service issued it on 330 million stamps. More than any other work of art, *LOVE* became the icon of the peace and love generation. As both a declaration and an exhortation, it was ubiquitous. "It's become my logo," says Indiana. "But most people have no idea who did it. My name has just disappeared."

Indeed, the famous four-letter word did not spell success for Indiana. He milked it artistically and churned out endless variations on the theme in thousands of paintings, prints, and sculptures. But his failure to copyright the design meant that he reaped few financial rewards from its wildfire proliferation: the millions of unauthorized stickers, coasters, matchbox covers, tiles, lamps, earrings, buttons, key chains, hippie patches, and wastepaper baskets. Rather than receive royalties, Indiana was royally ripped off. "The only thing it didn't come out on was toilet paper," says Indiana sourly. "And I'm rather surprised about that."

LOVE was bad news for Indiana in the art world too. Although the good-looking young Pop artist had been a hot item in New York since 1961, the visibility of his *LOVE* sign and his own permutations on it year after year overwhelmed his earlier work. Quickly tiring of the logo, the artist's peers judged its creator harshly as a crushing, repetitive bore. By the time he left New York in 1978 for the seclusion of a distant island off the coast of Maine, Indiana was considered a has-been.

Yet *LOVE* did succeed in turning its creator into a metaphor for his times. Having created the most enduring one-word expression of the sixties, Indiana saw it become carelessly commercialized in the decade that followed. And today – in the sexual revolution's darkest hour – Indiana is suddenly finding himself a victim of the conservative backlash. Love, in other words, may have been central to Robert Indiana's life, but it was also his undoing. Now love has found him again. And again it may undo him.

· · · · ·

On a quiet day in August last year, Detective Ernest W. McIntosh of Rockland, Maine, armed himself with a search warrant, boarded the Knox County Coast Guard boat, and traveled fifteen miles across Penobscot Bay to the little island of Vinalhaven. McIntosh's destination was the Victorian mansion of one Robert E. Clark, age 61, known to the outside world as Robert Indiana.

Inside the artist's three-story refuge, a former Odd Fellows lodge decked out with curios and memorabilia from the life and times of Indiana and of Maine alike, McIntosh and his men conducted a search and turned up their evidence. And by nightfall, they had their prey by their side, handcuffed and aboard the Coast Guard boat on its way back to the mainland. With Indiana was a portfolio of recent prints and love-inspired drawings, nine of them explicit studies of male genitals.

On arrival in Rockland, the artist was fingerprinted, photographed, and having refused to make a statement, released on $300 bail. But the charges against him are plain and quite public: two criminal complaints of engaging a prostitute and one of patronizing the prostitution of a minor.

In his request for a search warrant, Detective McIntosh stated that two men, ages 19 and 21, had told him that Robert Indiana had repeatedly paid them amounts ranging from $20 to $200 to pose nude and engage in sex during the modeling sessions. One of the men told the detective that Indiana wanted to draw his genitals and that this had led to oral sex. Moreover, such hanky-panky had allegedly been going on for years – ever since one of the men was an adolescent. One young man confessed that he "knew it was wrong but was doing it for the money." These accusations were leveled by him during the period in which he was being investigated for forging Indiana's checks.

If convicted of the misdemeanor of engaging a prostitute, Indiana could face six months in jail and a fine of $500. If he is found guilty of patronizing the prostitution of a minor, also a misdemeanor, he could be sentenced to 364 days in jail and fined $1,000.

As an open homosexual in the tiny fishing village on Vinalhaven Island (population 1,200), Indiana stuck out like a sore thumb – ever since he and his former lover staged their

ROBERT INDIANA 1990

breakups nightly for all of the town to hear. Indiana also seems to have left himself wide open to accusations from each and every unemployed young male islander he ever paid for services rendered. In fact, his vulnerability, his relative wealth, and his artistic renown may explain why he and he alone is facing these three misdemeanors. In a reversal of the standard police practice of dragging prostitutes through the courts and giving their clients a gentlemanly slap on the wrist, the Rockland police have no intention of charging the young man with prostitution. To do so, says Knox County district attorney William Anderson, "would only make the case against Mr. Indiana harder to prosecute."

Of course, the local papers – the *Portland Press Herald* and the *Maine Times* – and even the *New York Post* ran with the story. Despite the sad reality of Indiana's victimization, who cannot savor the irony of the charges against him? Ever since the nation entered the age of AIDS, America's moralist minority has been on a witch-hunt, and the name of Robert Indiana – whether he likes it or not – is closely identified with the free love movement. His being charged with paying for sex suggests that free love has become very expensive indeed.

· · · · ·

As Indiana awaits trial, he is visiting New York more frequently than at any time since he left the city thirteen years ago. But in New York, too, Indiana can see how his ideal of love has deteriorated. Over the last few years, a three-man artists' collective from Canada called General Idea has produced an image based on *LOVE* that substitute "AIDS" for "LOVE." As *LOVE* did, General Idea's revision speaks volumes about the world we live in, and whatever the group could get their hands on – magazines, wallpaper, scarves, the windows of the New Museum in New York, the sides of trams in Seattle and Amsterdam, a billboard in San Francisco, stickers, and dozens of paintings exhibited around the world – has been plastered with their tragic distortion of the face of *LOVE.*

In nineties neo-activist art-speak, General Idea's AA Bronson explains his group's motives: "We wanted to make AIDS a household word, something that anyone could get. And by spreading the image the way the *LOVE* logo was spread, we think we can deprive the disease of its exotic quality and depoliticize it. If you can get AIDS to look completely normal, you can get normal medical gears into operation that can deal with an epidemic."

Surprisingly, Indiana concurs, with a qualification. "It's what I would have done myself," he says, "because the association

of love with AIDS is inevitable, one of the ironic twists of coincidence. But I wouldn't have made it as grotesque as theirs – their *D* is grotesque."

Cigar in hand, his head wrapped in a scarf, the Robert Indiana of the 1990s is a strange mixture of country and city. He manages to be simultaneously well-mannered and awkward, pompous and candid, intellectual and superstitious, bone-dry and sopping wet. "Indiana was always more intelligent than most artists," recalls the critic David Bourdon, "but I can't remember a time, even in the early sixties, when anyone was crazy about his personality. He was cool and stand-offish, a cold fish." Indeed, part of Indiana's current isolation may be attributed to his arrogance. According to art-world personality Henry Geldzahler, Indiana is the only person who won't shake his hand.

If Indiana suffers from an image problem, it may have arisen from his lifelong history as an outsider, or it may be the afterglow of his former glory. Even his all-American stage name, Indiana, has a dated, hippie-ish ring to it. Fortunately, however, things have a way of reversing themselves, and Robert Indiana is beginning to receive the recognition due one of the key artists of the Pop era. Paintings and prints from his latest series, using the work of Marsden Hartley (who died in 1943 and was Maine's greatest modernist painter) as a focus, are being bought by museums around the country. Last year, Abrams published a 232-page monograph on Indiana. In December, there were three simultaneous exhibitions in New York – at the Marisa del Re and the Ruth Siegel galleries on 57th Street and at the Vinalhaven Press Gallery in SoHo. And in May, he held a print retrospective at Susan Sheehan Gallery in New York City, which was accompanied by a glossy catalogue raisonné of his prints from 1951 to the present and two versions of a new color etching, *LOVE 1991.*

Indiana's works are also making an appearance on the resale market, where they are fetching respectable prices. Two years ago, a *LOVE* painting went for almost $145,000 at auction in France, and now, *One Indiana Square* (commissioned in 1970 by the Indiana National Bank in Indianapolis for $10,000) is on the market for a mid-six-figure amount. Indiana is optimistic about his chances for a comeback despite the crash in the art market and the blip in his personal fortunes. He is also advisedly modest. "I'm not a million-dollar auction figure – let's put it that way," he says.

· · · · ·

Before he assumed the moniker of his home state in the 1950s and set about becoming a successful artist, Robert Clark was a rootless Depression-era only child born to Christian Scientist parents. At church, he says, he used to contemplate the GOD IS LOVE sign that hung on the pulpit. During the first 21 years of his life, Indiana lived in seventeen homes, shuttling across the state of Indiana from parent to bankrupted parent. After his ex-aunt murdered his grandmother, Indiana took shelter with his mortician uncle, moved here and there to study art, ran off to join the air force, which at least enabled him to study art under the G.I. Bill, and later traveled to Europe on a fellowship. Through it all, the young Robert Clark exhibited extraordinary stamina and a peculiar vision. By the time he moved to New York in 1954, he had educated and groomed himself to become an all-American poet and painter and an advocate of brotherly love.

In 1954, Indiana wrote, typeset, and published a poem whose first line was simply "Love." His early heroes were the great American writers Herman Melville, Walt Whitman, and Hart Crane and visual artists Charles Demuth and Marsden Hartley (whose paintings he admired for their adventurous use of letters and numbers). In the 1960s, Indiana lifted lines from the novels and poems of Melville and Crane that eulogized New York and painted them reverently into his Pop portraits of the city. Whitman's words, which also appeared in his early canvases, especially stirred the young artist. *I Hear America Singing* – with its Romantic evocation of good-hearted American people from different walks of life singing their "varied carols" and "strong melodious songs" in unison – was a pers-onal favorite. The sentiments of the poem are also a far cry from the harassed and marginalized position in which he finds himself today.

At the beginning, his studio in New York was on Fourth Avenue, looking directly into the loft of Willem de Kooning, whom Indiana says he could watch painting his great Abstract Expressionist canvases in the nude. (This was as close to Abstract Expressionism as Indiana ever wanted to come.) He supported himself by working in an art-supply store on 57th Street. One day in 1956 he sold a Matisse postcard to Ellsworth Kelly. Kelly, at age 33 a painter of ambiguous abstracts, had returned from Europe where he studied art under the G.I. Bill, as Indiana had done. The two struck up a special relationship (though they are no longer friends). "Ellsworth was the most important person in my life," Indiana claims. "And by being the most important person in my life, he influenced a little bit of art history."

Kelly persuaded Indiana to use bold, primary colors in a hard-edge format, as he did in his own ground-breaking paintings. "When I first knew him," recalls Kelly, "he was painting strange figurative things, with heads like eggs. I would try to influence him to go abstract."

Indiana did not go abstract for long, but with Kelly's support, his career did get under way. As soon as they met, Kelly told Indiana about a string of rugged old shipping buildings at Coenties Slip, down at the very tip of Manhattan, where he could find a decent loft for thirty dollars a month, and Indiana moved there. The ancient alley, which overlooked the East River along an undeveloped edge of Manhattan, had poetry enough for Indiana, having been immortalized by Melville in the opening of *Moby Dick*: "There now is your insular city of the Manhattoes belted round by wharves as Indian isles by coral reefs – commerce surrounds it with her surf.... Circumambulate the city of a dreamy Sabbath afternoon. Go from Corlears Hook to Coenties Slip, and from thence, by Whitehall, northward. What do you see? – Posted like silent sentinels all around the town, stand thousands upon thousands of mortal men fixed in ocean reveries." (Indiana's loft has since made way for a brown brick skyscraper on Vietnam Veterans Plaza, near the noisy South Street Seaport tourist site.)

By 1958, Indiana was painting large, bold geometric motifs, such as a Yin-and-Yang-like ginkgo leaf, on wood. These resembled Kelly's abstract compositions but also hinted at the stylized realistic forms – stars, banners, and road signs – of Indiana's Pop works to come.

• • • • •

A month or two after Indiana moved to Coenties Slip, Kelly followed, and a little subculture quickly arose that harbored many of the artists who would shape the sixties. Robert Rauschenberg and Jasper Johns shared a building around the corner from Indiana, and their close friend and collaborator, the composer John Cage, was on Corlears Hook, a little further up the waterfront. "It was comfortable there," says Cage. "Even though we were poor, we lived with such a view – from Brooklyn and Queens across to the Statue of Liberty – that life was enjoyable and not oppressive."

Kelly also installed Jack Youngerman and Agnes Martin in lofts on Coenties Slip. Martin brought her devotion to Gertrude Stein, and Youngerman brought his wife, the actress Delphine Seyrig, who after starring in Alain Resnais's *Last Year at Marienbad* bestowed an air of post-existentialist French chic on the grubby surroundings. In 1957, Indiana and Youngerman set up a life-drawing studio on the slip, and one of the young painters who used it was James Rosenquist, whom Kelly settled into the community in 1960.

Although there were divisions among the little band of artists, they were all unified in isolation from the swaggering Abstract Expressionist heroes of Greenwich Village by their softer, more sophisticated sensibilities and from the uptown art scene by their indigence. Only Johns and Rauschenberg had glimpsed success. Cy Twombly, whose scrawly gray paintings are now the toast of the auction houses, was forced to borrow Indiana's studio to paint in while Indiana was away at work. And Indiana, for his part, would often attend art openings uptown because he needed to eat.

In addition to their isolation, the hidden homosexuality of the subculture's prime movers prompted cliquish behavior — secrecy and ambiguity on one hand, exaggerated conformity on the other. Like Whitman, who wrote, "I dare not tell it in words, not even in these songs," more than one artist on the waterfront used code words and symbols to stand in for forbidden subject matter. By depicting the inside of the proverbial Closet, their art epitomized the conflicted gay sensibility of the day.

Indiana and Kelly became close, and there are many intimate line drawings by Kelly, a few of which show Indiana asleep. Indiana has framed them and hung them in a votive "Ellsworth Kelly room" on Vinalhaven. After a few years on the slip, however, the inevitable rifts and recriminations set in. Kelly "became very busy," says Indiana. "He just became obsessed with his career and didn't have time for me." Indiana, according to Kelly, "was a difficult guy with a chip on his shoulder. We had fights, terrible fights, and I stopped going to see him."

Johns and Rauschenberg kept their distance from almost everybody. To Indiana, the couple seemed like snobs, "very unfriendly." He says, "Jasper feels that I invaded his territory and there was an antagonism between Rauschenberg and Kelly because somewhere along the line Rauschenberg did something to Kelly and Kelly never let them into the building."

Indiana tells one of his favorite stories about life on the waterfront to illustrate his point: "One night, before my eyes," he says, "a ship collided with a tanker. They burst into flames, and the oil on the river was burning as well. The crews of the ships had to swim underwater to safety. The only person who died was a journalist covering the story who had a heart attack. The fire started under the Brooklyn Bridge, but because the East River is not a river but a tidal basin, the ship floated under the Manhattan Bridge, and that bridge caught on fire. And because of the subway tracks, the electricity was throwing sparks. I ran to tell Ellsworth Kelly, and on the way yelled out to Johns and Rauschenberg that the river was on fire, but

they ignored it. They came to their window, but they had a carefree attitude, a let-'em-die attitude."

Indiana himself, however, was sufficiently moved by the scene to portray it in his *Fire Bridge* painting, which shows the Brooklyn Bridge illuminated by a fiery, apocalyptic glow.

. . . . .

It wasn't until 1961 that anyone took much notice of Indiana as an artist. But that person was Alfred Barr, the Museum of Modern Art's director of collections, who had helped put Jasper Johns on the map two years earlier. Indiana was invited to participate in a little exhibition downstairs from the Martha Jackson Gallery, and Barr visited the show the day after it closed. He bought Indiana's *The American Dream*, a dramatic star-spangled canvas with a title lifted from Edward Albee's play and imagery lifted from pinball machines. It is a landmark piece in the development of Pop art — linking the "high" abstract art of Kelly to the "low" art of signwriting and echoing the hectic colors and energy of Stuart Davis and the startling frontality of Johns.

Soon, Indiana began to live The Dream. The Pop art onslaught was under way, and he was part of the gang. "Pop art was simply a reaction to the commercial mentality of America, and I was a peripheral figure," said Indiana on one occasion. Another time, however, he proudly declared: "There are six Pop artists. I am one of the six."

His work was part of "The Art of Assemblage" show at the Modern in 1961. The following year, he was invited to participate in the show that launched Pop — "New Realists" at the Sidney Janis Gallery — and he was picked up by Eleanor Ward for a solo show at her Stable Gallery, where his stablemates would include Andy Warhol and the Pop sculptor Marisol.

In 1963, he had an entire room devoted to his art at the Museum of Modern Art's "Americans" show. It was, he says, "one of the most important, most exciting things in my life." According to David Bourdon, "many artists, including Andy Warhol, were jealous of Indiana. They were jealous that he was in the 'Americans' show and that he was one of the most discussed artists in the show."

In many ways, Indiana's works provided the clearest examples of the Pop aesthetic. In a series of paintings of the numbers 0 through 9, now in the collection of Fiat chairman Gianni Agnelli, Indiana appropriated the figure 5 from a 1928 painting by Charles Demuth. The number-5 painting is a prime example of Pop art's voracious appetite for using preexisting graphics. (It was also a premonition of the appropriation epidemic of the 1980s.) Indiana's numerous series of number paintings and prints, moreover, are classic Pop because of their serial nature; like Warhol's silk screens and the elegant repetitions of the Minimalist artists, Indiana's numbers emphasize that a painting is a link in a chain of associations and that a work of art invariably gets its meaning from its context.

Among the "six" Pop artists, including Roy Lichtenstein, James Rosenquist, Claes Oldenburg, and Tom Wesselmann, nobody was more aggressive about getting to the top than Warhol. To promote Stable Gallery and give it a Pop art profile, Warhol suggested that he and Indiana collaborate on *Eat*, a movie to be named after one of Indiana's most blatant Pop paintings.

The two *Eat*s, Indiana's and Warhol's, actually have little to do with each other, just like Indiana and Warhol themselves; they exemplify the two extremes of Pop – the brassy and the banal. Indiana's *EAT* and its companion painting, *DIE*, both from 1962, are dazzling, diamond-shaped canvases with their colorful titles emblazoned across their girth, whereas Warhol's movie is monochromatic and monotonous. Shot at the end of 1963, his *Eat* shows Indiana in his loft on the slip eating a mushroom – for 45 long minutes.

Although Indiana calls the film "pure poetry," he has his doubts about Warhol's mastery of the medium. "While we were shooting it," says Indiana, "his camera was falling apart, he was putting it back together with paper clips, and I was thinking, God, why are we wasting our time? I didn't think it was very professional. Of course, it was many reels, and he didn't put them back in the proper order, so the film is jumping about ... Real pro, real pro."

Just before he died in 1987, Warhol quipped that his early films are perhaps better talked about than seen. Indiana agrees: "Without a doubt," he says. "Except for *Blow Job*."

· · · · ·

The words in Indiana's canvases made his work stand out from that of the other Pop artists. They were also the cause of acrimony among his friends. "There was a prejudice against using words," he says. "Most people don't like to see words. In the Muslim world, mosques are decorated only with gorgeous arabesque words. But our culture has a block against this. Yet I always considered myself a poet, and I always considered my art to be concrete poetry."

As Indiana's Pop style became more pronounced, his statements became more blunt, and lines of poetry were reduced to simple exclamations. Experimenting with punchy three- and four-letter words stenciled onto wood sculptures and paintings, Indiana inevitably hit on the real thing: he drew a black-and-white schema for a painting called *FUCK*.

According to Indiana, the person most upset by his use of words in paintings had been Kelly. So Indiana showed him his draft for *FUCK*. Kelly was, Indiana says, "absolutely horrified. He said that if I ever exhibited it he'd never speak to me again. I never exhibited it. But the damage was done."

"I don't remember it," counters Kelly. "I probably just said I don't care for it. I'm not a confrontational artist. I don't like to rub people's faces in it. It's a little bit like overkill. He wanted to be controversial."

Indiana was chastened, so he toned down and dreamed up *LOVE*. Indeed, the evolution of this pivotal work suggests that *LOVE* is a watered-down version of the former. "There's no question," says Indiana now. "That's the reason for the tilted *O*. It's an erection."

In 1964, *LOVE* became the most popular Christmas card that the Museum of Modern Art had ever published. When he was invited to design the card, Indiana painted three studies, and they became the beginning of the end. "Having done three small paintings," Indiana claims, "I didn't go on doing *LOVE* paintings because of the success of the Christmas card. I simply did it because I liked the *LOVE* paintings and they got bigger and bigger and more and more and more and it never stopped. I'm still doing *LOVE*."

After the card came the ring. In 1966, Indiana contracted a small firm called the Beautiful Bag and Box Company of Philadelphia to produce a hundred rings bearing his *LOVE* motif. These, says Indiana, quickly became the fashionable things for New York's richest ladies to wear. Then Indiana mounted an exhibition at Stable, an entire galleryful of *LOVE*. To promote the show, the gallery printed a *LOVE* poster and circulated it around town. Although the poster helped make the show a huge success, there was something missing from it that had an enormous effect on Indiana's future career – the copyright sign.

Around the same time, a well-known poster company also published a poster, which Indiana says omitted the copyright notice. And within weeks, he says, the cat was out of the bag. "When the rip-off people discovered that there was a print that I had been involved with that carried no copyright symbol, it killed my legitimacy as an artist.

"I sent off the necessary papers to the United States Copyright Office and was advised that a word cannot be copyrighted. I was ill-advised, [but] that was the advice I got, and I just became discouraged. I'm not litigious. I don't sue people. People who sue people are interested in money. Besides, I don't know who they all were.

"LOVE has since gone into a hundred different variations. You walk down the street these days and the word SALE is written SA on the top and LE on the bottom. But the really painful rip-off was Love Story." Indiana says that someone approached Erich Segal, author of the best-selling novel, and asked him if he felt any guilt about the similarity between the book jacket's design and Indiana's painting and Segal replied that the artist should feel honored.

According to art dealer Marian Goodman, whose Multiples company collaborated with Indiana on some of the artist's own editions, "There was really inadequate copyright for artists then — that came later. We tried to defend the copyright, but it couldn't be done because we were up against companies that were too big." Among them was a big cosmetics company that produced thousands of LOVE rings as a promotion.

"The rip-offs kept me from being a billionaire, although I would never have done those things anyway," says Indiana. "But they certainly soured the art world on the image of my LOVE. Only two museums ever acquired LOVE paintings, and I think that's immediately a result of people's just presuming that I had been responsible for all this junk that flooded the world."

Indiana's response was to be fruitful and multiply. With Multiples, he forged six twelve-inch, carved-aluminium LOVE sculptures (last year, one went for $35,000 at Christie's). For RCA, he authorized a LOVE record cover for Messiaen's Turangalila-symphonie. Then came a LOVE cross, a banner, a diptych, and a silk-screen edition in collaboration with Mass Originals, art collector Eugene Schwartz's company, in both a signed edition of one hundred and an unnumbered edition of thousands (which sold out at twenty dollars each). In 1970, Indiana made a twelve-foot, three-dimensional Cor-Ten steel version of LOVE that was sold to the Indianapolis Museum for $75,000. In 1972, he did an edition of six-foot polychrome LOVE sculptures. And in 1973 came the LOVE stamp, for which the U.S. Postal Service paid him an honorarium of $1,000.

As opposed to the rip-offs, he says, all of the above is art. "I don't call it junk. Nor do I call my original LOVE ring junk. It happens to be a very beautiful object. I still wear it."

· · · · ·

Stable Gallery closed in 1966, after rival galleries had skimmed its cream. "They lost everybody," Indiana says. "Andy left.

Marisol left. For six years I had no gallery." It was one of the things that finished off his career. "How marvelous it would be to have one important dealer in your life," he says wistfully. "This business in New York of the artists jumping from dealer to dealer I find absolutely repellent. That's one reason I stayed at the Stable Gallery too long. I, too, should have left. It was a sinking ship. But I didn't. I remained loyal until it just became impossible."

In 1972, he signed with the Paris dealer Denise René, who was opening a space in New York and wanted at least one American artist among her European ones. But that didn't last either. "Denise opened at a very bad time, when the recession began," says Indiana. "By 1978 she closed." By this time, Indiana was also losing his loft and had gone through a few lovers, notably the women's clothes designer John Kloss. What's more, the former Pop artist's career was also on the skids. "Fashion comes and goes," he says, "and I was no longer invited to be in the Whitney Biennials. I thought that having a show every six years, that scarcity and rarity might possibly work to my advantage. It didn't." So in 1978 he packed up and moved permanently to his vacation home on the distant island of Vinalhaven, Maine.

· · · · ·

Vinalhaven Island lies in the fog just out of reach of the prettiness of New England. The closest port is Rockland, and the nearest landmass to the east is France. The region is quintessential rural Maine. Robert Storr, a refugee from Maine who is now a curator of painting and sculpture at the Museum of Modern Art, calls it the Appalachians of the North.

Indiana hauled two trucks on twelve trips from New York to his new home. There were hundreds of canvases and prints and thirteen cats and dogs. His former Odd Fellows men's lodge is still undergoing restoration, and Indiana has been forced to sell his valuable Twomblys at Sotheby's to finance the repair work. Inside his creaky but comfortable château there is space for all of his art to be arranged according to period and media, as well as numerous studios and studies, libraries and living rooms.

Here Indiana worked with a handful of assistants — young men from the island, part-time fishermen — building sculptures, reading, and mapping out new pictorial work. He even devised a four-person chessboard; while he was designing it, he paid his assistants ten dollars an hour to play with him. And he sometimes became so absorbed in his life on the island and in renovating the lodge that he forgot about New York, even refusing to answer the telephone. "New York left me," he explains. "I became a nonperson. I never knocked on doors, and no dealer came to me."

Indiana slowly acquainted himself with the history of Vinalhaven and discovered that Marsden Hartley had once summered on the island. Near the end of his life, Hartley abandoned abstract art and occupied himself with landscapes, as well as with voyeuristic drawings of virile lobstermen sunning themselves on the beach and hunky, broad-shouldered versions of Cézanne's bathers.

Hartley had once cut a swath across Europe, from the salon of Gertrude Stein in Paris to militaristic, prewar Berlin. Most pertinent of all to Indiana's story is that Hartley had become deeply infatuated with a German officer who would be killed in the opening blasts of World War I. In 1914 and 1915, the painter expressed his heartbreak in his Berlin Series, nearly fifty paintings, all laden with symbolic military insignia, Iron Crosses, and flags painted in bold geometric patterns. As Indiana rightly recognized, they are imbued with the same heraldic spirit that characterizes his own work. With their boundless imagery of circles, triangles, checkerboards, zigzags, numbers, and letters, the original Hartleys could almost be Indianas.

Indiana was delighted to discover parallels between his life and work and Hartley's, and in 1989, he launched a new series of direct appropriations of Hartley's paintings, which he calls The Hartley Elegies. "They're a natural for me," he says with excitement. "They liberate me from the symmetry and strict formalism that I had been rather stuck in for some time."

At the same time, Indiana was inspired by Hartley's example to return to drawing from life. "I had for a long time wanted to bring the LOVE from the spiritual into the erotic," he says, and Hartley's work "suddenly spurred me to get back to drawing." While discussing one particular Hartley portrait, Madawaska, in which the male model is wearing nothing except a G-string, Indiana is enthusiastic: "I have always loved that painting because it was one of the first Hartleys that I ever experienced in person. I would love to redo that nude as an homage to Hartley and remove Mr. Hartley's inhibitions – and the G-string."

So began his drawings of phalluses. "And that," says Indiana, "is where the recent difficulties came from."

· · · · ·

To be specific, Indiana's recent difficulties began a year ago — when Jason Marriner, one of the young men who worked for him, called the Rockland home of Detective Ernie McIntosh.

McIntosh, 35, a father of three girls, was formerly the patrol deputy on Vinalhaven. According to Indiana, McIntosh "was the island cop, and he bears a grudge." In fact, the townspeople had petitioned to have McIntosh removed from the island two years earlier on the grounds that he enforced the law in an intimidating way.

Despite the petition (which was ultimately dropped), McIntosh denies holding a grudge against any of the locals, including Indiana. "I like Robert Indiana," he says. Yet he describes the island as "a vicious little town with rumors" and boasts that the petition against him was actually "a pat on the back." Indeed, upon leaving Vinalhaven, he was promoted to detective and placed in charge of child abuse.

In August, Marriner called McIntosh to ask him about "a friend of his" who had stolen some checks. Marriner wanted to know what the punishment would be if "his friend" was caught. In the course of their conversation, however, Marriner broke down and said that it was he who had stolen the checks from his employer. He also said that for a number of years Indiana had paid him to pose nude and to "perform oral sex upon him."

As Marriner spoke, Indiana's bank was investigating him for allegedly stealing and forging almost $7,000 in checks. Indiana declares that he would not have brought charges against Marriner. "I have never brought charges against anyone," he says. "It's really the bank and the state. If I had known that this young man had stolen the money I wouldn't have done anything."

Nevertheless, Marriner may have gotten wind of the investigation from an unknown source and panicked. He called McIntosh and that's why, in an attempt to explain away his alleged thefts from Indiana, he spilled the beans.

As the detective untangled the twisted love story, he talked to another former Indiana model, John MacDonald, who corroborated the charges and also claimed that "during the posing of [a] nude drawing, Indiana stopped" and made similar advances. As a result of the claims, Indiana's nude drawings were seized and are being held as evidence of prostitution.

The artist maintains that the prosecutors "have to prove their accusations, and as far as my lawyers are concerned, the drawings don't mean anything." He is nevertheless concerned that Maine is "a redneck state ... a very homophobic state," so he has opted for a bench trial (in which he will be tried before a judge without a jury). The case against him is now set to be heard this summer.

Charged with four counts of theft, burglary, and forgery, James Marriner is also awaiting trial. In the meantime, he consigned for sale a number of prints that Indiana had given him. They appeared at auction at Christie's New York in May.

For Indiana, love goes on. He recently installed a huge *LOVE* sculpture outside the Monte Carlo casino, and the Marisa del Re Gallery, his new New York dealer, placed another *LOVE* sculpture in front of the Grand Palais for the duration of the Paris Art Fair. There's a renewed interest in Indiana's early work; dealers and collectors are quietly scouring personal collections for Indiana's gems. And *The Hartley Elegies* are being taken seriously.

Naturally, love is central to Indiana's Hartleys — brotherly love, the love of art, and mourning for lost love. "The only thing I'm worried about," says Indiana, casting his eyes heavenward, "is, what is Marsden thinking?" ●

LEO CASTELLI 1986

The Leo Castelli Anniversaries

MANHATTAN, INC. FEBRUARY 1987
THE NEW YORK TIMES FEBRUARY 1992

In the future, art historians will write about postwar art in terms of its entrepreneurs. The tendency is becoming apparent at a time when the activity of art-world impresarios like Leo Castelli seems vastly more compelling than the art they promote. Well, at least it's as interesting to talk about.

Starting this week, Castelli, the world's best-known art dealer, is staging his 30th-anniversary exhibition in two consecutive parts at his Greene Street gallery. Meanwhile, in his West Broadway gallery, Jasper Johns (Castelli's first claim to fame and the artist whose sales have more than anyone else's kept Leo Castelli Gallery in the black) opens a show of four new paintings, collectively entitled *The Seasons*. Taken together, the two shows provide a good excuse to begin writing the history of the era that saw the breakdown of differences between the roles of artist and entrepreneur.

Curiously, both exhibitions are really personal retrospectives – encapsulating the same thirty years in a pair of nutshells. While Johns has produced four paintings that "quote" from the imagery of his own work since 1957, Castelli has borrowed art works that he sold to museums and private collectors in order to narrate a rebus-like tale of his own brilliant career since the same year. Like Johns, Castelli is exhibiting himself – "There's a great competition between Jasper's show and mine," he jokes.

From the start of his career, Castelli has been splashed over the papers in a way that makes the Mary Boone Gallery pale by comparison. A 1966 profile in *The New York Times Magazine* claimed, "When it comes to attention-getting there is simply no other gallery quite like Castelli's." Though now 79 years old, Castelli is again at the center of the art world. Similarly, the early work of Jasper Johns is once more being cited as a major influence on young artists, and Johns has belatedly been chosen to represent the United States at the Venice Biennale next year. (This comes 23 years after Castelli's first international coup, when Rauschenberg won the biennale's major prize.) In its replay mode, the art world is rotating faster than ever before – and Castelli is still pushing the buttons.

But New York's museums, he says, are not: they are too unadventurous, too slow to pick up on the ever-changing definitions of newness. And MoMA's support for contemporary art, according to Castelli, has waned since the days of Alfred Barr and Dorothy Miller. It's a subject about which he gets emotional, picking out the needles from his usual conversational haystack.

"MoMA has been very remiss," he begins. "The Whitney has done whatever they could with the lack of space that they have, and the lack of funds. The Guggenheim is a special case; we won't even mention them, except that they're not very much present in the contemporary field – spotty things here and there. We now have the Walker Art Center [in Minneapolis] and [the Los Angeles] Museum of Contemporary Art. But unfortunately we have in New York no museum that can show anything in depth. If you go to the Beaubourg in Paris, the important American artists like, say, Serra or Judd or you name it, are shown in depth. To see artists, contemporary artists, you have to go to Cologne and see the Ludwig collection – that's probably the greatest concentration of contemporary American art!"

Whether museums are responding negatively to the marketing of contemporary art, or the marketing of art has taken new turns in the face of the museums' neglect, unusual variations on traditional roles are turning up daily. Jasper Johns's latest canvases – representing spring, summer, fall, and winter – were all "placed" well before opening at Castelli's. Three were sold, in effect, out of the studio – to David Whitney, Asher Edelman, and S.I. Newhouse (*Vogue* devoted its first-ever foldout spread to the paintings last month) – and Johns kept one, *Fall*, for himself. So the series is now being borrowed by Castelli, just like the pieces for his own anniversary. Therefore Castelli is effectively transforming his gallery spaces into a temporary museum.

"Very little credit is given to the activity of the galleries – relatively little credit," says Castelli. "For instance, the new issue of *New York* magazine writes about all kinds of meritorious people, and in speaking about what happened in the arts in New York, not one gallery is mentioned. After all, what the galleries are doing here, beginning with us – or earlier, with Sidney Janis or whoever it was – to now and what happens in the East Village ... is just fantastic. It's really a great phenomenon, the galleries. And people have a sort of scare mentioning them because it's commercial. But if there are some galleries which are not commercial and just great entrepreneurs, it is certainly us. We spent more money and more effort than any museum and we have to do it by our own means. We have to be commercial because we have to make that money that the museums get as a handout from the corporations. I mean, that's a truth!" He sits back, nods angrily, then relaxes. Soon, it's all smiles. He must know that in thirty more years historians will say it all for him.

II

For more than three decades, Leo Castelli has been lionized as the king of art dealers, mythically endowed with the two qualities most prized in his profession — a good heart and sensitive ears. But this month, as he celebrates the 35th anniversary of his gallery and approaches his 85th birthday, the Castelli kingdom is being hit by the depression in the art market, and his prized qualities are being boosted by a pacemaker and a hearing aid. His dominance is also being shaken by old rivals and recent protégés, and by his former wife and best friend, Ileana Sonnabend, owner of the Sonnabend Gallery. Most devastating of all is that for ten years his gallery, which has three outlets in the SoHo section of Manhattan, has been hemorrhaging artists.

In other words, after 35 years as king of the art jungle, Leo Castelli may be nearing the end of his reign. Accordingly, the lineup of art dealers in New York has changed radically in the last few years and the major powers have consolidated their positions. "There are now four or five players on the scene, not including Ileana," Castelli says, referring to his ex-wife, whose gallery is overshadowing his as a forum for young artists.

"We have old-timer Arnold Glimcher and the newcomer Larry Gagosian, who are both really financiers," he says. "Gagosian's methods are a bombshell, with his well-done historical shows and marvelous catalogues. I wonder how he supports his fantastic splurges. Glimcher is a good businessman whose game is to get the best possible artists and estates, though he is not so successful with contemporary artists. Perhaps we still have to consider Mary Boone, who is an intelligent operator and not out of the game yet. And then there is myself."

In 1957, when he opened his gallery in his Upper East Side home, Castelli was a 50-year-old hanger-on in the French and American art scenes. He was also an Italian-Jewish refugee with a rich wife and a small collection of European and American paintings by artists and friends such as Alberto Giacometti and Jackson Pollock, which helped form his opening exhibition. Within a year he had secured his future by exhibiting the young Jasper Johns, and he has seasoned the art world ever since — with shows by Robert Rauschenberg, Frank Stella, Cy Twombly, and the most heavily promoted Pop, Minimalist, and Conceptual artists in the world. He became renowned for his benevolent business manner, his generosity and his willingness to share his artists with other dealers.

With stars like Andy Warhol in the Castelli constellation, the diplomatic, fun-loving dealer became a myth in his own right. "Leo Castelli is a man of genius," says Sam Hunter, a professor emeritus of art history at Princeton University who has organized exhibitions of the Castelli and Sonnabend personal collections. "Part of it was his being there, and part is his accommodating nature. He is a very good collaborator, and artists feel very comfortable with him."

. . . . .

Castelli is a firm upholder of his own legend. The current string of parties is only the latest in a series of commemorations, including exhibitions and publications for his tenth, 25th and 30th anniversaries. His milestones are marked with royal ceremony.

This month's jubilee began with a two-gallery show of large environmental paintings by Roy Lichtenstein, timed to open exactly three decades after the Pop artist's debut at the gallery. The celebrations continued with a champagne party, and a luncheon in honor of Lichtenstein for two hundred friends and clients, including the architect Philip Johnson, the Hollywood agent Michael Ovitz, the European curatorial duo of Norman Rosenthal and Christos Joachimides, the artist Larry Rivers, and the publishing and editing team of Sandra Brant and Ingrid Sischy.

There is also a display at Castelli's third gallery, where the dealer has papered the walls with a list of his galleries' programs over the last 35 years. The festivities continue till May, when there will be a fundraising party to benefit the Village Nursing Home AIDS Programs. No other art dealer has promoted himself with such aplomb, but Castelli holds his achievements in extremely high esteem.

Apropos of this self-esteem, Robert Rauschenberg has referred to his old dealer as an "egotistical maniac." And Paula Cooper, a dealer whom Castelli does not include among the major players, calls him "very myopic." She says: "He and Glimcher and Gagosian and Boone are involved in the battle of the machos, which doesn't have much to do with art. I like Leo, but he has never been very supportive or helpful to me, which colors my opinion. He's just involved with the galleries in his power axis."

As energetic and optimistic as ever, Castelli is determined that his flagging fortunes won't spoil his enjoyment of his "game." He discusses his gains and losses in the last few years candidly, and says that in 1989 and 1990, at the height of the art boom, the gallery's annual turnover doubled, from more than $10 million in 1987. But last year, during the crash, it dropped back to the 1987 level. He adds that for him the recession is "less bad than expected."

More bad than expected is the departure of many artists from his gallery, as well as the death of Andy Warhol in 1987. Ten artists in as many years have gone, amid speculation that Castelli's scrupulous business style fails to clinch the enormous deals they demand and that his devotion to the work of Johns and Lichtenstein, the gallery's chief money spinners, eclipses his efforts on behalf of the others. According to an artist who has been with the gallery for decades, "it's always Jasper and Roy, Jasper and Roy, and that's why everyone is leaving."

The heavy-metal sculptor John Chamberlain, who severed his twenty-year relationship with Castelli in 1983, says, "I left Leo because I kept feeling I was being neglected." Last month, the light sculptor Dan Flavin also left with some bitterness. "Flavin's defection was partly my fault," says Castelli. "It is possible I did not pay enough attention to him."

· · · · ·

Many who leave are landing at Pace Gallery, owned by the blue-chip art dealer turned movie director Arnold Glimcher. According to Glimcher, the reason for the migration may be that "we are very successful at placing sculptures and getting commissions," and Castelli agrees. Consequently, Pace Gallery now represents more than 25 artists and artists' estates, including two recent gains from Paula Cooper.

Five of Castelli's sculptors – Claes Oldenberg, Richard Serra, Donald Judd, Chamberlain, and Flavin – are now at Pace Gallery. Rauschenberg and Stella are only nominally tied to Castelli and are co-represented by Knoedler Gallery. Ellsworth Kelly shows mostly at BlumHelman Gallery, and Richard Artschwager has moved to Mary Boone.

"I've lost all the Minimal group," Castelli says regretfully. "I also wanted to keep the Pop artists together, but Andy died and then Oldenburg left." Julian Schnabel and David Salle, who were co-represented by the Castelli and Mary Boone galleries,

left them for the Pace and Gagosian galleries, respectively (though Salle continues to assign paintings to Castelli to sell). When the post-Pop generation emerged in the 1980s, Castelli was scooped by the Sonnabend Gallery. And all the young artists recently taken on by Castelli are being shown by him in conjunction with other galleries, like the trendy 303 Gallery in SoHo.

Leo Castelli is indeed a lion in winter, yet both Glimcher and Gagosian deny that they have designs on the Castelli throne. "Succession as Leo's heir doesn't appeal to me," says Gagosian. "Inheritance is not a particularly interesting form of transmission." Glimcher actually bristles at the notion: "I don't have to set myself up as an heir to anything. My gallery has been around since 1960, in Boston."

There was nevertheless a missed heartbeat when Gagosian – with whom Castelli shares the 65 Thompson Street gallery in SoHo as a collaborative venture – invited Roy Lichtenstein to hold his current exhibition at the Gagosian Gallery on Madison Avenue. Castelli was alarmed and told the artist that he would prefer that the show remained downtown. But, says Lichtenstein, "there has never been even an oblique offer from anyone for me to leave Leo's gallery, and I'm not considering it." In return, Castelli announced that the Lichtenstein luncheon was held "in praise of loyalty, which is so rare these days."

Leo Castelli says he is still on the lookout for new artists: "I feel I am getting old and creaky, and also I envy Ileana's success with young people." As for the speculation that his 35th anniversary may be a pretext for winding down his operations, he dismisses the suggestion out of hand. "What would I do?" he asks. "As it is, I'm bored on Mondays when I can't come into the gallery." •

ILEANA SONNABEND 1986

Sonnabend of SoHo

CONNOISSEUR SEPTEMBER 1991

Gilbert and George are up to their old tricks. This month, the English poker-faced Conceptual artists are reviving the performance that put them at the center of international art circles. Their act was hypnotically simple: wearing gleaming bronze body paint and identical suits, the "singing sculptures" climbed a pedestal and robotically mimed the lyrics of "Underneath the Arches" (an inane cockney ditty about a pair of tramps in the alleyways of London) — over and over, day in and day out, for almost a month. "Underneath the arches we dream our dreams away," they lip-synched, as they shuffled and jerked and swayed. That's performance art.

Twenty years ago, this offbeat performance inaugurated the Sonnabend Gallery in SoHo, and the duo became wildly and unexpectedly popular. The same thing happened to the gallery, a pioneer in then-sparsely populated SoHo. Now Gilbert and George are celebrating Sonnabend Gallery's twentieth anniversary by re-creating their historic histrionics, and for the event, Ileana Sonnabend is restoring her gallery space to its original condition. "Anybody who wanders in and hasn't been in the gallery for twenty years will think it's the same old show," quips George. "But for us, it's just like taking a sculpture out of the closet and dusting it off."

For Sonnabend, it's a way to relive one of the highlights of her fifty-year career as an art collector and dealer. Like many things about this legendary 76-year-old impresario, the opening of her New York gallery in September 1971 was sensational and scandalous, and people are still talking about the crowds, the fire trucks, and the strange spectacle of singing sculptures. The opening act was also a gamble that paid off nicely, for Gilbert and George have since entered the top rank of British artists and infiltrated museums everywhere — including Manhattan's Solomon R. Guggenheim Museum, where they staged a massive retrospective exhibition of their works in 1985.

This month, the gallery is full of activity: Stefano Basilico, one of the Sonnabend's co-directors, is looking for a table for Gilbert and George to climb up and down on; it has to be a bit closer to the ground than the one they used twenty years ago. Walls are coming down. And Sonnabend's daughter, Nina Sundell, is spending a lot of time in the back room and on the telephone. September marks her entry into the family business, as she and her mother are setting up Sonnabend-Sundell, a graphics company dealing in editions by Sonnabend's artists and others.

. . . . .

Ileana Sonnabend has long been renowned for being the Geiger counter of the art world and for rooting out new artists the way a poodle discovers truffles. But she is also famous for being half of one of the great partnerships in the story of modern art. Her extraordinary success is the result of good taste developed over more than half a century of looking at art and her preference for the new and unknown. With her former husband, Leo Castelli, she discovered Jasper Johns and showcased Robert Rauschenberg, promoted Pop art (in his gallery in New York and then in her gallery in Paris), and crowned their achievements by introducing ever-newer waves of art — Minimalism, Conceptualism, performance, Neo-Expressionism, and most recently, a post-Pop hybrid of all the above.

After an amicable divorce from Castelli in 1959, she married Michael Sonnabend, an amateur classics scholar, moved to Paris, and opened a gallery where she and her new husband exhibited Rauschenberg, Johns, Andy Warhol, James Rosenquist, and a bunch of other Americans (along with a handful of European artists). In Europe, the Sonnabends and their artists were given a decidedly mixed reception. "She was a strong person with a broad vision of what she wanted to do in Paris," says the French art critic Pierre Restany. "She shell-bombed us with information about Pop art, which was very important, because Paris at that time was very reticent. But there was also great antagonism — not between French and American artists but among the art dealers — because Paris had lost the art market to New York and they were quite resentful."

Sonnabend's artistic campaign was initially as controversial as the Pop art she peddled, and ultimately as triumphant. So great was their success in Paris that in the early seventies the Sonnabends expanded, opening galleries in Geneva, Switzerland, and New York. Once back in New York, they were also bold enough to position themselves squarely in Leo

Castelli's lap, or rather, one floor above his new gallery space in the SoHo warehouse building at 420 West Broadway. (Sitting in the quiet of Castelli's office nowadays, one can hear the crowds stampeding through Sonnabend's overhead.)

Considered one of the most powerful art dealers in the world, Ileana Sonnabend is reaping the benefits of years of taking chances. And in SoHo she is revealing a far more confrontational taste in art than that of the diplomatic Castelli (although she is also more secretive about her dealings). Of the pair, it is she who is currently considered more adventurous and canny. And because of her stature in the art world, there are few willing to speak out against her. Through all her gallery's changes of location and direction, Sonnabend has managed to hold on to many of her original artists, including Rauschenberg, whom she shares with Castelli (although personal differences with Rauschenberg have recently brought their business dealings to a standstill).

Indeed, Sonnabend is famous for giving her handpicked group of artists enough rope and encouragement to plaster her gallery walls and ceilings and hide under the floorboards — literally — if that is how they want to pronounce the name of art. Her artists have also primped, preened, and blasphemed, publicly masturbated and ejaculated, cut, pasted, and copied, and in almost every other way taunted and flaunted the artistic status quo (some have even done it with a paintbrush).

When, for example, she and rival dealer Mary Boone were both in pursuit of the hip, young artist Ashley Bickerton, he chose to go with Sonnabend because of her gallery's liberalness. As he recalls, "I asked myself one question: five years down the line, if I want to shit in the corner of the gallery, put up a plaque, and call it a show, who out of Mary and Ileana would let me do it? The answer was obvious, and that's why I'm here."

Any doubts about Sonnabend's courage will be dispelled by an exhibition of sexually explicit new works by Jeff Koons she has scheduled for November. Koons's paintings and sculptures depict him with his new bride, the Italian porn star-cum-politician Cicciolina, in the kind of embraces more commonly seen in the peep shows of 42nd Street than in a gallery space belonging to the grande dame of SoHo. Sonnabend lauds them as "beautiful painted dreams," although she also admits that they are "daring." She says, "If Jeff can risk it, then I can too," and adds with a giggle, "Maybe it won't please Senator Helms. But who can please everybody?"

· · · · ·

Unlike her dashing and mercurial former husband, Ileana Sonnabend is a shadowy, saturnine figure, and nothing about her appearance suggests her extraordinary background and immense wealth. There are no flashing jewels, and her plain, olive smocks (she must have one for every day of the week) clothe her like a sack of potatoes. With the exception of her passion for opera, her professional and private worlds revolve around contemporary art and are fused in a way that is essentially bohemian. She is a perfect complement to her artists: whereas Gilbert's and George's lives are their art, Sonnabend's art is her life.

She is also a massive hoarder, with warehouses of Art Deco furniture, expensive photographs, and historic works of art. (When she loans works from her collection to museums, she fills their galleries and leaves roomfuls more in storage.) The part of her collection that recently toured Europe and Japan was insured for more than $30 million, yet Sonnabend maintains — and quite convincingly too — that nobody knows the full extent or value of her holdings, including herself. (She is currently negotiating an extended loan of her collection to the Guggenheim Museum.)

Despite her riches, Sonnabend describes herself a gypsy, "a geographical and cultural nomad," and often says that she has no home. For the last twenty years, however, she has been firmly planted in a pair of converted hotel suites on lower Fifth Avenue near Washington Square and lives, as she works, with Michael Sonnabend and Antonio Homem, her gallery director. "I came from a wealthy background, and I lost everything," she says. "I learned a moral lesson from that. I became quite detached from things, which simplified my life and gave me a lot of freedom. The money I have now I spend on the artists."

According to Homem, 51 years old and recently adopted by the Sonnabends, "Ileana and Michael live totally by their own rules, which have nothing to do with the rules of the world. They are totally devoid of snobbishness and live very much the way adolescents live — with videos and books and records all around. There are a few works of art [by Rauschenberg, Warhol, Anselm Kiefer, and a photo mural by Gilbert and George] and some fine Art Deco furniture that is used as though it were hotel furniture." Yet nobody is ever invited there.

Everybody, on the other hand, is invited to the gallery, where the sweetly smiling Mrs. Sonnabend can be seen wading through her day — talking softly on the phone, casually turning the pages of art catalogues, waving to visitors like a benign pope, and cracking witty asides to her staff. She is short, stout, and stooped, and shuffles about like Gilbert and George in measured rheumatic hydraulics. Homem is her antithesis in every way. He streaks through the gallery, talks up a storm with anyone who will stop to listen, and keeps the energy level exceedingly high, if not actually nervous. Michael Sonnabend seems to never come near the place.

And Ileana hates being photographed. When she does submit, she looks painfully embarrassed. "I think my personal appearance is of no importance," she explains. "It's one's way of looking at life, which is interesting. This attitude probably goes back to childhood. I had an elder sister who was more beautiful than me, and I reacted against that by developing in other directions."

. . . . .

Ileana's sister, Eve Schapira, met Leo Castelli, a sporty, 25-year-old insurance clerk, in 1932, when he was transferred by his father, a banker, from Trieste, Italy, to Bucharest, Romania. The fact that Eve was married didn't stop her from flirting with Castelli, nor did it keep him from sending roses and coming to her home to meet her father, Mihail Schapira, one of Romania's wealthiest Jewish industrialists.

Inside the big family house, Castelli recalls, "they were talking all the time about Ileana," who was 17 at the time, away at school, "and by no means as pretty as Eve but infinitely more attractive." Ileana says she "was a typical upper-class, slightly banal girl" but that while her older sister and mother went shopping, she used to visit museums and spend hours contemplating the art. Castelli found her "a very bright, very wonderful girl to spend one's time with, whereas with Eve it was the usual social chitchat." Yet Ileana had nothing to compare him with. When she first laid eyes on Leo, she says, "I thought I wouldn't mind at all marrying him."

They married a year later in a secular ceremony, when Ileana was 18. His wedding present to her was a small Matisse, and their wedding, instead of being the end of the adventure, was only the curtain raiser. In 1935, Leo assumed a position at the Paris branch of the Banca d'Italia, the Castellis moved there, and the following year their daughter Nina was born.

In Paris, they met art collector and furniture designer René Drouin, through his socialite wife, a friend of Eve Schapira's. Sonnabend recalls Drouin as being "like a French Leo," and the two men became business partners backed by Mihail Schapira. In 1939 they started a gallery on the ritzy Place Vendôme. It opened with one painting by Pavel Tchelitchew, an Art Deco armoire by Leonor Fini, a mirror by Meret Oppenheim, and furniture designed by Drouin; its inaugural

exhibition took place on the eve of World War II. When it closed, the Castellis left town for the summer and never returned. Paris filled up with the German Army, and according to Castelli, "it was quite obvious that, being Jewish, we would have ended up in some oven in Auschwitz if they had caught us." Ileana Castelli would not return to Paris for another two decades, but when she did, it was as Ileana Sonnabend – and with an explosive American artistic agenda.

. . . . .

The reason for Ileana's split from Castelli in 1959 was, according to art-world gossip, his pecadilloes. But Castelli claims that the outbreak of war and the occupation of Paris served to mend what had already become a deteriorating union by the late thirties. "We had some trouble pretty early on in our marriage, in Paris and also in Romania," he explains. "She was flirty, I was flirty, we were not exactly homebodies – but there was nothing really serious until she got involved with our doctor and decided that she wanted to leave me and get married to him. At the end of 1938 we separated for a time. I pursued my activities and in the spring opened the gallery, in which she no longer participated. It had become my affair and I don't know what she was doing at the time. Then the war brought us together."

They fled Paris to join Ileana's father in the south of France and charted an escape route through Portugal. "We did it all on our own," Castelli says. "We had money at our disposal. Her family was very, very wealthy, so there was money to do whatever we needed to do."

They arrived in New York by a circuitous route with Nina (then five), 22 suitcases, a little dog, and their daughter's nurse. Ileana's father installed them in a hotel suite and subsequently bought them a townhouse on East 77th Street – the building where, fifteen years later, the Castellis opened their gallery.

Castelli joined the U.S. Army and served in Europe in the intelligence division. In Paris he met with Drouin and arranged to be his representative in the U.S. After that he worked as a knitwear salesman for a New York firm backed by Ileana's father. At 40 he was still looking for a career.

Ileana, meanwhile, was studying psychology at Columbia University. She failed to complete her studies but met Michael Sonnabend, a small, elfin man who became a good friend of the Castellis. "He appeared in our lives when I was away during the war," recalls Castelli. "And he was around all the time. I think he is a brilliant sort of 'gutter philosopher' – in the sense that he doesn't care about wealth, riches, social connections.

We liked him very much. Ileana liked him very much. But I don't know why she married him."

Michael Sonnabend became a regular fixture at the Castellis' summer house in East Hampton in the 1950s, as did the de Koonings – Willem and Elaine – Jackson Pollock and Lee Krasner, Franz Kline, the art critic Harold Rosenberg, and the art dealer Sidney Janis. Also in residence was Ileana's mother, Marianne, who had gotten divorced and remarried – to the eccentric painter turned occultist John Graham (who later took up with Ultra Violet, one of Warhol's cronies). And Nina Castelli, a teenager by this time, had her friends around too. She recalls that "everyone was yelling and carrying on and having great Abstract Expressionist arguments. It was fabulous, like Parnassus, being surrounded by people that you knew were the most significant, brilliant, and fun-to-be-with people in the world."

Interspersed with the fun was, typically, the melodrama. "I remember the despair of Jackson Pollock," Ileana says about one night the artist announced his intention to drive into the sea and drown himself. "He was in a terrible state of nerves. Leo and de Kooning and Elaine and I followed in a car and fetched him out. I stayed in the car, but I was very upset by the episode." Castelli remembers her hiding delicate vases before the artists arrived. "I was shy and withdrawn," says Ileana. "And by 'withdrawn,' I mean voluntarily withdrawn. It was too intense."

In 1951, Castelli and the painter Jack Tworkov organized the "Ninth Street Show," a large survey exhibition in what would today be called an alternative space – a building in Greenwich Village that was facing demolition. Among the more than 60 second-generation Abstract Expressionist artists in that show was 26-year-old Robert Rauschenberg, who was to feature prominently in the fortunes of the Castellis – together and separately. Ileana in particular took a shine to the young artist. "The first time I saw Bob was at that 'Ninth Street Show' in 1951," she told historian Calvin Tompkins. "Here was this young man, so handsome, laughing and happy – quite a contrast to some of the others."

This was when she began to collect art, including works by Pollock and Rauschenberg, while Leo collected the dues owed him by Drouin and brought over a few pieces of contemporary French art from Paris. These became his inventory, and in 1957, he took the plunge and opened a gallery in his home, using Nina's former bedroom as the office. Although she remained in the background, Ileana contributed her money and taste.

"Ileana was crucial to Leo's being Leo," says Judith Goldman, author of a Castelli biography-in-progress. "And they remain soulmates. Theirs is an intellectual and emotional bond that no one can cut." Sonnabend simply says of her husband's preeminence at that time, "Leo was more mature and he had more star quality, so it was natural that he was the star."

"Leo likes to do things fast," says their daughter, "but Ileana likes to imagine the consequences and work out the outcomes. They used to discuss tactics and strategy. Temperamentally, he was tactics and she was strategy." ("Our children don't always know us," is Ileana's response.)

. . . . .

Castelli's greatest early successes were with Rauschenberg and the young, previously unknown Jasper Johns, whom he and Ileana discovered by accident in Rauschenberg's studio. For a few years in the 1950s, the two artists shared a building downtown, and in April 1957, two months after the Leo Castelli Gallery opened on 77th Street, the Castellis visited Rauschenberg as part of an elaborate setup. Neither Castelli nor Rauschenberg had wanted to show too much interest in the other, so it fell to the painter Paul Brach, who was already in Castelli's stable, and the composer Morton Feldman to orchestrate the meeting. It was a big occasion – Rauschenberg's mother sent ducks, and Rauschenberg cooked them on the hotplate in his studio.

But nothing went as planned and the seeds of the notorious Rauschenberg-Johns rivalry and the Rauschenberg-Castelli resentment were sewn. When Castelli heard that Johns, an artist whose work he had spotted in a group exhibition, was somewhere in the building, he visited Johns's studio, became elated, forgot about Rauschenberg, and left filled with plans for Johns instead. Rauschenberg was speechless. Many accounts of this episode have the distraught artist subsequently running to the gallery and being consoled by Ileana, who promised him a show soon after Johns's.

But this version is contradicted by Johns, who says that he actually swung the deal for his friend. "I have heard Leo's report and I've heard Ileana's and I've heard Bob's and none of them jibes with my own memory," says Johns. Johns remembers a party two months after the studio visit: "Leo said that he was going away for the summer and that when he came back he thought he might like to give me a show and he would be very interested to see what I had done. And I said, 'What about Bob?'"

Rauschenberg maintains that as far as Castelli is concerned, he has played second fiddle to Johns ever since. "I think that Ileana and Leo did not appreciate my work, though they did not depreciate it either," he says. He says he's not angry with Castelli, yet calls him an "egotistical maniac" and complains that the dealer currently owes him $980,000 in commissions. He has also recently transferred his business from Castelli to rival Knoedler Gallery in all but name. "I didn't leave him," Rauschenberg says. "I'm still in that gallery, but I'm mostly showing at Knoedler. I felt that Castelli lacked interest in my work."

Sonnabend says that the whole saga is "sickening" and that the classic anecdote of the studio visit is false. "Bob always felt that he was a victim no matter what. Whether he has reasons or whether he invents reasons makes no difference as long as he can feel sorry for himself. It's his character." She refers to Castelli's generous gift of Rauschenberg's *Bed* painting to the Museum of Modern Art two years ago. She and Leo first saw *Bed* during that fateful studio visit; in 1989 it was valued at $10.5 million. "Bob was very touched that Leo gave that painting. At that party he was very emotional, and we are still very close."

Castelli is blunter. Rauschenberg "knew right from the beginning that I was more involved with Jasper than I was with him, so that's a case of jealousy," he says. "I always favored the kind of work that Jasper does, the type of personality that Jasper is." He says that Ileana, on the other hand, "tended to like Rauschenberg more than Jasper because her taste goes more toward expressionist painting. She, for instance, handled those Germans, like Baselitz and Kiefer and Immendorff and so on, which I would not be interested in." (Appropriately, when she left Castelli and moved to Paris in 1960, Rauschenberg became the backbone of her new gallery.)

Ileana and Leo and Jasper and Bob split apart around the same time. Leo fell for the late Antoinette Fraissex du Bost ("Toiny," whom he eventually married). "I was at a loss after my divorce," Ileana says. Johns and Rauschenberg had a bitter breakup, and Rauschenberg moved to Florida. Then the rivalries set in for real. Johns, who is normally silent on such matters, states, "I suppose I learned more about painting from Bob than I learned from any other artist or teacher, and working as closely as we did and more or less in isolation, we developed a strong feeling of kinship. When that ended, each of us seemed to develop – where there had been none before – some sense of self-interest."

And he offers a similar comment about Leo and Ileana. "I have the feeling that at a certain point Leo wanted to manifest his own taste more clearly and make it known that it was his. I would say that it was when they split up. That's very hard to read because it's difficult to tell what was going on in a situa-tion like that. But if you follow what Ileana has done since, she's certainly made strong decisions that have nothing to do with Leo's taste."

. . . . .

As soon as Ileana was away from Castelli she started expressing her own preferences – especially for Rauschenberg. After she was remarried to Michael Sonnabend, Ileana says, they "went to Europe to escape New York and the art-scene gossip." Within a year they moved to Rome, where they tried unsuccessfully to do business with an Italian gallery that was showing Rauschenberg's friend Cy Twombly, and then to Paris, where they rented a space suggested by Drouin.

Rauschenberg had just held an exhibition in Paris that coincided unfortunately with the outbreak of the Algerian revolution, and according to Sonnabend, he felt totally neglected and unappreciated in France. So the Sonnabends decided to work as agents for him there. "If it weren't for Rauschenberg, I would never be here now," Ileana says. "I didn't really want to become a dealer, but we became successful and we had to stay."

She credits Michael Sonnabend with thinking up the idea of opening their gallery in Paris. He also gets credit for promoting the gallery in novel advertisements in magazines and on posters around town as well as in catalogue introductions. She says he engaged many of the visitors, including such luminaries as André Breton, the elderly founder of Surrealism, in lengthy discussions about Pop art. According to art critic Pierre Restany, however, Michael Sonnabend was actually "just a nice man who had no power. He couldn't wait for the dog to piss so he could take it out for a walk."

The Sonnabends and Rauschenberg became devoted friends. Rauschenberg reminisces about the time he was stealing sand from a construction site in Paris to make art for a show that was opening the next day and Ileana was his lookout. He also recalls that when a piece was to be in an exhibition and was delayed, the uncrating became part of the opening. "Ileana is a kind, tough person who fluctuates between a silly little girl and an iron marshmallow," he says.

Ileana eventually outgrew her girlish reticence, and a hard-nosed businesswoman peeked out from behind "the Ileana Sonnabend kind of smile," as Andy Warhol cautiously described it in his *Diaries*. Ethel Scull, who with her husband, Robert, bought mountains of art from the Castelli and Sonnabend galleries in the 1960s, warns that "people should be aware that Ileana, being very quiet and sweetly smiling, is really a very intelligent woman. She plays the role of not knowing much, but she's actually terribly clever and has a good eye. She has always picked the best art of her artists, and nobody can get their hands on it. She makes collectors terribly upset."

About her history as a dealer, Sonnabend claims to have forgotten most of the details. "I don't plan," she says. "I do what I do hoping it will turn out all right. I never think of the future and I never think of the past. I don't remember blunders, though I am sure that I have made a lot of them. If you make blunders and they are not retrievable, then you have to think of the next thing to do to be successful." The impression she gives is that she is more comfortable with official glosses than with the truth.

Undoubtedly, Ileana's greatest triumph in Europe was when Rauschenberg won the Grand Prix at the 1964 Biennale of Venice — an award Castelli and Sonnabend were accused of politicking for because of the new esteem it bestowed on American art in Europe and the benefits that flowed to both of them as a result. In fact, Sonnabend was frequently cited in these years as Castelli's European general (although it was she who had first seen and collected the work of such artists as James Rosenquist and George Segal), and conspiracy theories about their business partnership have never ceased.

In Paris, however, Sonnabend represented American Pop art against its French opponents — without Castelli. Pierre Restany was her main antagonist, and they fought on the front lines. He accuses Sonnabend of wooing critics to win their support. "My problems with her came to a head in 1968, when she was Arman's dealer," he says. "It was the time of the big student protests and also the 1968 Venice Biennale and the Documenta, and the French artists closed their pavilion in Venice as part of the protests. Arman was the only artist who would not close his room because he said he was living quite well off the capitalist system and wished to do even better. She wanted him to close because she wanted to show that she, too, was left-leaning, and she criticized me for trying to influence him to stay open. So she attacked me in the café at Documenta and got quite aggressive. I didn't want anything to do with her for years after that." Restany nevertheless admits that Sonnabend "accelerated the rhythm of history."

Sonnabend hasn't seen Restany in twenty years. "You know, it's one of those things," she laughs. "What I don't like I don't see."

. . . . .

Wisely, her list of artists in Paris was peppered with European names, and Sonnabend quickly hit on the recipe that has ensured the success of her galleries ever since — a mix of art from both continents. With the young Italian dealer Gian Enzo Sperone, she exhibited her American artists in Italian galleries, and reciprocated by taking on some of his "Arte Povera" artists from Turin. She also showed the photographs of Bernd and Hilla Becher, a German couple (an edition of their work is the first project of Sonnabend-Sundell), as well as installations by Christian Boltanski and Anne and Patrick Poirier from France, the Minimal and Conceptual artists from Castelli's gallery, and a handful of Californians, including John Baldessari. At the same time, her Pop artists were sold heavily to galleries and mus-eum collections across the entire European continent.

On this side of the Atlantic, she opened initially on Madison Avenue in 1970 (and held on to the space for years afterward for the display and sale of Art Deco furniture), while running her gallery in Paris for another ten years. Then, in 1971, she found her current space in SoHo — and invited Gilbert and George to perform the opening honors.

They were followed in 1972 by Vito Acconci, who in his famous *Seedbed* performance lay beneath the floorboards while his masturbatory gasps and groans were amplified through loudspeakers in the gallery. She also exhibited the photographs of Cecil Beaton, George Hoyningen-Huené, and Deborah Turbeville when they were considered too lightweight for serious artistic tastes. And until he went to Knoedler in 1987 on a $1 million one-year contract, Rauschenberg remained an integral part of the gallery.

. . . . .

"I had the idea that the gallery had a function to inform," Sonnabend says. "When I find something of interest that is totally unknown, I want to make it known. I wanted to break up the isolationism that existed here at that time. I wanted to show the multiplicity of interesting things and not just one kind of art. I also thought that the galleries and museums didn't do enough." Her finds, however, are almost exclusively white and male.

Castelli had exclusive New York representation of the American artists she was showing in Paris (with rare exceptions such as Rauschenberg), so Sonnabend tried to poach artists from other galleries. When she approached Sol LeWitt with an offer, John Weber, his dealer, was upset. Sonnabend recalls, "John came in very angry. I said, 'Yes, I very much like Sol LeWitt and I like Robert Ryman.' And he said, 'So what's wrong with the others?' "

She made her next round of big bids in the early 1980s and netted the German Neo-Expressionists, including Baselitz, A.R. Penck, and Jörg Immendorff, who were ripping open the art scene in Europe. "No one else was doing it, so it had to be done," she explains. She also entered into negotiations with Brice Marden. But Marden, who had worked as Rauschenberg's assistant, says, "She used to treat him like shit. I mean, she doesn't pay people."

She lost most of her Germans soon after discovering them — they went to Mary Boone when Boone became engaged and married to their long-standing German dealer, Michael Werner (Boone subsequently lost them when she and Werner separated). Sonnabend also lost the touchy Anselm Kiefer, one of the biggest sellers of the decade, who was being hounded for shows by Sonnabend, Boone, and Marian Goodman. Sonnabend had purchased more than fifty of his works (and was selling them from her back room, although she never exhibited them), and then, according to her, lost him because of a single verbal indiscretion. (Neither she nor Kiefer will elaborate.) Luckily for her, however, Neo-Expressionism was waning by the mid-1980s, and she was fast on the scent of the next big thing.

The next big thing sprouted right under her nose in New York's dinky East Village art scene. Among the second wave of East Village artists, Haim Steinbach and Jeff Koons were embracing cultural icons in a hard-edge Pop way that stood out strongly against the messy and telegraphic subjectivity of the Neo-Expressionists and graffitists.

Sonnabend picked up a handful of East Village artists and turned them into stars virtually overnight. Four — Koons, Bickerton, Meyer Vaisman, and Peter Halley — made their debuts with her in a massively attended show in 1986, and Steinbach followed in a two-gallery show with Sonnabend and Jay Gorney, his East Village dealer who was busy hightailing it to SoHo.

The New York art establishment did not know what to make of Sonnabend's newest fancies. The crotchety critic Kay Larson, for instance, wrote in the May 1987 issue of *New York* magazine that Steinbach "shows himself to be a perplexing and intriguing artist [who] daringly presents cultural clichés wrenched from their contexts and compacted to a high density." Three months later, she denounced his work as "plodding commercialism."

Antonio Homem says that the reaction to the gallery's new finds "was the same as to the Pop artists in the 1960s. They are seen simultaneously as *enfants terribles* and as classic artists." Sonnabend agrees, but waves her hand to show that she doesn't let this, or anything else, get to her.

Nor does the current recession seem to be causing her to lose any sleep. Homem claims that the gallery's major collectors are still buying and that he and Sonnabend don't look at their finances "as long as the rent is paid. There were a lot of people buying and selling at auction and pushing the prices up," Homem says. "I always thought that when a recession happened, these funny people would stop buying and we'd be left with the others. And that is exactly what is happening now. Nobody is buying things to try to sell them tomorrow for twice the price."

"I've been through many recessions," Sonnabend says. "There have been others and there will be more."

. . . . .

The Sonnabends summer in a rented apartment in Venice and often sit at their favorite café, outdoors in the Piazza Santo Stefano. Here Ileana mentions that compared to when she started out, the public for art is huge, and this sets Michael off. He starts to expound on art as the new religion and on how the art world will keep growing: "My opinion is that the schools have turned out five hundred times more students of the history of art than ever in the history of the world. Every collector that I see at [Sonnabend's] — all those people were sucked up into art history as against theology, as against religion. You have no idea.

"Now let me tell you something else ..." But it's hot and his wife yawns. Such are their days together, and one can imagine this pair of old bohemians sitting and talking endlessly, like Gilbert and George's tramps. "Underneath the arches," they could be singing, "we dream our dreams away." ●

Part Six

Show Business

Hollywood's Portraits of Artists

THE NEW YORK TIMES FEBRUARY 1988

What do Edward G. Robinson, Alec Guinness, Daryl Hannah and Dick Van Dyke have in common? Apart from being artists in the entertainment sense, they have also played artists in the artistic sense. And as Hollywood and the New York art world move closer together in the 1980s – with their star systems, the big prices and instant fame that awaits hot new discoveries – Hollywood has started to take the art world seriously (or humorously, as the case may be). Kirk Douglas's portrayal of Vincent van Gogh in *Lust for Life* has always been a classic for art-theory students – for whom it embodies all the clichés of the angst-ridden artist. In fact, some bidders at auctions where astronomical sums were paid for *Sunflowers* and *Irises* have admitted that their interest was fueled by Hollywood's singular portrayal of van Gogh.

And in the aftermath of art as a major element of such movies as *Legal Eagles* and *Wall Street*, an aggressive portrayal of artists – as dreamy romantics, counterfeiters or glamorous bohemians – is the hook of more than half a dozen new movies currently in development or poised for national release.

Just as Andy Warhol's movies of the 1960s prefigured today's interest in the downtown artist scene, many of the new movies are treating the art world in classic ways. Biographies and farce predominate. And the artists are cut from the same cloth. They are invariably bug-eyed maniacs or dandyish phonies. They tear through the world like shooting stars and lead lives that are scandalously impoverished or extravagantly rich. Indeed, money – or the lack of it – is the root of their existence.

Among the new wave of art movies, the first scheduled arrival is Alan Rudolph's *The Moderns*, opening in April. Rudolph's most lavish production to date, the film stars Keith Carradine as an art forger in the bohemian Paris of the 1920s and takes an extremely black view of the pretensions of modernism.

It is a modernist painter, Georgia O'Keeffe, who is topping the charts as Hollywood's newest discovery. Concurrent with the national museum tours of her work, there are no less than three movies being developed about this new-found American heroine. Her early life in New York with the photographer Alfred Stieglitz and her years in isolation in the deserts of the west are now suddenly ripe for the big screen. O'Keeffe's new biographers – art historians eighties-style – include United Artists, Steven Spielberg's Amblin Entertainment company, and an independent co-production of Viacom Productions and the actress Jane Alexander's Altion Productions.

If O'Keeffe's historical importance runs the risk of being overrated by all this attention, however, the rest of the art movies do little to restore sanity. They include: a few "Jack-the-Dripper" scripts about Jackson Pollock, as well as a movie of Tama Janowitz's East Village extravaganza, *Slaves of New York*. By next month, M-G-M hopes to have a director for an art-world farce called *The Three C's*. (The C's stand for Color, Composition, and Carnovsky – the movie's oddball artist-hero. But within the art world, the Three C's is a nickname for the three Italian New Wave painters of the early eighties – Chia, Cucchi, and Clemente.)

The director Bobby Houston is already laying the soundtrack to his new art-world feature, *Trust Me*, with the British pop star Adam Ant as an unscrupulous art dealer. The 79-year-old French director Marcel Carné is preparing an epic movie about his country's Impressionist painters. In Australia, Paul Cox's latest movie, *Vincent*, about van Gogh, has already opened. And there are two Andy Warhol stories circulating. One, called *A Way of Life*, depicts the zany goings-on inside the Warhol Factory. And the second, which has been in negotiations between the actor-producer Warren Beatty and the author Jean Stein for more than a year, is the story of Edie Sedgwick, Warhol's most famous groupie. (In Hollywood, people are asking if the star of *Shampoo* is planning to don the artist's blond wig.)

The most inspiring thing about the art scene, say a number of the filmmakers, is the glaring similarity between Hollywood and the 1980s art scene. Alan Rudolph explains that his film, *The Moderns*, "is as much about Hollywood as it is about art. It's about trying to get your work sold – which is something I understand." The director Ivan Reitman said that *Legal Eagles* (his ill-fated 1986 movie that depicted a love affair between two lawyers who share a client in the artist played by Daryl Hannah) was set in the New York art world because it "has made stars out of artists, and art has become part of fashion, nightclubs, and music." Most of the art displayed in the film came via Arnold Glimcher, owner of New York's trendy Pace Gallery.

• • • • •

Bobby Houston, the director of *Trust Me*, says that his film takes place in Los Angeles's art world, "not because of any point I want to make about art but because of the resemblances between the art industry and the film industry. The art world is a mini-version of the movie world. They are both closed circles, and all the players know one another. Only difference is that in L.A. the art business is a service industry to the movie business." And Adam Ant, an art dealer on screen but a former art student and present-day art collector in real life who has a small Picasso and a Stanley Spencer among his holdings, adds that art has become interesting because "paintings have become a currency. With all the corporate interest in the art world, as in Hollywood, it is now a really big business."

Michael Kohn, whose Hollywood art gallery is the setting for a number of movies, including a new Roger Corman production, believes that the trend is a natural consequence of the early-1980s art boom. "All the money and heat generated by the New York scene five years ago is finally dribbling down into popular art forms like movies," he says.

Despite the recent avalanche of interest, some of the most powerful producers of movies and television are extremely wary of the rush to portray the art world on film. "I get proposals about the art world every two weeks," says Douglas Cramer, executive vice-president of Aaron Spelling Productions. "But other than to work an art scene into a series, I don't do anything about them because they are very tough sales at the networks. The networks don't feel that the art world and any particular art subjects have the mass appeal for television movies." Cramer, who is also a prominent art collector, found this out for himself when two of his own ideas, for movies about Mark Rothko and Pollock, were turned down.

Such indifference is prompting some film makers to deny that there is any new fashion at all. Instead, they insist, their movies are about "human nature," and art is just the backdrop. Says Ann Biderman, the screenwriter for *The Three C's*: "My story is not about art, but obsession." Chris Bomba, a vice-president of creative affairs for M-G-M, says "the art world is not a trend, like the Vietnam movies. It's more like a coincidence. It is just a 'plus' to the stories, as it has not been exploited in recent memory." And James Ivory, the director of

Slaves of New York, says that "while our characters are struggling young artists who haven't yet made it big, they could just as well be young Off Broadway actors."

• • • • •

The new batch of films caters unashamedly to an audience that is fascinated by the downtown glamor of art in the 1980s. This is the world over which Warhol presided. Twenty-five years ago, the Pop artist was a pioneer in the "crossover" territory that links the art world to Hollywood. While his movies were never commercial successes, they did bridge the gap between art and entertainment and also set up the art world's first-ever star system. Even more important, Warhol's movies were prototypes for many of the independent film productions of today.

In 1963, a starstruck Warhol shot his first attempt, *Tarzan and Jane Regained ... Sort of* in the Beverly Hills Hotel. It starred a few of Warhol's friends who went on to become his "superstars," as well as his fellow Pop artist Claes Oldenburg, and Dennis Hopper. Five years later, Paul Morrissey took over the task of directing, and Warhol became a mini-producer. But having spent $1.2 million on *Bad* in 1977 and still not winning acceptance in Hollywood, he canned his ambitions.

Then, just months before his death last year, Warhol reevaluated his prospects and announced his intentions to reenter the movie production field. He purchased an option on five of the stories in Tama Janowitz's collection, *Slaves of New York*.

The artist also expressed interest in the rights to Stephen Koch's novel *The Bachelor's Bride*, a story about a charismatic artist of the 1960s who combines qualities of both Robert Rauschenberg and Warhol himself, but they remain unsold. And recently, Fred Hughes, president of Warhol Enterprises, sold off the rights to *Slaves of New York* to Merchant Ivory productions. Shooting is slated to begin next month.

When it comes to painters and sculptors on the screen, says the art historian and film buff Max Kozloff, "there are very few depictions of serious artists in movies. They are always looked upon with a mixture of derision and admiration, probably because they devote their lives to an apparently higher, intangible vision. The only worthwhile and believable one of the lot is Gulley Jimson in *The Horse's Mouth*," he adds, referring to the painter portrayed by Alec Guinness (who, as screenwriter, crafted the character from Joyce Cary's novel).

Film makers have always tended to view artists as anachronisms. Moreover, the most notable directors of art-world genre movies, such as Warhol, are most likely to have been artists

ARNOLD GLIMCHER 1993

themselves, artists who abandoned their early attempts, or film makers with an exceptional familiarity with the art world. For example, Vincente Minnelli's *Lust for Life*, about the darling of today's auction houses, may be the best-known artistic biography on film and has probably inspired more than one young soul to take to the brush. But less well known is the fact that Minnelli himself studied Post-Impressionist painting at the Art Institute of Chicago. Given his depiction of the desperate van Gogh, it is not surprising that Minnelli threw still lifes overboard in favor of movie pictures.

. . . . .

Even more influential on the history of art in the movies is the director Jean Renoir, who introduced the artist-as-forger theme in his 1931 film *La Chienne*. Shot in Montmartre – the SoHo of the prewar years – it depicts a hapless painter whose works are appropriated by a forger and sold to a guileless public. *La Chienne* was completed just twelve years after the death of the director's father, the Impressionist painter Auguste Renoir. A blow to the reputation of the entire artistic profession, this film became the blueprint for scores of postwar Hollywood movies: ever since *La Chienne*, art and forgery have been irrevocably linked in the popular imagination.

Renoir's film was remade by Fritz Lang in 1945 and retitled *Scarlet Street*, with Edward G. Robinson cast as the henpecked, exploited artist. In later variations on the theme, generations of shrewd artists have come to the realization that their work would be more valuable if only they were dead, and this breakthrough in their otherwise unexceptional artistic development has given rise to a slew of situation comedies in which dastardly artists, like Dick Van Dyke in *The Art of Love*, have elaborately staged their own disappearance.

The fraud genre satirizes the supposed authenticity of today's painting and sculpture, and reflects the public's suspicions about modern artists. Since *La Chienne* and *Scarlet Street*, our faith in artists has never been the same. Indeed, who today can honestly deny entertaining any suspicions that art is a fraud, that artists are fakes and that the art world is little more than counterfeit culture?

It was with some delight that Alan Rudolph enlisted the services of David Stein, once jailed for art forgery, to stimulate the masterpieces shown in *The Moderns*, re-creating the paintings stage by stage to meet the demands of the plot. A latter-day plagiarist, Mike Bidlo, whose career is a deliberate affront to the idea of authenticity, was spotted among the handpicked audience at a preview of the film in January. Bidlo's reproductions of paintings by Picasso, including the *Demoiselles d'Avignon*, *Three Women* and *Guernica*, were exhibited last month at the Leo Castelli Gallery under the title "Picasso's Women."

Lately, Hollywood's perception of art has earned an eighties-style twist. In *Wall Street*, a film totally laden with glitzy new art, the corporate raider Gordon Gekko brags that art is "capitalism at its finest!" (Likewise, in *Terms of Endearment*, the financial safety net of the two leading ladies is a painting – a Renoir, no less.) But if art is winning back the appreciation of today's audiences, it is largely because it has become a valuable commodity.

According to the painter James Rosenquist, who makes a cameo appearance in the art-auction scene in *Wall Street*: "Audiences are starting to become very sophisticated. After yuppie things like expensive cars, apartments, and clothes, they want art. In *Wall Street*, the art is portrayed as just another poker chip. It's become like drug money."

In the world at large, art is now a bewildering paradox: if art equals money, it is at the root of all evil. But then again, isn't art supposed to be the peak of human and cultural expression? In the 1980s, this dilemma looms larger than ever before, and today's film makers have a lot of material on their hands. In the distance from *Scarlet Street* to *Wall Street*, from forgery to commodity, art has become a worthy Hollywood target. And in 1988, there are no signs that the shooting will stop. ●

SYLVESTER STALLONE 1977

The Stallone Collection

Connoisseur DECEMBER 1991

For fifteen years, Sylvester Stallone has gloried in a celluloid career and multimillions of dollars, thanks chiefly to Rocky and Rambo, his pair of comic-book warriors. But the real Stallone is a thoughtful soul who has educated himself about art and is serious about the possibility of heroism in modern life. Like the story of Rocky Balboa, Stallone's rise makes for a good, old-fashioned morality tale about a fighting man who drags himself, bruised and bleeding, out of the gutter. But Stallone is nowadays a pampered movie star who lives alone behind electronic security gates above Beverly Hills. He is fabulously popular among the blue-collar folk, yet is one of the Republican party's major donors, a member of its elite Team 100 club. And despite the big-budget movies with enormous casts, the private Stallone gets his kicks by locking himself in his garage with a forty-watt bulb, paint, and a palette knife and spilling his guts on canvas.

An art lover, Stallone, 45, has put his money where his mind is and estimates that he has spent $25 million on nineteenth- and twentieth-century paintings and sculptures since *Rocky* hit the jackpot in 1976. But although his commitment to art is genuine and longstanding, many of his prizes have become casualties of the actor's fits of pique and landed back on the market only months after he purchased them. In the process, he has acquired a reputation for paying too much for particular works. According to New York art collector Stuart Pivar, who sold Stallone a *Pietà* (1876) by the nineteenth-century French academic painter Adolphe William Bouguereau for a high $1,785,000 and was sued for it in 1989, "Stallone's efforts at art collecting have ended in a flurry of lawsuits. I have no sympathy for him or his connoisseurship."

Not long after he started to collect, Stallone was shown a painting by leading New York Abstract Expressionist Willem de Kooning, "and I did one of the most naive things that I ever did in my life," he says now, "which is why I should never listen to anybody. I was shown a six-foot de Kooning from around 1955, a real classic – big, huge. And I was looking at it at someone's apartment and it was, like, $80,000, and as I was about to sign the check, I thought, 'Oh, my God, this is my first big acquisition.' I had this local security guard with me at the time, so I said to him, 'By the way, what do you think, Tony?' And he goes, 'Well, I wouldn't put that piece of shit in my dog house.' 'Excuse me?' I said. He said, 'What are you talking about? It's a mess. I could do better than that. It's like a shower curtain.' And the lady said, 'I beg your pardon. This is a valuable piece. It's a de Kooning. Trust me.' To make a long story short, it was sold for about $4 million about five years later. I try to block it out of my memory. It was a bad move."

Stallone has the courage of his convictions now, though he always had faith in his own creations. The character of Rocky, for example, originated in the Stallone psyche in the early 1970s, when the out-of-work actor made paintings of a hulking silhouette against an oppressive city skyline. A few years later, Stallone realized the Rocky fantasy when he sold his script to Hollywood, insisting on acting the title role himself, even though he stood to earn more if he bowed out and let Ryan O'Neal have the part. And in the 1980s, victoriously on the other side of superstardom, he created his monumental canvas *Rocky I* by cutting up his original script, collaging it into the figure of Rocky, and burying it in layers of paint.

Side by side with the heroic, there is the comic Stallone, increasingly in evidence in recent years and in such movies as the soon-to-be-released mother-and-son buddy movie in which he plays a bachelor forced to share his career with his mother – played by Estelle Getty from the TV sitcom *The Golden Girls*. (Stallone did not write this script.)

. . . . .

Stallone's collection of more than two hundred pieces used to be displayed in the 35,000-square-foot converted warehouse that housed his movie company, White Eagle Enterprises, in Santa Monica, California, sometimes behind velvet ropes and always interspersed with his own paintings. Immediately apparent to even the most casual visitor was Stallone's predilection for passionate and dramatic subjects – not only in the art he bought but also in his own. Says his former art advisor, Barbara Guggenheim, "His collection was shaping up to be quite good. He especially loved heroic and larger-than-life-size figures and animals fighting animals. He'd read the classics. That's where he gets his material and his inspiration."

Then in 1989, White Eagle merged with Carolco Pictures, and Stallone moved out of his offices. It was at this time that he started to deaccession his collection – although he still has more paintings than space for them. Surrounding his own canvases at home is an assortment of paintings and sculptures, including a pair of portraits of Stallone by Andy Warhol and another by the painter LeRoy Neiman (of the actor as Rocky), who is popular in California. There is also a Diego Rivera work on paper; a huge, rough-hewn bronze figure by Émile-Antoine Bourdelle; an enormous, painted bronze heart by Jim Dine; bold, even bombastic, paintings by the German-American Neo-Expressionist Rainer Fetting and the Russian emigrés Komar and Melamid; and an Anselm Kiefer with straw and a lead wing.

Like many bodybuilders, Stallone exhibits a special love of statuary. He has Rodin's *Eve*, two balloony bronzes by Botero, and a small, valuable collection of fine nineteenth-century bronzes by Antoine-Louis Barye that were among the first objects he acquired. He also owns a few bronze sculptures by New York artist Robert Longo, who is a particular favorite of Stallone's because he paints and sculpts, Stallone says, "like a director ... very movielike figures ... almost like animation." There is a larger-than-life-size bronze of Stallone that gestures melodramatically toward the depths of his swimming pool. (This work, by former New York Academy of Art professor Martine Vaugel, was commissioned by Stallone in 1986 as a double portrait of himself and his then wife, Brigitte Nielsen. When their marriage hit the rocks, Nielsen was cut out of the piece.) There is a little bronze by Thomas Schomberg – the sculptor responsible for the enormous *Rocky* statue that was placed on the front steps of the Philadelphia Museum of Art in 1985 for the filming of *Rocky III* and was left there until the museum removed it to a nearby sports stadium. And at the baby-grand player piano in his living room sits a life-size acrylic gorilla.

. . . . .

Dozens of newly acquired canvases are stacked against walls in various rooms in his hilltop mini-mansion, still more hang in his beach house in Malibu, and Stallone also keeps churning out his own. Artistically, he is an Expressionist. His inspiration comes directly from his heart, and from the groin.

"All my paintings are done out of angst, anger, happiness, or something," he says, pointing to one of the graffiti-like canvases he painted during his breakup with Nielsen, the Danish-born star of *She-Hulk*. The work is filled with tortured shapes and scrawled words. "It is pure, unadulterated rage," says Stallone, and it was executed without paintbrushes. Instead,

he uses palette knives, spray paint, and his bare hands. "I like the smashing effect," he says. "It's a little cruder."

He likens his artistic style to his acting technique. "Acting has nothing to do with dialogue," he says. "Dialogue only interferes with the conveyance of true emotion. You could take the alphabet and scream it out or make it hysterically funny. It's the intonation that lets you know how a person is feeling, and the words mean nothing. The same in painting, where color means nothing. The feeling of the painting tells you what color to use. If you understand what your painting is, really understand, you don't just push the slop around. You're painting this ... emotion. You're not thinking about red or green. You grab tubes and – boom! It's done."

Stallone keeps a copy of a Joseph Campbell book by his side as he paints: "I take a quote from it, like, 'He who says he knows, doesn't, and he who says he does not know, knows,' and I get that in my brain and I hit the canvas." He also keeps the lighting dim, "so I am forced to push the colors a lot harder than normal. I have a full-on street fight with that canvas. I go to war." It takes him a few paintings to get going, he says, but then – boom! It's done.

Last year, he showed slides of his work to New York art dealer Leo Castelli. "The response wasn't exactly overwhelming," Stallone says. For his part, Castelli can't remember what the pictures looked like but says he "liked Stallone very much as a person. He was very innocent and sincere despite his success and very warlike films."

. . . . .

Stallone's career as a painter started in the late 1960s, when as a 19-year-old acting student/traveling man, he exhibited a handful of paintings in bus terminals in Florida to raise funds for his fares. Those works – a primitive mix of Surrealist and Expressionistic styles painted on readymade canvas boards – varied from abstracts to a painting of a Watusi warrior copied from a record cover, to a picture of Edgar Allen Poe, to one of "a woman's legs, arched, with a city coming out of her soft spot, which was a little rough to sell at a bus terminal," says Stallone. He sold three of them for fifteen to twenty dollars each.

Nothing interesting happened for another twenty years – until 1989, when he was introduced to Scott Hanson of the Hanson Galleries, on Rodeo Drive in Beverly Hills. "I didn't originally intend to show Stallone's work," says Hanson. "I was just interested to meet him. I expected to meet Rambo or some variation on Rambo. But he was articulate and had developed a very sophisticated eye."

Stallone showed Hanson his paintings of Hollywood's "fallen idols" – Marilyn Monroe, James Dean, and Errol Flynn among them – in which the figures are posed beside clocks set at, say, six o'clock or ten o'clock, a device intended to represent the different stages of the stars' lives. "We all have a clock, our peaks and valleys," says Stallone, "and I try to show the professional peaks in the paintings." Hansen liked Stallone's work and booked him for a show in September 1990.

The art business in Los Angeles is a very different proposition from the one in New York. There are not as many famous artists on the West Coast, serious collectors are fewer, and the prices for art are lower. The other thing about the L.A. art scene is the increasing number of celebrities who are exhibiting their landscapes and still lifes – even when the little numbers are almost visible through the paint, figuratively speaking.

Hanson Galleries has managed to thrive in this environment, and since originally opening in San Francisco in 1974, Hanson has opened five other branches in California, two in New York, and one each in New Orleans and Maui. In Beverly Hills, he exhibits the work of Peter Max, Ernest Trova, and Mark Kostabi, prints by Robert Rauschenberg, and ceramics by Picasso. He also moves large quantities of editions by such New York artists as Christo and Jim Dine to the Japanese. "We cater to a middle audience – a broader one," Hanson explains. "As compared to the avant-garde art world on the East Coast, where there may be fifty or so major collectors who are flying around the world collecting art, we have forty thousand clients. Our average client buys seven times over a three-to-five-year period, and many are first-time buyers."

Around the celebrity artists – the Gene Hackmans, Buddy Ebsons, and Donna Summers – a new class of patrons is being cultivated: their agents, managers, and lawyers, who feel they have to support their clients' artistic aspirations by buying their art. They turn the openings into Hollywood evenings. Aided by the press releases distributed by his agency, Stallone's opening was a crush. Yet Hanson maintains that "in Sly's case, his attorneys and agents got here on opening night, but the show was already completely sold out. Nobody bought any works out of obligation."

Hanson sold more than thirty paintings, all of them priced from $10,000 to $40,000 (they went to the songwriter Lamont Dozier, former Carolco Pictures co-owner and *Rambo* executive producer Andy Vajna, and assorted fans, from car dealers to doctors), and the flood of requests for his art has still not abated. There are orders from Europe and Japan, and Stallone was booked to mount a show at Tokyo's trendy Seibu Museum,

which he was forced to postpone by his shooting schedule. A painting by Stallone hangs in the brand-new New York restaurant Planet Hollywood, in which he is a partner, and he is now preparing his second sell-out show for Hanson.

Delighted by his success, Stallone says, "It's one thing when someone slaps down six or seven dollars for a movie ticket. But when they lay down thirty or forty thousand dollars, it's an amazing validation. I think it's better than any feeling than I've had in a performance."

. . . . .

Stallone is obviously on the pinnacle of Beverly Hills, but when it comes to the big-time New York and international art markets, he thinks he was taken for a ride. To begin with, there was the irritating matter of Mark Kostabi, the publicity-crazed New York painter whose PR stunts have been notoriously spiteful. Stallone purchased two of his works, including a painting of two lesbians. Now he says he finds Kostabi contemptible. "He is the most unhappy, miserable being on the face of the earth. He's kind of like the dog who soils the carpet because he thinks that it's better to be beaten than to get no attention at all. He is that desperate."

One evening, Stallone turned on his television set and saw Kostabi being interviewed. He was making fun of people who buy his work, calling them idiots. "I couldn't believe it," says Stallone. "He named me." He said that Stallone only buys Kostabis that have "tits and ass." So the next day, Stallone sold off his Kostabis, claiming that "I would be a masochist if I kept them." (Not to be outdone, Kostabi went to work on two paintings of Stallone, one of them titled *Tits and Ass*, which depicts a naked Stallone ripely endowed with a pair of breasts.)

Then there was the Kiefer episode. Stallone says he learned about 46-year-old Kiefer, the German Neo-Expressionist, from his lawyer, Jake Bloom, who with his wife, Ruth, is a prominent collector of contemporary art. (She is co-owner of the Myers/Bloom Gallery in Santa Monica, in a building owned by Stallone.) And once he had discovered the artist, Stallone was keen to obtain one of his paintings. "He desperately wanted a Kiefer," says Barbara Guggenheim.

Guggenheim located a massive canvas, *Wayland's Song (with Wing)* (1982), from the Saatchi Collection in London, that was being sold in this country by Irena Hochman, a private dealer, at the time of Kiefer's 1988 Museum of Modern Art retrospective in New York. Prior to 1988, one Kiefer painting had gone at auction to The Limited's Leslie Wexner for half a million dollars, and Eli Broad, the prominent California collector, had paid $1 million for a 1973 "masterpiece." Both figures were considered extremely high.

Hochman showed Saatchi's piece to Stallone, who fell for it on the spot and left the negotiations to Hochman and Guggenheim. "It was a very brief visit," Hochman recalls. "He loved the painting." Hochman says she doesn't know what Guggenheim charged Stallone. What Stallone says is that with Guggenheim's commission, he paid about $1.75 million.

But after he took possession of the painting, it started "shedding" — flakes of paint and pieces of straw fell from it, and once when the piece was transported with its leaden wing attached, it threatened to rip open the entire canvas. Rumors started circulating that he had paid too much for it.

"The Kiefer is a big question mark," Stallone now says of the painting. "I paid far and away the most anyone ever paid for a Kiefer painting. It outdistanced the market by about $750,000." Yet, when he bought it, he insists, "they were telling me this was world class, the most incredible thing I'd ever own."

He and Guggenheim put it back on the market only months after purchasing it, and no one would touch it. The painting now hangs in a vestibule near his front door. "In the long run, maybe it's fate," he says philosophically. "Maybe me and this Kiefer are destined to float off in the sunset together. Maybe I'll carry it out on a shield. I don't know. But I'm starting to actually like it."

. . . . .

His collection dates back to 1976, when Stallone used his purse from *Rocky* — $225 million in box office receipts alone — to start buying. It began humbly and unpretentiously with purchases of Barye bronze sculptures and a candelabrum he had long admired in the window of Gorevic & Son Inc. (then on Lexington Avenue in New York, across the street from where Stallone used to live). The grease spots on their store window, he tells Charles and Roger Gorevic, were made by his nose. By the time Stallone visited them to buy, the Gorevics say he was accompanied by "three or four bodyguards and a bunch of girls running after him for autographs." But they add that the pieces he bought in the 1970s for $10,000 may be worth more than $100,000 today.

Like Rocky, he initially struck out alone and followed his own inclinations. Then he worked briefly with a West Coast art advisor, Tamara Thomas, and in 1984 he hired Guggenheim. He became a high-stakes speculator and bought and sold fine paintings by Monet ("What I like to call the master shot of his haystacks," he says), Dali, Magritte, Chagall, Delvaux, and what

he dubs an "X-rated" nude Rodin sculpture, *Iris*.

Guggenheim earned a lot from Stallone. And on the strength of his patronage, she became one of the best-known art advisers in New York, with a number of prominent clients on the West Coast, including TV producer Aaron Spelling and his wife, Candy, and had truncated dealings other entertainment types, such as actress Lily Tomlin and CEO of Fox Inc. Barry Diller. She is an elegant operator who had been on extremely close terms with former CBS chairman William S. Paley, Goldman Sachs partner Arthur Altschul, British artist R.B. Kitaj, Derek Johns (formerly of Sotheby's London and the founder of the Embassy Club), Robert Bookman of Creative Artists Agency (CAA), and Mohan Murjani, former owner of Gloria Vanderbilt jeans.

And she was visible as the longtime girlfriend of Stuart Pivar, a pal of Andy Warhol's. "I met her either through the Warhol-Pivar connection," Stallone recalls, "or through my agency, because she was dealing with a few people there — Michael Ovitz, Ron Meyer, Ray Stark." (CAA head Ovitz has been involved with Guggenheim on and off for years, and Stark was her mentor in Hollywood from the start.)

Pivar and Warhol, by turns an extravagant and penny-pinching pair of eccentric millionaire collectors, would hit New York's flea markets and auction houses almost daily. Pivar's name frequently appears in Warhol's *Diaries*: Warhol describes him as "full of knotted nerves," and asks, "Why is Stuart looking for other girls, with Barbara so in love with him and she's pretty and intelligent and now is even making lots of money?"

Pivar owns industrial-plastic companies, "not a very glamorous kind of thing," he laments, "so what I do all day is collect and advise." A nineteenth-century buff, he is the author of the catalogue raisonné of Barye's sculptures and a founder and chairman emeritus of the New York Academy of Art, a Beaux Arts-type school on Lafayette Street, which he says is "by far the biggest recipient of funds from the Warhol Foundation — a few hundred thousand dollars a year."

Around the time Stallone and Guggenheim teamed up to build Stallone's multimillion-dollar collection, Pivar was also doing business with the actor. He says he arranged for the artisans at his New York Academy to make a replica of an unobtainable Barye sculpture for Stallone, for which Stallone would make a tax-deductible donation to the Academy. Yet according to Warhol's *Diaries*, "Stuart Pivar is casting bronzes for Stallone and he doesn't know what to do because he just saw an *original* of the one he's casting going at auction for cheaper than he's casting the *copy* for Stallone for [*laughs*], so he doesn't know what to do, he's afraid Stallone will see it, too." (Pivar simply dismisses the *Diaries*.)

Guggenheim and Stallone became fast friends. She took a percentage in commission on their deals. "He bought some really terrific things," she says, "and wasn't collecting what other people were. It fit his personality. He was also taking advantage of undervalued markets, as well as well-established ones." She bought him Delvaux's *Les Extravagances d'Athènes* for $325,000 (he sold it three years later for nearly $1.5 million), a Bourdelle *Hercules* for $304,000 (they sold it for $1.6 million), and Magritte's *Les Bons Jours de Monsieur Ingres* for $178,000 (which they resold for more than half a million dollars). In all, Guggenheim estimates that her purchases and resales earned him more than $3 million in profits.

. . . . .

In 1989, however, Stallone and his collection became the subject of litigation when he and Guggenheim were sued by Anthony d'Offay Gallery in London and when Stallone in turn sued Guggenheim and Pivar. At the heart of the disputes were two paintings – the Bouguereau *Pietà* and *Oedipus and the Sphinx (After Ingres)*, a valuable 1983 work by the British artist Francis Bacon.

Stallone bought the Bacon before he met Guggenheim and the Bouguereau *Pietà* in 1988. Depicting the Virgin Mary and the dead body of Christ surrounded by a band of angels, the *Pietà* cost him $1,785,000 and came from Pivar's collection. Pivar, who had purchased it "for a low six figures" in France fifteen years earlier, had had it restored and had been trying to sell it for years. (Prior to Stallone's interest in the piece, pop star Michael Jackson had shown interest in buying either the *Pietà* or another Bouguereau in Pivar's collection. But Pivar was never home when Jackson called to see the paintings, so Jackson went elsewhere.)

Extremely proud of both his Bacon and his Bouguereau, Stallone announced that he would never part with either. Early in 1989, however, smarting from his Kiefer experience, he told Guggenheim to put both paintings on the market. "He stopped collecting," according to Guggenheim, "because he was perspicacious enough to think it was time to cash out. He had a sense that the market had crested." Stallone says, "I started to get a little tired of the pieces" and explains that he decided to "invest in newer, younger artists instead of buying blue chip, because I don't think that does anything to promote the growth of art. It's like selling the same car over and over again and no one gets to build a new model."

He packed the Kiefer, Bacon, Bouguereau, and a few other paintings off to New York for Guggenheim to sell. She priced the Bacon at $2 million and found a buyer for it in dealer Anthony d'Offay. D'Offay, lacking the funds, cut in his colleague Massimo Martino, an art investor who owns Danae Art International Inc., which is incorporated in Panama and headquartered in Lugano, Switzerland. Hoping to flip the Bacon for as much as four or five million dollars, d'Offay anxiously awaited its delivery.

As the events are recounted in the suit brought by d'Offay and Danae against Stallone and Guggenheim, no sooner had the buyers declared their interest in the Bacon than New York art dealer Larry Gagosian approached Stallone with a better offer of $2.07 million. In his legal defense, Stallone verifies this. Gagosian, however, denies it and claims that Stallone approached him, asking him to sell the painting and not the other way around. Gagosian also says that he could have gotten much more than $2.07 million. He already had a buyer – Keith Barish, the movie producer and chairman of Planet Hollywood and for years an important collector and client of Gagosian's. Learning of the competition from Gagosian, d'Offay increased his offer to $2,125,000 in cash.

At this point, things got messy. Stallone calls it "a major case of miscommunication" and claims that he had already made a deal with Gagosian and Barish. But Guggenheim says, "I felt honor bound for d'Offay to get it because I had made a deal. My reputation was at stake."

Stallone was in Cincinnati filming *Tango and Cash* when Guggenheim told d'Offay that the Bacon – which was in storage in New York – could be his. D'Offay sent her a check; she deducted her commission of $55,000 and sent her own check to Stallone's office, where it was deposited in his absence. She told Stallone, according to him, that the sale had been made and that the Bacon was on its way to d'Offay in London, so when he learned that the painting was actually still in New York, he saw red. His lawyers returned a check to Guggenheim, she refused it, the sale came to a standstill, and the Bacon stayed locked in its warehouse. Barish and Gagosian dropped out. "He couldn't deliver," Barish says of Stallone, "so what could we do?"

Stallone was embarrassed, and on August 7, exactly one month after d'Offay's original offer, he dismissed Guggenheim as his art adviser. And on September 1, d'Offay and Danae sued the pair of them for the painting, damages, and legal fees.

"I should have been a little bit more observant," Stallone says today. "I should have listened to my conscience, and I should have been a little less frivolous with my delegating of authority – meaning Barbara. And from that time on, I have handled all my matters myself. I don't use an agent. Not at all. I had some good times with Barbara. I had some bad times." Worse times were to come.

Stallone's accountant at the time, Tony Low, who had also worked for Guggenheim, was being told that Stallone had been overcharged for the Kiefer. And now Stallone and Guggenheim were badly at odds over the Bacon. So Low tried to go through the books to see if Guggenheim was getting kickbacks on her purchases. (He found nothing.) When it came to the Bouguereau, however, he remained sure that things were amiss. After all, Guggenheim had obtained it from her boyfriend, Pivar, sold it to Stallone without his ever having seen it, induced him to pay a record price for it, and then taken a commission of $85,000 on the sale.

Pivar and Guggenheim counter that the sale of the *Pietà* was the only sale Guggenheim ever made from Pivar's collection. They also point out that $1,785,000 compares favorably with prices fetched for other works by the artist. (The collector Fred Koch paid more than a million dollars each for two Bouguereaus four years before Stallone's purchase, and New York's Borghi & Co. Fine Art Dealers are currently asking $1.8 million for the artist's *Petites maraudeuses*.) Moreover, Pivar says that when he purchased the work, he set a record price for Bouguereau, that the *Pietà* was of great sentimental value to the painter himself, who drew inspiration for it from the untimely death of his son, and that it had fetched the highest price that Bouguereau ever got for a painting in his lifetime. "It's Bouguereau's masterpiece," proclaims Pivar.

Low continued to be suspicious and cast about for someone to appraise the *Pietà*. He was introduced to Bruce Gimelson, an antiques/autographs/paintings appraiser, as well as the host of *What's It Worth*, a live phone-in appraisals program that was on Manhattan Cable TV's channel J. Low hired Gimelson to look at the painting under a black light and to make a written estimate of its worth. Gimelson's findings, dated August 18, 1989, were grim.

First of all, he said, the canvas had been slashed. Furthermore, "25 to 30 per cent of the painting has been restored or retouched, and it has been relined under enormous pressure resulting in an unnatural flat appearance." Gimelson also declared that the Christian subject matter of the painting was not popular and that when Bouguereau's paintings reach more than five to six feet in height, "the already shaky market in his works declines." He concluded that he doubts "if it would exceed $300,000 at a well-attended auction."

Stallone felt betrayed by Guggenheim – and was heard to say that he "wanted to rip her head off and shit down her throat." And Gagosian, who was observing the action from the wings, possibly hoping to win the actor as a client, invited Stallone to move the *Pietà* from the Manhattan warehouse where Guggenheim had stored it to the Gagosian Gallery on Madison Avenue. There it was seen by the pop star Madonna and her art adviser, Darlene Lutz.

When Madonna saw the *Pietà*, she fell in love with it, although Lutz was cautious. "Its faults read from across a football field," says Lutz. "I had also heard it wasn't in great condition. It looked beautiful but had extensive restorations, more than ten per cent. Knowing Bouguereau's market and the subject and the size all meant that the asking price of $1,785,000 was too high." Lutz says she had an independent condition report made on the painting. It approximated her own, and she advised Madonna to offer less than half a million dollars. Madonna did and was turned down. Through all this, Lutz says that Stallone "felt embarrassed and humiliated. He was being made to look like he was not an astute collector."

That October, the journalist Stuart Greenspan, who was an old school friend of Guggenheim's from Columbia University and associate of Pivar's for fifteen years, wrote an article in the *New York Observer* based partly on information provided by Lutz. It claimed that Stallone was a collector with a "decidedly checkered taste," that Bouguereau was a "bombastic" painter, that Pivar had purchased the *Pietà* for "$20,000 ... just a few years ago," and that "Gagosian ... if he is trying to get his foot into Mr. Stallone's door, ought just to take a loss ... because $1.75 million for a Bouguereau ... is just ridiculous." Pivar and Guggenheim were shocked that Greenspan, who was suffering from AIDS and had only months to live, would turn on them. Pivar nevertheless threatened to sue him and the *New York Observer*, and on November 15, Greenspan published a correction, retraction, and apology.

But Stallone had heard enough and called his lawyers. On December 26, with d'Offay's suit over the Bacon painting still unsettled, Stallone sued Guggenheim and Pivar for fraud, negligent misrepresentation, breach of fiduciary duty, and breach of contract. (Guggenheim says she learned about the suit when she picked up the newspaper.) Based on Gimelson's appraisal, Stallone claimed that the *Pietà* was "substantially damaged and had several large slashes in it" and charged that Guggenheim "acted willfully, maliciously and oppressively, and with a conscious disregard of the rights and property of the Plaintiff." He also sued fifty unknown defendants named John Doe who may have been behind her other acquisitions or sales for him and claimed a total of $35 million in all causes of action.

Today, the actor/painter/art collector and rather frequent litigant says he sued because there was suddenly a controversy around the *Pietà*: "I asked if the allegations were true, and I'm waiting for a response, and nothing happened. So a little pressure had to be applied."

Guggenheim found herself an attorney on the West Coast. She hired entertainment lawyer Bert Fields and countersued Stallone for defamation. She says she felt too saddened to work, and Pivar says the suit almost ruined her. "I'll tell you one thing," says Stallone. "Everyone was really reveling in the babbling of all the other dealers, saying that there's one less person ... less competition."

Fields hired four condition experts and consulted a Bouguereau expert, Mark Borghi from the Borghi gallery, who all soundly contradicted Gimelson's appraisal. And Gimelson himself amended his appraisal and said that what he thought were slashes in the painting were folds. Beside himself with anger, Pivar called Gimelson on his TV show and confronted him on the air. "He's an appraiser of books and old kettles," explains Pivar hotly, "and he defamed Bouguereau's masterpiece!"

The dust settled last year. Guggenheim's and Pivar's lawyers were able to demonstrate that the *Pietà* was not damaged or restored more than is acceptable in a nineteenth-century painting, and Stallone agreed to accept another Bouguereau, the patriotic *Alma Parens*, also from Pivar's collection, in exchange for the *Pietà*. According to Stallone, Pivar said, "Do you love this one better?" And Stallone said, "Actually, I do love this one better. Let me take it, and you take this one back." They traded and settled in October.

The suit over the Bacon was also settled in October. Stallone and d'Offay held a silent auction in which they both bid for the painting. D'Offay lost it (but was financially reimbursed).

Guggenheim was allowed to keep her commission on the sales of both the Bacon and the *Pietà*. And Pivar, who can't decide if he lost or won, gallantly declares that "if the truth be known, *I* won because I ended up with the better painting." (Both paintings are, however, currently on view at the Borghi gallery; the *Alma Parens* is priced at $2.8 million, the *Pietà* for a little more than half of that.)

During the heat of the litigation, Guggenheim was seen in public displaying affection with Fields — who, in addition to being a lawyer, writes pseudonymous novels about the sexual escapades of a racy West Coast attorney. Casting a novelist's

eye over the resolution of the entire drama, Fields says coolly, "Everyone got something. Barbara got what I consider a complete vindication. Stuart got a splendid painting from Stallone, and Stallone got a new Bouguereau from Stuart. D'Offay got a big check, and all the lawyers got their fees. But I got the most valuable thing of all. I got Barbara." They married in February.

And Stallone got to bring home the Bacon. "I have it. It's going on that wall," he says, gesturing to the one blank space in his house. "It's an incredible painting," he adds. "How it almost got away from me, I'm not sure at all."

. . . . .

Today Stallone is back in the art-world ring. He suffered a few knockouts, but as proof of his commitment to art, he is scouring the galleries again this season, often accompanied by Ruth and Jake Bloom, and buying quantities of works by young or unknown artists. Like Rocky, he lost his first fights but is gamely coming back for more. There may be endless sequels. ●

JEFF KOONS 1991

Jeff Koons and the Art of Public Relations

THE NEW YORK TIMES OCTOBER 1991

Although it doesn't open until November 16, Jeff Koons's exhibition at the Sonnabend Gallery in the SoHo section of Manhattan is already a *succès de scandale*. The sculptures and paintings all depict the plain-looking artist with his glamorous new wife, the Italian former porn star and Radical Party parliamentary deputy, Ilona Staller, more famously known as Cicciolina.

In the show's hard-core sexual tableaux, the newlyweds wear little clothing, exhibit even fewer inhibitions, and leave nothing to the imagination. They also display an anatomical prowess that looks like a mix of Hieronymous Bosch and Dr. Seuss. When the exhibition opens, there will be guards at the doors, and anyone under eighteen will be turned away.

While both Koons and Cicciolina make a point of espousing sexual freedom, they also stand to capitalize on recent debates about art and obscenity. So far, their ploy is a success, and profiles of the artist and his bride in *Connoisseur* and *Vanity Fair* are already celebrating what promises to be his newest media breakthrough. While there is an eighty-year tradition for stunts like Koons's, his new show (of factory-crafted sculptures of glass, marble and wood, and machine-made paintings derived from photographs) is a public relations triumph overshadowing all his previous attempts at notoriety.

The 36-year-old post-Pop artist has rarely been out of the face of the art world since he made his widely publicized SoHo debut at Sonnabend in 1986. Since then, his works have been acquired by museums around the world, including the Museum of Modern Art in New York, and prices for them have exceeded $400,000. A few years ago, he bought advertisements in art magazines and billboard space around Manhattan that trumpeted his forthcoming exhibitions as well as his blossoming affair with Cicciolina.

Then, when the pair exchanged vows in Europe last summer, their picture graced the cover of the Italian weekly magazine *Oggi* and, according to the artist, "somewhere around a thousand" articles followed. Hungry for more, he says he also tried to get *People* magazine to cover the wedding. (The magazine passed.)

Koons says he does not seek publicity for its own sake but so that he can "better prepare the public for what my work is about." In recent years, as he has become increasingly successful, he has mutated from being an attention-grabbing telephone salesman to a seemingly soulless creation who speaks in a low, robotic monotone. He shies away from direct questions and speaks in non sequiturs: "I don't think being effective in the world and taking responsibility to be effective is cynical. If you don't do it, someone else will."

Jeffrey Dietch, a New York critic, curator and art advisor, supports Koons's disclaimer. "Koons is not looking for publicity," he says, "despite the fact that he has probably got more press than anyone since Warhol. He's looking to communicate his aesthetic views. It's incidental that everything he does makes for a good news story."

With the exception of the artist Mark Kostabi (who, like Koons, emerged in the East Village art scene in the early 1980s and also, through his subject matter, frequently mocks the people who buy his art), nobody is more aggressively seeking to imitate Andy Warhol as the joker of the art-world pack than Koons. "I try to communicate that you don't need to be intelligent," he said in a recent telephone interview from Munich, where he lives part of the year. "Just to be clever is enough."

Like Warhol's, Jeff Koons's professional persona suggests that to be seen is to exist. He employs two clipping services and an assistant to collect the enormous number of articles published about him from around the globe. ("I do it to get the best possible picture of myself," he explains.) Like Warhol too, he uses cartoon characters and appropriated imagery in his art, and for this he is at present appealing a pair of lawsuits brought against him for copyright infringement.

. . . . .

Next month's exhibition may be the baldest attempt yet by an artist to stake a claim on the mass media's imaginary Mount Olympus. But Koons is far from alone among artists making moves in the world of public relations. In the last five years art and general-interest magazines have been filled with ads that show artists. They are of two kinds: there are those paid for by artists who are promoting their careers, and those that feature an artist promoting some fashionable consumer product. In the mainstream marketplace, artists make effective and attractive salespeople with a keen understanding of visual drama and sufficient name-recognition to lend an edge to mundane products like T-shirts and drinks. Many artists are also hiring press agents.

The liaison between art and public relations, far from being a sign of postmodern decadence, is actually as old as modernism itself. For decades, artists have ventured into advertising and merchandising in magazines and store windows. Originally, mixing art with public relations was a way to circumvent the elitism of the art world. Today, however, it is testimony to the profitable convergence of postmodernist irony and aggressive marketing.

In 1909, the Italian art impresario Filippo Tommaso Marinetti published his first Futurist manifesto as a paid advertisement in the Paris newspaper *Le Figaro*. The next year, a band of Futurist painters and poets dropped 800,000 fliers from the top of the Clock Tower in Venice into the crowds below, and numerous other Futurist pronouncements were published in newspapers and magazines throughout Europe throughout the 1910s and '20s.

By excelling at what Marinetti called "the art of writing manifestoes" and appropriating the format of political bulletins, the Futurists modernized the ways artists got their ideas across. They put forth the radical proposition that the distribution of an artist's work was as valuable as its content. And they guessed, correctly, that to capture an audience, artists would have to compete with such expanding mass communications as books and magazines, photography and cinema, radio and the telegraph. In fact, they brilliantly anticipated a new, modern phenomenon – the great hordes of art consumers.

· · · · ·

Nowadays, of course, capturing that art audience is big business. For museums, the practice of hiring corporate public relations firms to publicize their fragile masterpieces proved its effectiveness long ago. But for individual artists, adding promotional stunts concocted by press agents to the sales efforts of their dealers is fairly new. (Some artists even use an agent to hook a dealer.) Only recently have the country's biggest public relations companies – Hill & Knowlton, Ruder Finn, and Howard J. Rubenstein among them – begun accepting artists as clients. They charge around $5,000 for a year's promotion, or $2,000 for a specific exhibition.

In 1984, the Los Angeles Pop artist Ed Ruscha hired Livet Reichard, a small New York artists' public relations company. Within a couple of years, Ruscha's movie-star good looks were seen in ads in magazines and on bus shelters all over the United States. He modeled a suit in an ad for Barneys New York, and was invited by the photographer Herb Ritts to become the first "celebrity" sitter for the Gap. Better still, a retrospective of his paintings – arranged by Anne Livet, president of Livet Reichard and a former curator – toured museums in Europe and California. The company spares the artist a lot of footwork. "There's a certain amount of business that comes with being an artist," says Ruscha. "But as time wears on, having a PR agent means I can take more vacations."

Livet Reichard circulates press releases, makes deals, and lines up clients with galleries and collectors here and abroad, and receives works of art as payment (which are then sold privately to avoid competition with the artists' galleries). In addition to Ruscha, Livet Reichard represents the Conceptual artist Joseph Kosuth, whose collected writings are being published this month by MIT Press as a result of a deal clinched by Anne Livet. The company also helped launch the career of Nayland Blake, a San Francisco artist who will have an exhibition next March at the Mary Boone Gallery.

· · · · ·

It was another Futurist, the painter and designer Fortunato Depero, who first saw the potential for the store windows on Fifth Avenue to double as little art galleries, and claimed them as "Futurist." In 1939, Salvador Dali decorated Bonwit Teller's windows. Marcel Duchamp followed suit in Paris two years later. And in 1961, Warhol held his very first exhibition behind Bonwit Teller's glass.

Today store windows are an actual alternative to the gallery system – for what are galleries, after all, but glorified shops? According to Gene Moore, the display director of Tiffany & Company, who has hired artists (including Robert Rauschenberg, Jasper Johns, and Warhol) to decorate windows at Bonwit Teller and Tiffany's since the 1950s, "artists use store windows as PR for themselves. They also make sales from them."

Back in the 1930s, Depero also said that "the art of the future will tend strongly towards advertising" and designed a ground-breaking series of ads for Campari (which are the predecessors for the recent Absolut Vodka campaigns designed by Warhol, Keith Haring, Ruscha and dozens of other artists).

In 1974, the post-Minimalist artist Lynda Benglis bought a two-page ad in *Artforum* magazine and displayed herself wearing nothing but a pair of sunglasses and a dildo. (This was before anyone had heard of Cicciolina.) She claims that the image was intended as a takeoff of the media at a politically volatile time.

"Artists became sensitive to media manipulations largely because of Watergate," she says. "Nixon's resignation alerted a lot of us to the media's power and methods." The image also turned her into the subject of an instant art-world controversy.

A handful of others also bought ads for themselves in *Artforum*. Today, ads by artists that promote themselves appear in magazines all over the world and also on television. Last year Marilyn Minter, a painter, bought time on *Nightline*, *David Letterman* and *Arsenio Hall* to advertise her forthcoming exhibition. Minter says she found it cheaper than advertising in the art magazines.

In the mid-eighties, shrewd advertising companies recognized that the idea of art as a commodity had reached critical mass, and started to seek out artists to endorse their merchandise. Led by a campaign for the Japanese fashion house Comme des Garçons featuring artists in Comme threads photographed by Timothy Greenfield-Sanders, they helped turn artists into celebrities.

But to many of the artists who toy with advertising, Jeff Koons among them, "selling out" is a virtue, a backhanded way of stirring artistic rebellion. It is a post-Pop, post-punk pose that defies the traditional notions of what artists and art should be — poor and unknown. Peddling an image of themselves in the manner of a movie star not only promises to make artists famous; it also allows them to thumb their noses at the assumption that art is somehow above the marketplace.

· · · · ·

Moreover, superstars like Koons are dealing with a mob audience that, despite the recession, is clamoring for artistic gratification. What the Futurists knew, and what Picasso understood when he painted the sensationalistic *Guernica*, is that artists have to orchestrate media blitzes if they want to take their messages to the masses.

But the art historian Rosalind Krauss draws a distinction. "Artists' interest in using the media against itself was formerly subversive and parodic, beginning with Dadaism," she says. "Koons, on the other hand, is not exploiting the media for avant-garde purposes. He's in cahoots with the media. He has no message. It's self-advertisement and I find that repulsive."

Some art lovers are also offended by practices that flout clichés about poverty-stricken artists and notions of art as a privilege reserved for the few. But public relations is here to stay. Sensationalism and merchandising keep art-world debates heated, while also alerting audiences to underlying commercial interests in the art world. Public relations is also good for business and great for certain artists, although the question remains of whether it's good for art. Ultimately — or as soon as next month — Jeff Koons may discover that unadorned self-promotion is less successful at raising the art world's eyebrows (or its libido) than its hackles. ●

LOU REED 1994

The Velvet Underground presents Andy Warhol

THE VILLAGE VOICE JULY 1990

Around the time Andy Warhol discovered the Velvet Underground, Lou Reed and John Cale were selling their blood for money. But when they left France last week, guest stars of the Cartier Foundation's Andy Warhol exhibitions, their wrists were wrapped in gold Cartier watches.

Throughout his entire career, Warhol appealed to the transformative powers of gold – in tacky gold pictures of shoes, Marilyns, and splotches of oxidized piss. When it came to the Velvet Underground, however, his Midas touch was a bit limp. Warhol's stint as producer of the Velvet Underground in 1966 left the band members as poor as he found them. "Andy's commercial art work supported the shows," says Reed, "but nobody got any money from any of our records until two or three years ago." Unfortunately Reed's and Cale's saga doesn't end there. *Songs for Drella*, their recently released song cycle about Warhol, is also failing to spin yarns into gold.

It was gold that decided the Cartier Foundation to mount a Velvet Underground exhibition (through September 2 at the Cartier Foundation, Jouy-en-Josas, France). Initially, the Foundation wanted to sponsor the Paris showing of the large traveling Andy Warhol retrospective organized by the Museum of Modern Art. But in the light of sanctions against South Africa, gold – the setting for Cartier's glittering image since 1847 – has recently become the source of a garish image problem.

In 1986, Cartier's involvement with a handful of unsavory South African companies became the target of a piece by Hans Haacke, *Les Must de Rembrandt*, exhibited in Dijon, France. As Haacke cited in the work, Cartier is part-owned by Rothmans International, which in turn is part of the Rembrandt Group, which owns a large stake in GENCOR, a major South African gold miner that has been declared an "enemy company" by the National Union of Mine Workers in South Africa for its brutal treatment of miners. Haacke also stated that in 1984, as Rothmans's stake in Cartier increased from 21 per cent to 46 per cent, Cartier announced the formation of the Cartier Foundation for Contemporary Art, the implication being that contemporary art is a smoke screen for the company's less pretty handiwork in South Africa. (In defense, Cartier's president, Alain-Dominique Perrin, told me that he counted seventeen errors of fact in Haacke's research.)

Last year, as the Cartier Foundation was angling to sponsor the Andy Warhol retrospective at the Pompidou Center in Paris, the center staged a survey of Haacke's works, including *Les Must de Rembrandt*. And from here, gold started to wreak its terrible transformative powers. According to Perrin, a staffer at the Pompidou Center informed Cartier that the museum "didn't want South African money." Bernard Blistène, the curator-in-chief in charge of the Warhol retrospective at the Pompidou, corroborates the story, saying that an entire committee at the museum decided against Cartier's offer. "There was a real contradiction in accepting funding from Cartier when we had a show last year by Hans Haacke that criticized the connection between Cartier and South Africa," says Blistène. "We would look ridiculous if we took their money. In any case, we didn't really need it." Deciding to mount its own Warhol exhibitions in the foundation's grounds and exhibition spaces thirty minutes outside Paris, Cartier withdrew its offer.

Marie-Claude Beaud, director and curator of the Cartier Foundation for Contemporary Art, quickly swung into action and created Cartier's own Warholfest entitled "The Andy Warhol System: Pub [short for 'publicity'], Pop, Rock." Her solution was three-fold: she netted "Success Is a Job in New York," the touring show of Warhol's pre-Pop art. She lassoed MoMA's show of 85 Warhol screen prints in return for Cartier's commitment to sponsor the show's tour through Czechoslovakia, East Germany, Hungary, Yugoslavia, and Poland. And she hit on the idea of a show of Velvet Underground memorabilia comprising photographs, films, record covers, T-shirts, handbills, and posters.

To her credit, the Cartier Foundation's three exhibitions emphasize crucial aspects of Warhol's work that are overlooked by the big show at the Pompidou. The prints exhibition, moreover, will present art lovers in the Eastern bloc with a curious new business-art triumvirate: Warhol Enterprises, MoMA, and Cartier. All this, plus the surprise reunion of the Velvet Underground for five hundred invited guests from the international mass media and art world, made for an uproarious public relations triumph. (When I asked if the Velvet Underground was being used to burnish Cartier's image, Reed replied, "I performed at the Nelson Mandela concert in London one or two months ago, so I'm not worried about my credentials.")

Twenty-five years ago, not even Warhol would have imagined that Cartier would sponsor a rock band that wrote songs about heroin, sadomasochism, and transvestism, that used trash cans as drums, incorporated electronic feedback into its melodies, and whose records were banned. But everything has been transformed by some strange alchemy since 1966, when corporate sponsorship of contemporary art was tested for the first time (interestingly, it was a show of "Pop and Op" sponsored by Philip Morris).

Today, the children of the counterculture are Cartier's chicest customers. Publicity, not silence, is golden. And the Underground is strictly for miners only. ●

Bibliography

MAGAZINE AND NEWSPAPER ARTICLES

Unless stated, all publications are New York based
and/or English language editions

1993 162 "Cumulus From America," *Parkett* 35, Zurich, Winter (prev. unpubl. paper given at
the panel discussion "The Critic in the Mirror" at the Whitney Museum in 1986).

161 "Art on the Barricades," *Outrage* 113, Melbourne, October (publ. in full in this volume
as "The Activist Art Revival"; see Books no. 9, below).

160 Keith Haring book review, *Art & Text* 43, Sydney, September.

159 "Richard Prince, Art's Bad Boy, Becomes (Partly) Respectable," *The New York Times*,
Arts & Leisure, May 17.

158 "The Poet of Water and Stone," *The New York Times Book Review*, May 3.

157 "Leo Castelli in His 85th Year: A Lion in Winter," *The New York Times*, Arts & Leisure, February 16.

1991 156 "A Seeming Paradox," *The New York Times*, Letters, Arts & Leisure, December 8.

155 "Educating Rocky," *Connoisseur* (cover story), December.

154 "Time is Money," *Connoisseur*, November.

153 "The Art of Public Relations and Public Relations of Art," *The New York Times*,
Arts & Leisure, October 27.

152 "Marden's Metamorphosis," *Connoisseur*, October.

151 "SoHo's Avant-Guardian," *Connoisseur*, September.

150 "Love Story," *Connoisseur*, August (ed. version repr. in *Outrage* 106, Melbourne,
March 1992, cover story).

149 "How MTV Plays Around The World," *The New York Times*, Arts & Leisure, July 7.

148 "James Rosenquist," *Parkett* 28, Summer.

147 "Ellsworth Kelly," *Interview*, June (publ. in full in *Artstudio*, special Kelly issue, Paris, March 1992).

146 "Love/Aids/Riot/Fuck," *Culture* magazine, Sydney, June 17 (includes reprints of
nos. 143 and 144, below).

145 "Cindy Sherman, Old Master," *Art & Text* 39, May.

144 "Love: Robert Indiana," *Interview*, April.

143 "Fury: Marlene McCarty," *Interview*, April.

142 "The Norton Museum," *Flash Art* (News), Milan, March-April.

141 "Rauschenberg Recalls Warhol as the Pioneer," *The New York Times*, Letters, January 18.

140 "Peter Nagy," *Flash Art*, Milan, January-February.

139 "Wexner Center, Ohio," *Flash Art* (News), January-February.

138 "Canary Islands Museum," *Flash Art* (News), January-February.

137 "The Art of the Deal: Jeffrey Deitch," *Interview*, January.

1990 136 "Robert Rauschenberg," *Interview*, December (repr. *Tension* 24, January; and
Atelier magazine, Tokyo, Spring 1991).

135 "Life Size in the Holy Land," *Flash Art* (News), November-December.

134 "AIDS Guerrillas," *New York*, November 5-12 (repr. in *HQ* magazine, Sydney, March 1991).

133 "Ozone Schmozone: Alan Belcher," *Interview*, November.

132 "Art Down Under," *HG* (formerly *House and Garden*), Sydney, November.

131 "Mike Kelley," *Flash Art*, October.

130 "More Andy," *The New York Times Book Review*, August 26 (repr. in *Tension*, March-April 1991).

129 "Joe Weider—The Brains Behind the Brawn," *Interview*, September.

128 "The 'Indomitable Spirit' in Miami," *Flash Art* (News), Summer.

127 "The Golden Underground," *The Village Voice*, July 3-10 (repr. in *Art & Text* 37, September).

126 "Jasper Johns," *Interview*, July (repr. in *Tension* 23, November).

125 "Rover Thomas," *Interview*, June.

124 "Mike Kelley," *Interview*, April.

123 "The Merits of Merz," *HG*, March.

122 "Jenny Holzer, *Flash Art*, March-April.

121 "Sandra Bernhard," *Interview*, March.

120 "Post-Pop Art," *Art & Design*, London (ed. repr. of "Introduction," *Post-Pop Art*,
see Books no. 6, below).

119 "Athens (review)," *Artscribe*, London, January-February.

118 "Bronx Revival," *Vogue*, January (repr. in *Wellspring* 2/6, Sarasota, Fl.).

1989 117 "Interview: Roy Lichtenstein," *Flash Art* (cover story), September-October (repr. in *Tension* 22,
August-September 1990).

116 "In France, the Remembrance of Things Present," *The New York Times*, Arts & Leisure, August 27.

115 "Lichtenstein's Latest is a Perfectly Pop Thing to Do," *The New York Times*, Arts & Leisure, July 9.

114 "Return of the Native," *Time Out's 20-20*, London, July.

113 "Charlotte Moorman," *Yoko Only* newsletter 25, July.

112 "Tribal Dreamings for a Jaded Art Market," *The New York Times*, Arts & Leisure, May 21
(repr. in parts in *The Sydney Morning Herald*, January 13, 1990).

111 "The Impresario of Punk," *Tension* 14, May.

110 "Spotlight: Haim Steinbach," *Flash Art*, June.

109 "East Side Story," *Vogue*, May (repr. in *Studio Voice* 10, Tokyo, October).

108 "Mad Max's," *Fame*, May.

107 "Art for Art's Sake," *The New York Times*, Arts & Leisure, March 12.

106 "Face to Face to Face with Cindy Sherman," *New York Woman*, March (repr. in *Tension* 17).

105 "Yoko Ono's New Bronze Age at the Whitney," *The New York Times*, Arts & Leisure, February 5.

104 "Carnegie International," *Flash Art*, January-February.

103 "The Resurrection of Jean-Michel Basquiat," *Fame*, January.

1988 102 "Rose's Colored Glasses," *Fame*, December.

101 "We Are the Word—Jenny Holzer," *Vogue*, November.

100 "Anselm Kiefer—Painter of the Apocalyse," *The New York Times Magazine*,
October 16 (syndicated).

99 "Stella," *Fame*, premiere issue, November.

98 "Interview: Richard Prince," *Flash Art*, October.

97 "Object Lessons," *HG*, October.

96 "Bigger Crowds Head for Smaller Spaces," *The New York Times*, Arts & Leisure, July 17.

95 "Making Faces—Scavullo's Portrait Factory," *7 Days*, June 22.

94 "Robert Mapplethorpe's Climax," *Tension* 13 (cover story), June (uncredited version publ.
in *American Photographer*, January).

93 "Sonnabend's Shadow," *The Village Voice*, May 24.

92 "Cultural Geometry," *Flash Art*, May-June.

91 "What's New in Australian Art," *The New York Times*, Arts & Leisure, April 24.

90 "Lights, Action, Easel," *The New York Times*, Arts & Leisure, February 21 (syndicated).

89 "Instantly Notorious," *The New York Times Book Review*, January 10 (repr. in *Tension* 13, June).

88 "Gossip and Glory," *Follow Me*, Sydney, January.

1987 87 "Gilbert & George & Everyman," *Parkett* 14 (cover story), December.

86 "Speech Acts—Tokens of the 1980s," *Eau de Cologne*, Cologne, November.

85 "Interview: Donald Baechler," *Flash Art*, October.

84 "How Europe Sold the Idea of Postmodern Art," *The Village Voice*, September 22 (repr. in
Australian Art Monthly, Sydney, November).

83 "My Art Belongs to Dada," *The Observer Magazine*, London, September 6.

82 "Paul Taylor Plays with Sherrie Levine," *Flash Art* (cover story), Summer (repr. in Books no. 7, below).

81 "Samuel Beckett and Vito Acconci," *Review of Contemporary Fiction*, Indiana University,
Summer (ed. repr. of no. 14, below).

80 "Changing in Midstream," *Manhattan, inc.*, May.

79 "Interview: Donald Judd," *Flash Art*, May.

78 "Where the Girls Are," *Manhattan, inc.*, April.

77 "Andy Warhol—The Last Interview," Flash Art (cover story), April (repr. in full in *Flash Art*
Russian edition, 1989; in part in *The National Times*, Melbourne, and in Books nos. 7 & 8, below).

76 "Conversations with Art Dealers: Metro Pictures," *Flash Art*, April.

75 "Jannis Kounellis," *Flash Art*, April.

74 "Stampede," *Manhattan, inc.*, March.

73 "Art Dealers: Akira Ikeda," *Galeries*, Paris, February-March.

72 "The Castelli Museum," *Manhattan, inc.*, February (repr. in *X-Press*, Sydney, September;
and *Wolkenkratzer*, Frankfurt, March-April).

71 "How David Salle Mixes High Art and Trash," *The New York Times Magazine*, January 11
(syndicated *The International Herald Tribune* and others; repr. in *Tension* 14, September 1988).

1986 70 "The Hot Four," *New York*, October 20-27 (repr. in *X-Press*, November 1987;
and *Artstudio* 11, Paris, with an introduction by Ann Hindry, Winter 1988).

69 "Dial 1-718-Next Wave," *Manhattan, inc.*, November.

68 "A Vox on You," *Manhattan, inc.*, October.

67 "The Disney State," *File* magazine, Toronto, and *Art & Text*, Melbourne, joint issue, Summer.

66 "Editorial," *File* and *Art & Text* joint issue, Summer.

65 "The Return of Conceptual Art," *Parkett* 9, July.

64 "Boone's Groom," *Manhattan, inc.*, June (repr. in *Tension*, March; and
Safe, Amsterdam, April, 1987).

63 "Intro column," *The Face*, London, June.

62 "Intro column," *The Face*, May.

61 "Café Deutschland: Art in Germany after Neo-Expressionism," *ARTnews* (cover story), April.

60 "Malcolm McLaren: Pop's Smoking Pistol," *Vogue*, April.

59 "Interview: Joseph Kosuth," *Flash Art*, April (repr. in *Collected Interviews with Joseph Kosuth*,
see Books no. 5, below).

58 "She's A Mod," *Manhattan, inc.*, March.

57 "Interview: Hans Haacke," *Flash Art*, March.

56 "New York (reviews)," *Flash Art*, March.

55 "Conversation with Art Dealers: Nature Morte," *Flash Art*, March.

54 "A New Avenue for Art—Madison," *Vogue*, February.

53 "Interview: James Lee Byars," *Flash Art*, January.

52 "Robert Mapplethorpe and the Material World," *Follow Me*, January.

1985 51 "Kramer vs. Kramer," *Manhattan, inc.*, December.

50 "Mixmasters," *Art & Text* 19, Melbourne, November (repr. in *GS* magazine, Tokyo).

49 "Wet Paint," *Manhattan, inc.*, November.

48 "Interview: Cindy Sherman," *Flash Art*, November.

47 "Art After Modernism (book review)," *Flash Art*, November.

46 "Intro column," *The Face*, October.

45 "Sturm und Trash: Jiri Georg Dokoupil and the Cologne art scene," *Interview*, October.

44 "Intro column," *The Face*, September.

43 "Ventriloquists' Dummies," *The National Times*, Sydney, September 13-19.

42 "Fallout Art," *Vanity Fair*, July.

41 "IsolAustralia," *Domus*, Milan, May-June (repr. of Catalogues no. 15, below).

40 "Clemente Comes of Age," *Vanity Fair*, March.

39 "Andy Leaks to the Press," *Vanity Fair*, February.

38 "Civilisation and Its Discontents," *Flash Art*, January (repr. in *Tension*, September).

1984 37 "A Culture of Temporary Culture," *Art & Text* 16, December (repr. of Catalogues no. 14, below).

36 "On Photo-Rhetoric," *Bulletin*, Institute of Modern Art, Brisbane (repr. of Catalogues no. 13, below).

35 "Today a DJ Saved My Life (editorial)," *ZG*, London, and *Art & Text* 15,
joint issue "Double Trouble," September.

34 "Pirates and Mutineers," *Express*, New York, August, (repr. of Catalogues no. 7, below).

33 "John Nixon: Self Portrait," *Express*, August (repr. of Catalogues no. 8, below).

32 Panel contribution of art writing at the Festival of Adelaide published in *Artlink*, Adelaide, July.

31 "Editorial," *Art & Text* 14, July.

30 "Transavantgarde International (book review)," *Art & Text* 14, July.

29 "Juan Davila," *Outrage*, Melbourne, May (repr. of Catalogues no. 10, below; repr. also in *Studio International*, London; *Hysterical Tears*, Books no. 3, below; and *The Advocate* magazine, Los Angeles, January 21, 1986).

1983 28 "From Deserts the Profits Come," *Art Press*, Paris, October.

27 "Art News," *Vogue Australia*, Sydney, October.

26 "Items on the Menu," *Art & Text* 10, July.

25 "The Instrumentality of Dick Watkins," *Art & Text* 12/13, July.

24 "Querelle" (with Adrian Martin), *Tension*, May (repr. in *ZG*, 1984).

23 "The Men of Tom of Finland," *Stuff*, Melbourne, April.

22 "POPISM: The Art of White Aborigines," *Flash Art*, May (repr. in *On the Beach*, premier issue, Sydney, Autumn; and "Maria Kozic and Tsk-Tsk-Tsk," Tasmanian School of Art Gallery, Hobart).

21 "POPISM," *Real Life* 9, New York (repr. of Catalogues no. 5, below).

1982 20 "Biennale of Sydney," *Artforum*, October.

19 "Pool Talk (editorial)," *Art & Text* 8, "Pool-Side Issue," December.

18 "Interview: Rosalind Krauss," *Art & Text* 8.

17 "Angst in My Pants," *Art & Text* 7, September.

16 "Antipodality," *Art & Text* 6, July.

15 "Self and Theatricality: Samuel Beckett and Vito Acconci," *Art & Text* 5, March.

14 "Learning the Art," *The Age*, Melbourne, January 29.

1981 13 "Lip-reading: On Feminist Publishing," *Meanjin*, Melbourne, December.

12 "A Portrait of an Artist," *The Age*, October 31.

11 Editorial, *Art & Text* 3, September.

10 "Melbourne Galleries," *The Age*, August 7.

9 "Contemporary Art and its Audience," papers from panel organized and published by the George Paton Gallery, Melbourne.

8 "The Strategy of Presence," *Art Network*, Sydney, July.

7 "Howard Arkley's Muzak Mural," *Bulletin*, Institute of Modern Art, Brisbane, July (repr. in *Howard Arkley* catalogue, Monash University Gallery, Melbourne, 1991).

6 "Australian 'New Wave' and the 'Second Degree,' " *Art & Text*, premiere issue, April (repr. in Books no. 1, below).

5 "On Criticism (editorial)," *Art & Text* premiere issue.

4 "Jenny Watson's 'Mod'ernism," *Art International*, Lugano, Switzerland, January-February.

1980 3 "Dance: Graham Murphy," *The Examiner*, Launceston, June 20.

2 "Sydney Dance Company," *Island* 3, Hobart.

1 "Clement Greenberg and 'Postmodernism' – An Interview," *ART and Australia*, Sydney, December.

CATALOGUES

1988 20 Leo Castelli Gallery, "142 Greene Street, Last Show" (Kelly, Lichtenstein, Serra, Stella), New York, October.

19 *Impresario: Malcolm McLaren and the British New Wave* (see Books no. 4, below).

18 City Gallery, "La Boheme," Melbourne, May-June.

1986 17 42nd Biennale of Venice, Australian exhibition, "Imants Tillers."

16 Triennial of India, Australian exhibition, "Jenny Watson—Mirror, Mirror," Delhi.

1985 15 Commune di Venezia, "IsolAustralia," May-June, Venice.

1984 14 Los Angeles Institute of Contemporary Art and the Olympic Arts Festival, Los Angeles, "Australia: Nine Contemporary Artists," June-August.

13 University of Melbourne Gallery, "John Dunkley-Smith, On Photo-Rhetoric," September-October.

12 University of Melbourne Gallery, "Dale Frank," August.

11 Roslyn Oxley Gallery, "Robert Rooney," Sydney, March.

10 Festival of Adelaide, "Juan Davila," March.

1983 9 Matt's Gallery, "Imants Tillers," London, October.

8 Roslyn Oxley9 Gallery, "John Nixon: Self Portrait."

7 Roslyn Oxley9 Gallery, "Pirates and Mutineers."

6 University of Melbourne Gallery, "Tall Poppies," June (exhibition and catalogue by Paul Taylor).

1982 5 National Gallery of Victoria, "POPISM," Melbourne, June (exhibition and catalogue by Paul Taylor).

4 Institute of Contemporary Art and the Serpentine Gallery, "Eureka: Artists from Australia," London, March.

1980 3 National Gallery of Victoria, "On Paper" (a repr. of National Gallery of Victoria, below).

2 National Gallery of Victoria, "Aspects of New Realism."

1 The Tasmanian School of Art Gallery and the Fine Arts Gallery, University of Tasmania, Hobart and the Queen Victoria Museum and Art Gallery, Launceston, "Recent Tasmanian Sculpture and Three-Dimensional Art," September-November (exhibition and catalogue by Paul Taylor).

BOOKS

1995 9 Ed. Paul Taylor, *After Andy: SoHo in the Eighties*, Schwartz City, Melbourne (collected articles and interviews with intro. by Allan Schwartzman, including Articles nos. 161, 159, 157, 155, 153, 152, 151, 150, 136, 134, 130, 127, 126, 118, 117, 112, 109, 106, 105, 101, 100, 99, 94, 90, 89, 84, 82, 80, 78, 77, 72, 71, 70, 64, 58, 57 & 39, above; also includes prev. unpubl. "Interview with Tony Shafrazi" [1988]).

1990 8 Ed. Russell Ferguson, Karen Fiss, William Olander and Marcia Tucker, *Discourses: Conversations in Postmodern Art and Culture*, MIT Press, Cambridge and the New Museum of Contemporary Art, New York (publication of discussion panel "The Society of the Spectacle," with Greil Marcus, Richard Hell, Jon Savage and Stephen Sprouse, New Museum of Contemporary Art and the Fashion Institute of Technology, New York).

1989 7 The Editors of Flash Art, *Flash Art XXI Years*, Giancarlo Politi Editore, Milan (includes Articles nos. 77 & 82, above).

6 Ed. Paul Taylor, *Post-Pop Art*, MIT Press and Flash Art Books, Milan (with a new introduction).

5 Ed. Patricia Schwarz, *Collected Interviews with Joseph Kosuth*, Patricia Schwartz Verlag, Stuttgart.

1988 4 Ed. Paul Taylor, *Impresario: Malcolm McLaren and the British New Wave*, MIT Press and the New Museum of Contemporary Art (with exhibition and essay).

1985 3 Ed. Paul Taylor, *Hysterical Tears*, Greenhouse-Penguin Books, Melbourne (with introduction repr. from Catalogues no. 10, above).

1984 2 Ed. Jean-Louis Pradel, *Art 83/84*, Chene and Jacques Legrand S.A., Paris, English and French volumes (essay repr. from Catalogues no. 6, above).

1 Ed. Paul Taylor, *Anything Goes: Art in Australia 1970-1980*, Art & Text, Melbourne (with new introduction and essay repr. of Articles no. 6).

●

Paul Taylor 'After Andy: SoHo in the Eighties'

First published in Australia in 1995 by Schwartz City

a division of Bookman Press Pty Ltd, 325 Flinders Lane, Melbourne, Victoria 3000 Australia.

National Library of Australia cataloguing-in-publication entry

     Taylor, Paul: 'After Andy: SoHo in the Eighties'

     ISBN 1 86395 049 4

Designed by Ian Robertson, Melbourne.

Production and printing by Griffin Colour, Adelaide.

Publication assisted by the Australia Council,
the Australian Government's arts funding and advisory body.

Paul Taylor is best known for conducting
the last interview with Andy Warhol. A regular contributor
to *Vanity Fair, Manhattan, inc., Fame, Connoisseur* and
Interview magazines as well as *The New York Times, Flash Art*
and *Parkett*, he edited *Anything Goes: Art in Australia 1970-1980*
(1984) and *Post-Pop Art* (1989). Before taking up residence
in New York City in 1984, he founded the Australian journal
Art & Text in 1981 and curated the landmark "POPISM"
exhibition at the National Gallery of Victoria in 1982.
Among his other activities in New York he curated the
exhibition "Impresario: Malcolm McLaren and the British New
Wave" for The New Museum of Contemporary Art in 1988.
He is described by famed New York gallerist Leo Castelli
as writing "groundbreaking articles" and by Grey Art Gallery
director Thomas Sokolowski as "deflating the windbags and
unmasking the succubi of the art world in the raucous 1980s."
He was a frequent speaker at museum panel discussions
and in 1986 was Australian Commissioner at the Biennale
of Venice. Paul Taylor died of an AIDS-related illness
in Melbourne in 1992.

Timothy Greenfield-Sanders is a New-York based
photographer best known for his portraits of Manhattan and
Hollywood celebrities. Solo exhibitions of his work have taken
place at Leo Castelli and Mary Boone galleries, and in 1991 at
the Modern Art Museum of Fort Worth, Texas.

Allan Schwartzman has written extensively
about art for *The New Yorker, Manhattan, inc., Interview*
and *The New York Times*.